The College History Series

VASSAR COLLEGE

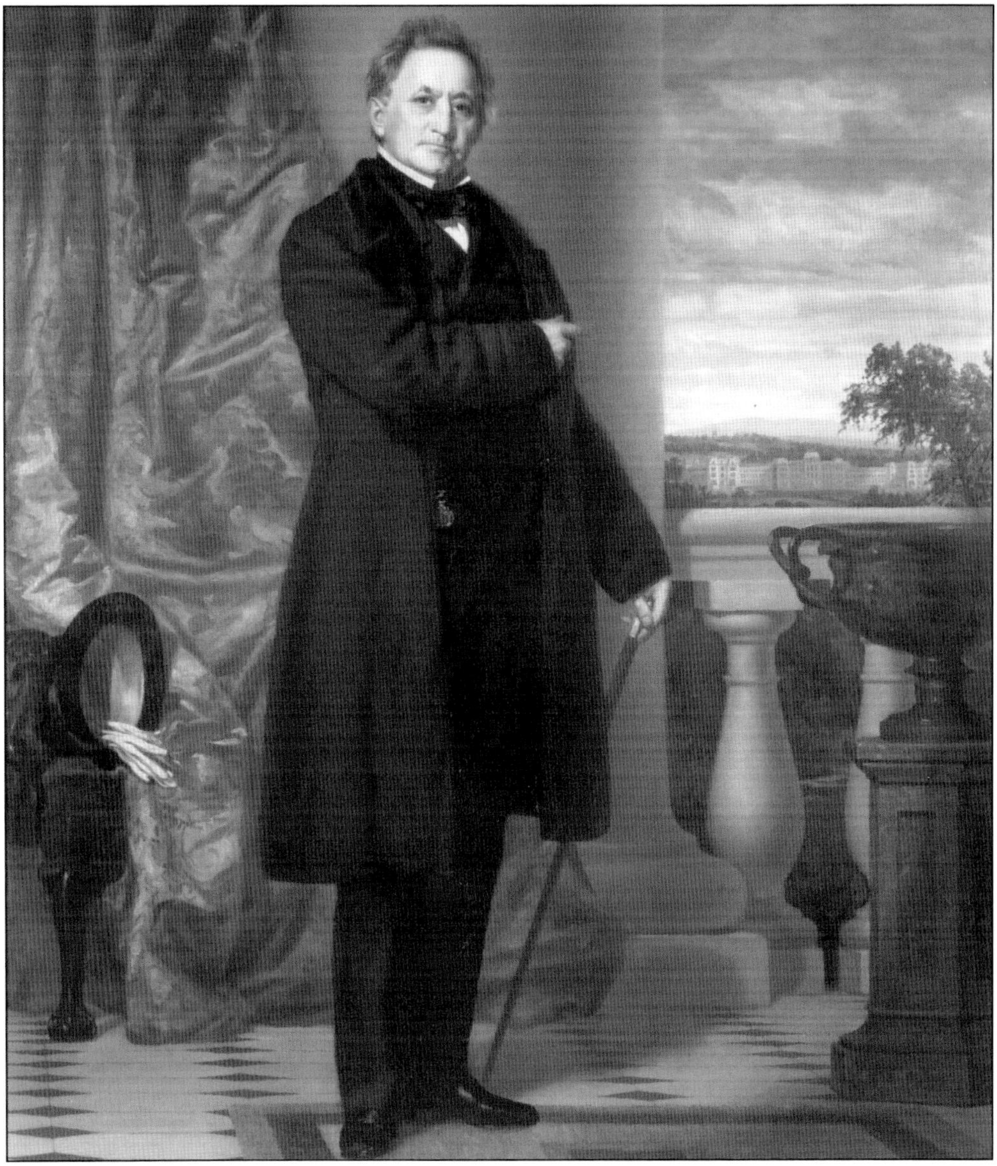

A Portrait of Matthew Vassar, Oil on Canvas, Charles L. Elliott (1861). "It occurred to me that woman, having received from her Creator the same intellectual constitution as man, has the same right as man to intellectual culture and development." Such were the founder's words to the new board of trustees at its first meeting in 1861. In this painting, Vassar points to Main Building, designed by prominent New York architect James Renwick Jr. The building was modeled on the French Tuileries, which Vassar, who had immigrated from England at age four, admired when he visited Europe in 1845. On that trip, Vassar was inspired to build a monument for posterity that would honor the Vassar family and "be of benefit to mankind." Conscious of his moment in history, Vassar commissioned Charles L. Elliott, a pupil of John Trumbull, to paint a portrait. He also commissioned Benson Lossing—a prominent author, engraver, and historian on the board of trustees—to write the commemorative book *Vassar College and Its Founder*, signed copies of which were sent to trustees. (Courtesy Frances Lehman Loeb Art Center.)

The College History Series

VASSAR COLLEGE

MARYANN BRUNO AND ELIZABETH A. DANIELS

ARCADIA
PUBLISHING

ISBN 978-0-7385-0454-4

Published by Arcadia Publishing
Charleston, South Carolina

Printed in the United States of America

Library of Congress Catalog Card Number: 00-111390

For all general information contact Arcadia Publishing at:
Telephone 843-853-2070
Fax 843-853-0044
E-mail sales@arcadiapublishing.com
For customer service and orders:
Toll-Free 1-888-313-2665

Visit us on the Internet at www.arcadiapublishing.com

Dedicated to the founder, Matthew Vassar,
and to the Vassar Classes of 1941 and 1982.

CONTENTS

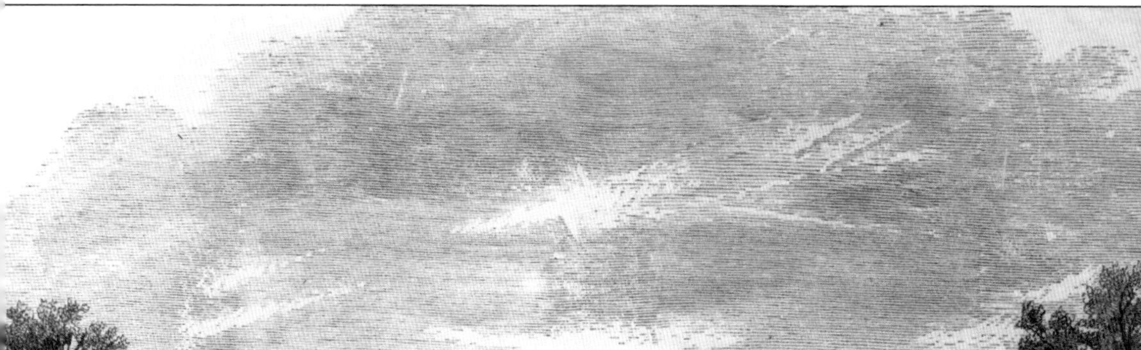

AN ENGRAVING OF THE COLLEGE CAMPUS AND BUILDINGS FOR THE FIRST CATALOGUE, 1865. Benson Lossing rendered this engraving of the early campus for use in the first catalogue in 1865. Main Building (center) was built between 1861 and 1865, the year the college opened. To the left of Main Building is the observatory, designed by physics professor Charles Farrar and completed in 1864. The Calisthenium and Riding Academy, which was designed by Poughkeepsie architect J.A. Wood and completed in 1866, is to the right of Main Building. Not shown is the Gate Lodge, designed by James Renwick as the college's formal entrance on Raymond Avenue. The carefully wrought site shown here is a far cry from the "treeless plain," a phrase said to describe the condition of the former fairgrounds when Vassar purchased the property from farmer William Davies in 1860. Main Building provided living accommodations for students, administrators, the faculty, and servants. It also housed a dining room, a chapel, an art gallery, a library, large drawing rooms and parlors, music rooms, and storage space.

Introduction:
Twice Breaking Precedent

With no previous experience as an educator, 69-year-old Matthew Vassar founded and endowed Vassar Female College in 1861 after a wrenching struggle of deciding how use his wealth to benefit mankind and bestow honor on his family. His decision to create a women's college resulted in the most unexpected accomplishment in the career of this feisty Poughkeepsie brewer and civic leader. First inspired by his niece, feminist schoolmistress Lydia Booth, Vassar was also encouraged after her death by an ambitious newcomer in Poughkeepsie, Dartmouth-trained educator Milo P. Jewett. Vassar left his imprint on history by creating a college where women could have the same educational advantages that their brothers could have at Harvard or Yale. Once he had made the decision, the founder applied for a charter for the college and invited 28 men to serve on his board of trustees. Thereafter, he spared no effort in bringing his dream to fruition.

There were no precedents in 1861 for endowed liberal arts education for women, a fact Vassar pointed out to his board when he addressed them for the first time in January that year. Then, after having sought the best advice available, Vassar actualized what astronomer Maria Mitchell, the first professor hired, called his "magnificent enterprise." The college opened on September 26, 1865, with 353 students, including a Civil War widow, 9 professors, and 20 teaching assistants. Vassar stipulated that standards should be high to allow women to "advance." He charged his trustees, "I wish to give one sex all the advantages too long monopolized by the other."

To follow the progress of Vassar College in these photographs is to discern the growth of higher education for women in America. As the decades unrolled, the college responded to women's changing needs. From its earliest years, leading scholars offered women rigorous, challenging courses and opportunities for independent achievement. In the late 1960s, with 100 years of educational leadership for women under its belt, Vassar broke new ground again as the first women's college to develop coeducation. The photographs in the last chapter of this book reflect both the continuities and changes in campus life as the 139-year-old Vassar moved toward the millennium.

One

Creating the College: 1861–1885

In 1855, Rev. Milo P. Jewett, a newly arrived Dartmouth graduate interested in education for women, purchased from Matthew Vassar the Cottage Hill Seminary in Poughkeepsie after the death of proprietor Lydia Booth, Matthew Vassar's niece. Jewett—who had learned that Vassar was leaning toward founding a college for women rather than joining his nephews in endowing a hospital—used his eloquent powers of persuasion to help the founder make the right decision. Rewarded for his efforts, Jewett was elected the college's president at the first trustee meeting in 1861. At that meeting, Vassar presented to the board his endowment gift of $408,000 along with a deed to 200 acres of land. Almost immediately, James Renwick Jr. was employed to design the multipurpose Main Building, which was erected and outfitted between 1861 and 1865.

Following a disagreement with the founder in 1864, Jewett resigned and was succeeded by fellow trustee Rev. John H. Raymond, who organized the college, its staff, and curriculum. In 1867, the trustees sought and received permission to remove the word "female" from the college's name. Sarah Josepha Hale, influential editor of *Godey's Ladies' Book*, had insisted the word had Darwinist overtones and must go.

On June 23, 1868, as he was making his yearly address to the board of trustees in the Trustees Room in Main Building, Matthew Vassar slumped into the arms of trustee Benson Lossing and died. After a respectful interval, the trustees met again and heard the final paragraph of his address, in which Vassar was bidding them a fond farewell.

In the college's early years, high school education for young women was still largely unavailable, and two-thirds of the early candidates were unprepared for Vassar's rigorous classical and scientific curriculum. Accordingly, the trustees established a preparatory division, which continued until 1890. Raymond died in 1878, and Rev. Samuel Caldwell became president. Not up to the job, Caldwell submitted his resignation in 1885. The college was off to a tentative start.

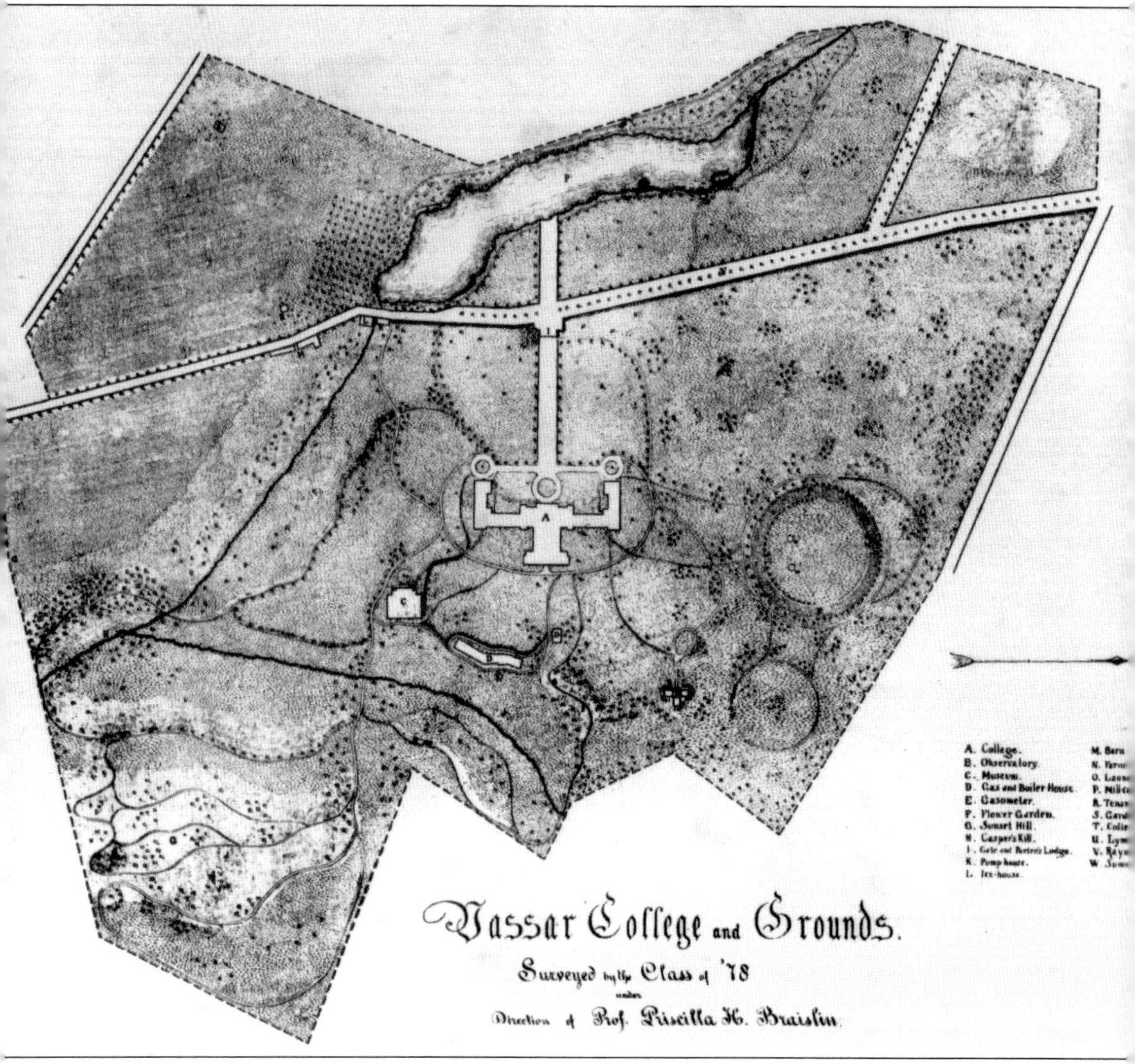

A Survey of Vassar College and Grounds. The students of Prof. Priscilla H. Braislin in the Class of 1878 put their understanding of mathematics to work in preparing this survey for publication in *Historical Sketch of Vassar College* (1876), which was submitted as an exhibit during the national centennial of 1876. Professor Braislin, like many other Vassar professors over time, was committed to sending students to the sources (in this case, surveying the campus on which they lived) and demanded that her students take individual responsibility for their own work.

MATTHEW VASSAR AND HIS DOG "TIP" AT SPRINGSIDE. In 1850, Vassar employed landscape architect Andrew Jackson Downing to develop his country property south of Poughkeepsie. After Downing's death, Vassar dropped his plans to make a showplace of Springside, instead using his fortune to endow his college. There he put into play many of the ideas about landscaping and environment that he had reaped from Downing. (Courtesy Frances Lehman Loeb Art Center.)

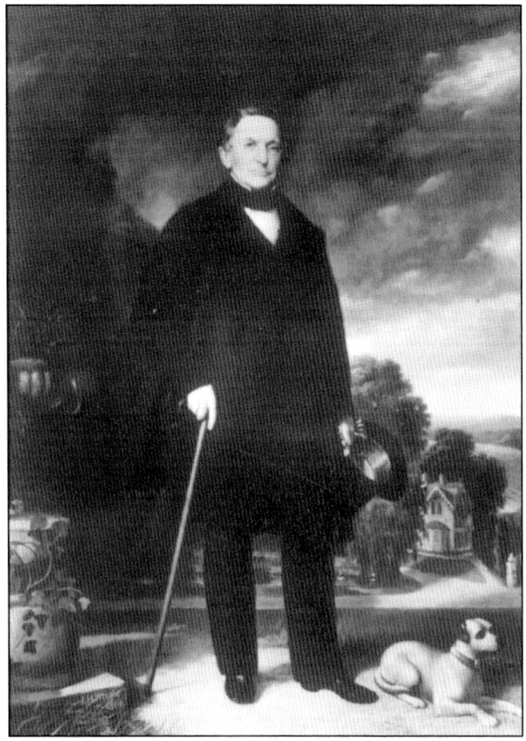

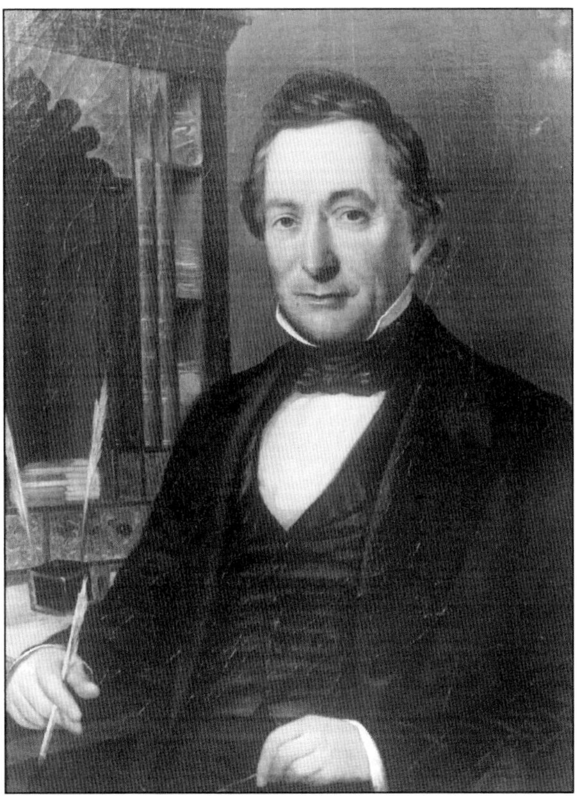

MATTHEW VASSAR, MAN OF LETTERS. This portrait by an unknown painter dates to the 1850s, when Matthew Vassar was president of the Poughkeepsie Lyceum of Literature, Science, and the Mechanic Arts. On December 3, 1852, Vassar opened the season's program, which included a speech by Ralph Waldo Emerson. On May 17, 1867, at the request of students, Emerson spoke again at Vassar College. The students, however, felt that Emerson talked down to them in the speech. (Courtesy Frances Lehman Loeb Art Center.)

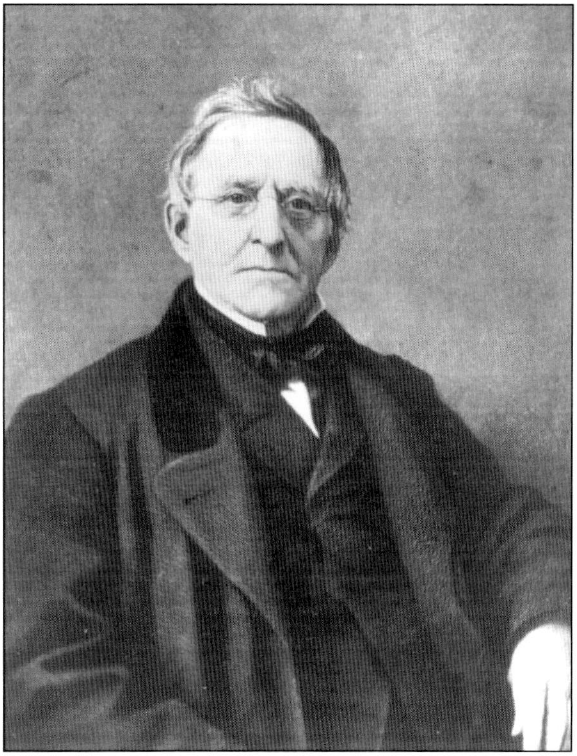

Matthew Vassar (1792–1868), Founder of Vassar College. At age four, Matthew Vassar came with his parents and siblings from northern England to Poughkeepsie in Dutchess County. When he was 14, he ran away to escape being apprenticed to a tanner. Two years later, he returned with $150 in his pocket and personal ambition to make something of himself. Joining the family brewing business, he rose rapidly to become one of Poughkeepsie's richest and best-known citizens.

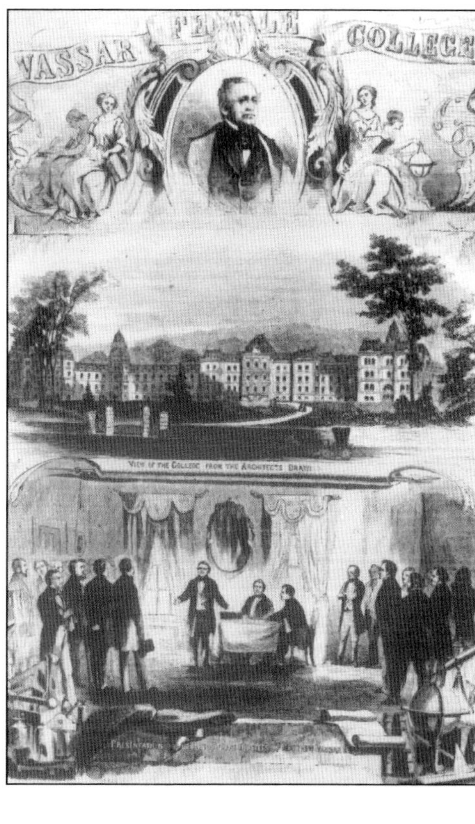

The Presentation of Funds to the Trustees. This engraving from the March 30, 1861 edition of *Harper's Weekly* was typical of the press's interest in the new college, which attracted notice in publications in America and abroad. The view of the college is from an architect's drawing. The presentation of funds in a tin box (securities amounting to $408,000) took place at the Hotel Gregory in Poughkeepsie on February 19, 1861.

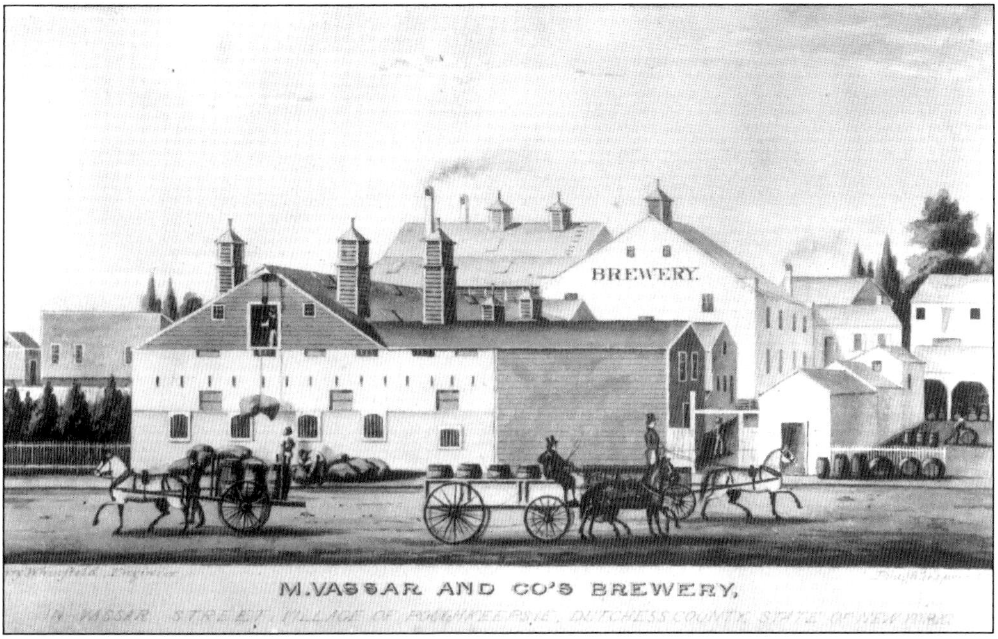

THE M. VASSAR AND COMPANY BREWERY. The Vassar brewery was the largest of its kind in the United States. The building shown here was located on Vassar Street in Poughkeepsie, opposite Matthew Vassar's townhouse. Vassar accumulated his fortune from the brewing of ale, the buying and selling of real estate, and from other enterprises. (Painting by Henry Whinfield, 1834; courtesy Peter Van Kleeck.)

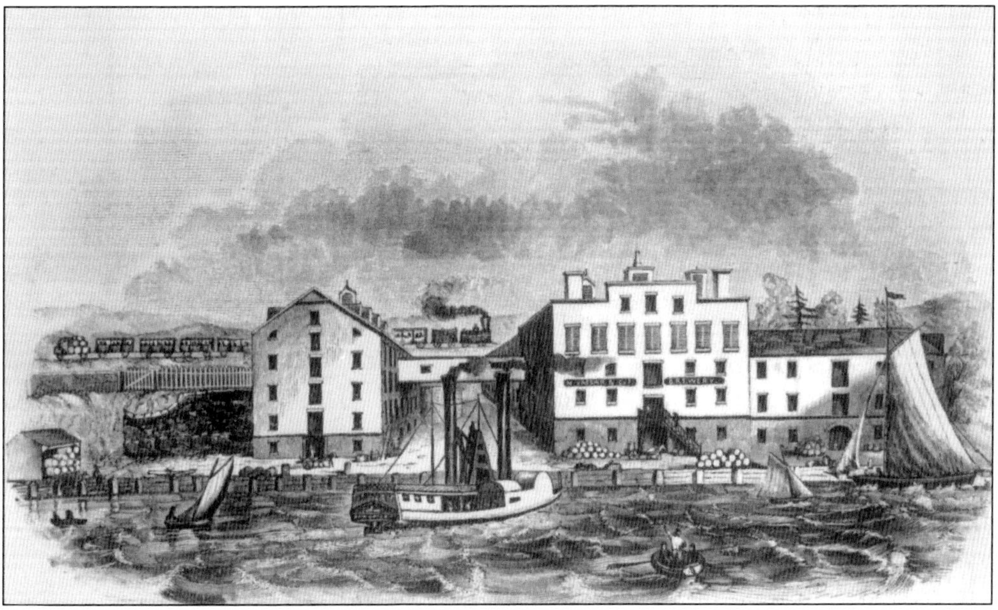

THE VASSAR BREWERY ON THE HUDSON RIVER. In 1836, the Vassar brewery moved to the Hudson River, about two blocks from the Vassar Street building. The waterfront building was four stories high, 200 by 50 feet, and capable of producing 50,000 barrels a year. By 1836, M. Vassar and Company had two other branches, one in New York City and one in Lansingburgh, New York, near Albany. (Engraving by Benson Lossing.)

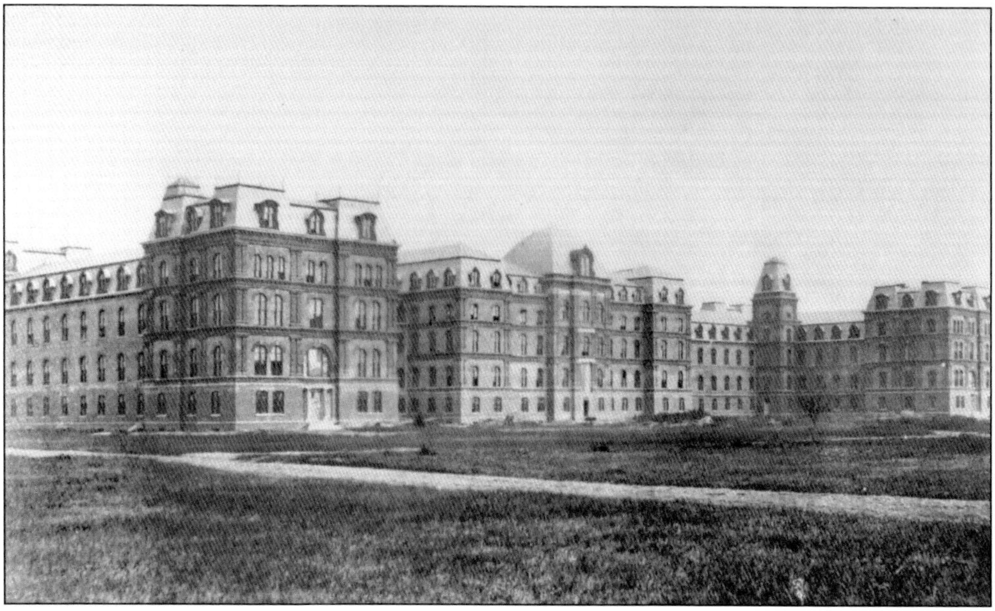

Main Building, Vassar College. After looking along the eastern banks of the Hudson River for a site, Vassar finally decided to build his college on farmland two miles east of Poughkeepsie. This site was far enough away from prying eyes to provide sheltered surroundings, but close enough for convenient access to the city and river.

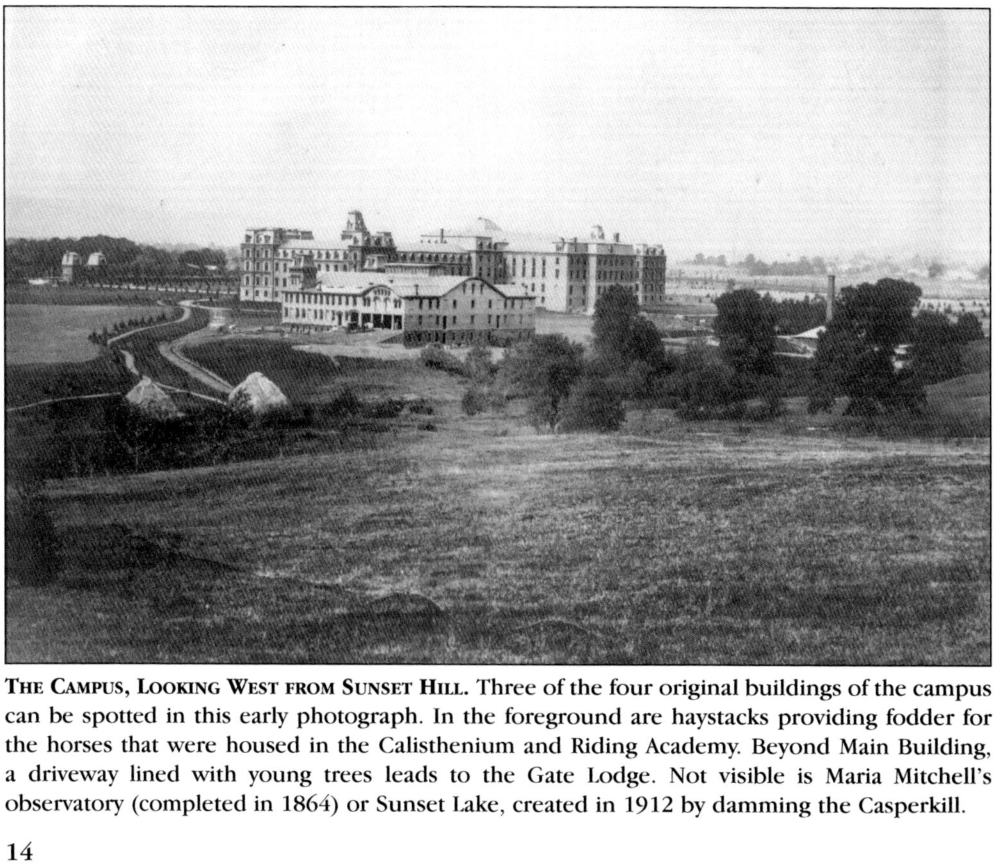

The Campus, Looking West from Sunset Hill. Three of the four original buildings of the campus can be spotted in this early photograph. In the foreground are haystacks providing fodder for the horses that were housed in the Calisthenium and Riding Academy. Beyond Main Building, a driveway lined with young trees leads to the Gate Lodge. Not visible is Maria Mitchell's observatory (completed in 1864) or Sunset Lake, created in 1912 by damming the Casperkill.

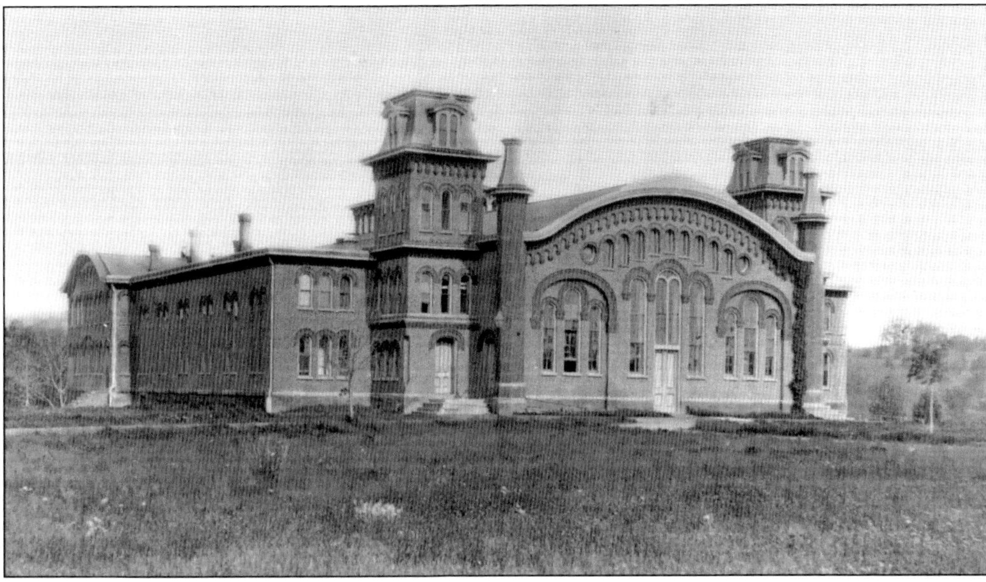

The Calisthenium and Riding Academy. Matthew Vassar, who believed that women should exercise in all seasons, solicited advice for planning an athletic program from Dio Lewis, a health practitioner in Massachusetts. Lewis's program of Swedish exercises and aesthetic dancing was subsequently instituted in the Calisthenium, Vassar's first gymnasium and the first gymnasium in a women's college in the United States.

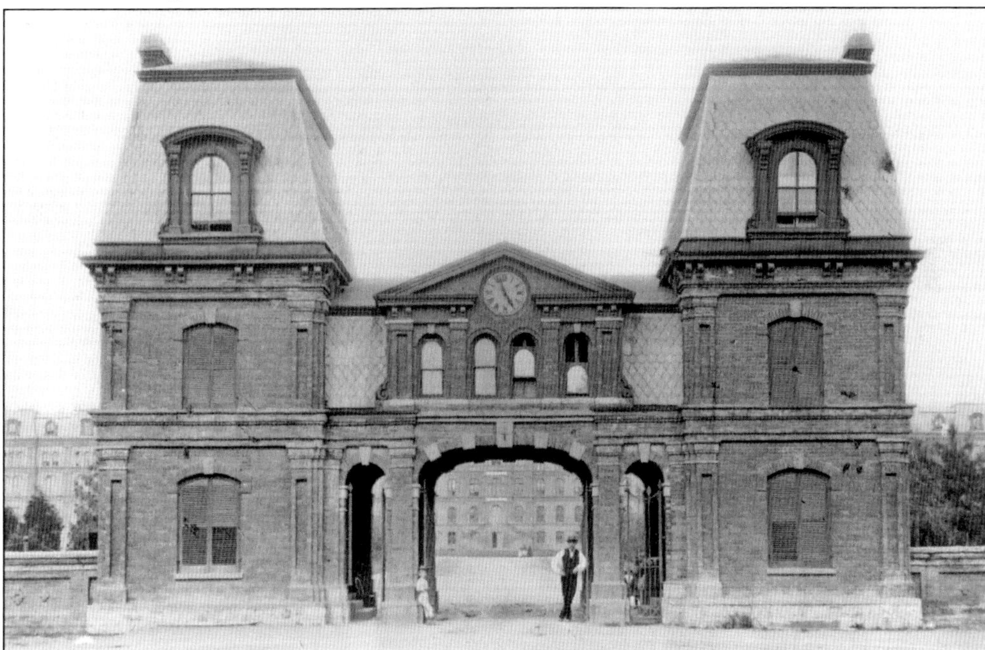

The Vassar Gate Lodge. Designed by James Renwick Jr., the Gate Lodge stood as a sentinel of the campus from 1866 to 1913, when it was razed to make room for Taylor Hall and a new entrance that would accommodate motor cars. The porter standing at the gate may well be the aptly named Mr. Lockit, gatekeeper for many years. Visible through the arch is Main Building with its original entrance stairs.

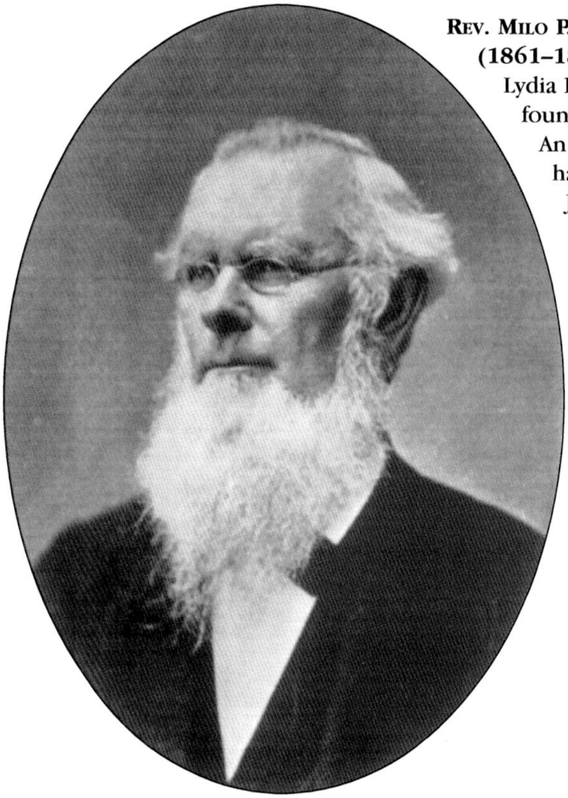

Rev. Milo P. Jewett, Vassar's First President (1861–1864). Milo P. Jewett and Vassar's niece, Lydia Booth, were strong influences on the founder's decision to endow the college. An educator from Alabama, where he had founded Judson Female Institute, Jewett took over Lydia Booth's Cottage Hill Seminary after her death in 1855. Elected president of Vassar at the first meeting of its board, Jewett resigned in April 1864 after a clash of will with Vassar.

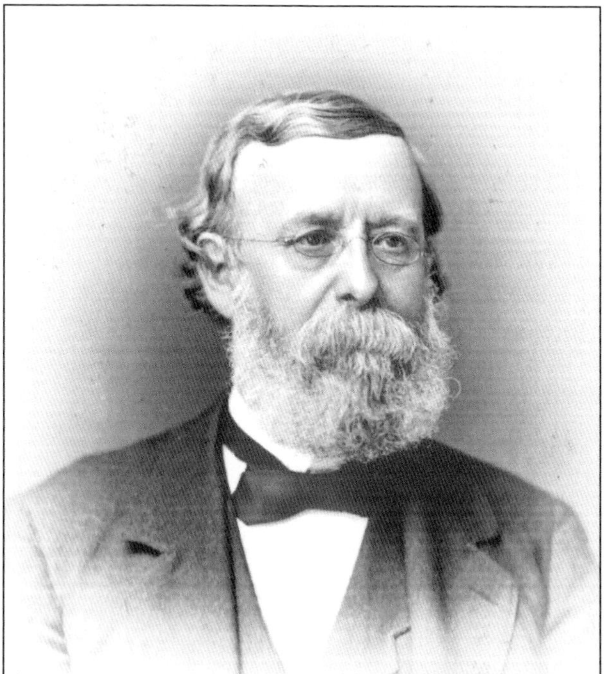

Rev. John Raymond, Vassar's Second President (1864–1878). Rev. John Raymond, a charter trustee, accepted the presidency of Vassar Female College in April 1864 after Jewett's resignation. On the eve of the opening, he wrote his wife in Brooklyn, "It seems like a dream, the sudden transmutation of this great lumbering pile of bricks and mortar, which hung on my spirit like a mountainous millstone, into a palace of light." Raymond died in the summer of 1878.

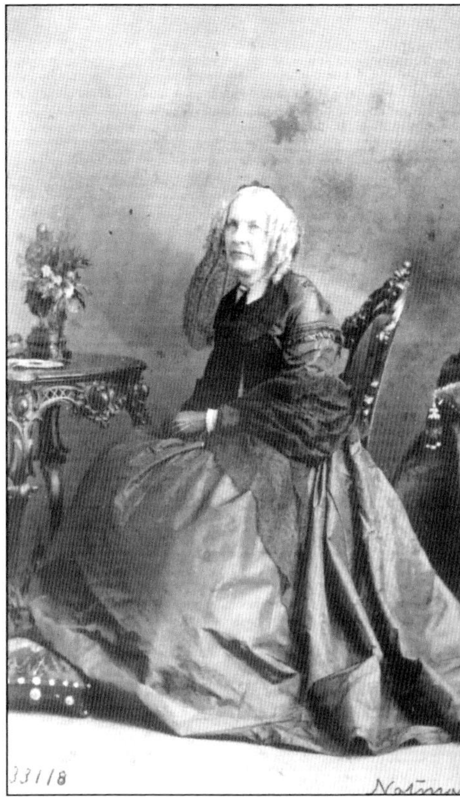

HANNAH W. LYMAN, LADY PRINCIPAL (1865–1871). Canadian by birth, Hannah Lyman was a stylish woman, as suggested here by her elegant hairdo and elaborate dress. Her job was to make Vassar College function like a family that would protect the students *in loco parentis* (in place of a parent). She drew up rules and regulations and presided over a battery of about 20 women teachers, who doubled as corridor mistresses.

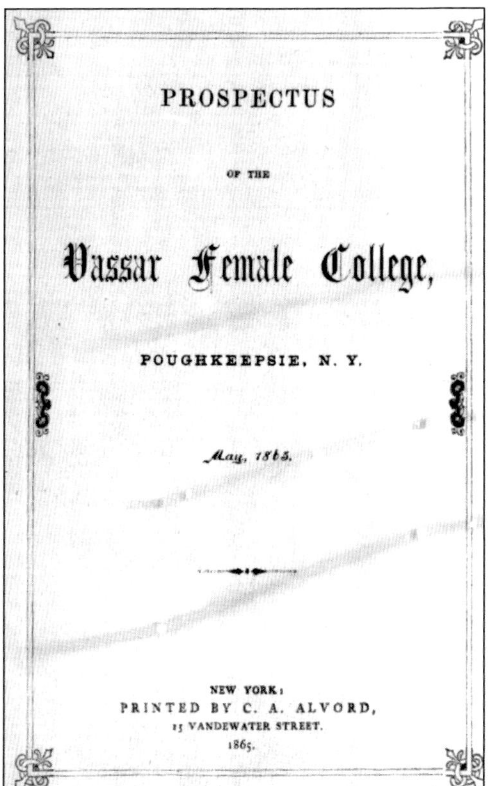

PROSPECTUS

OF THE

Vassar Female College,

POUGHKEEPSIE, N. Y.

May, 1865.

NEW YORK:
PRINTED BY C. A. ALVORD,
15 VANDEWATER STREET.
1865.

THE PROSPECTUS OF VASSAR FEMALE COLLEGE. President Raymond wrote a prospectus advertising requirements for admission to prospective students: Students must be 15 years old and prepared to pass entrance exams in subjects required for entrance. The curriculum was modeled on requirements at the men's colleges. The prospectus also emphasized that the daily lives of young women would be regulated by the lady principal's sensible rules.

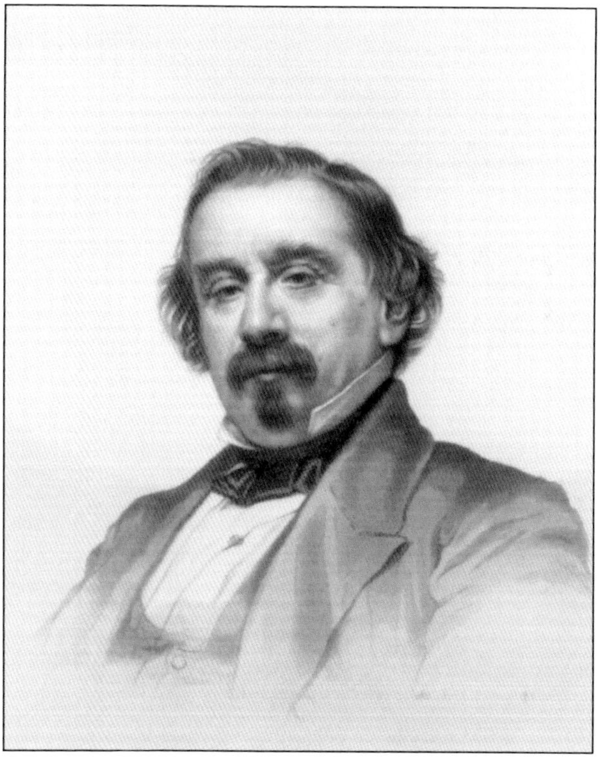

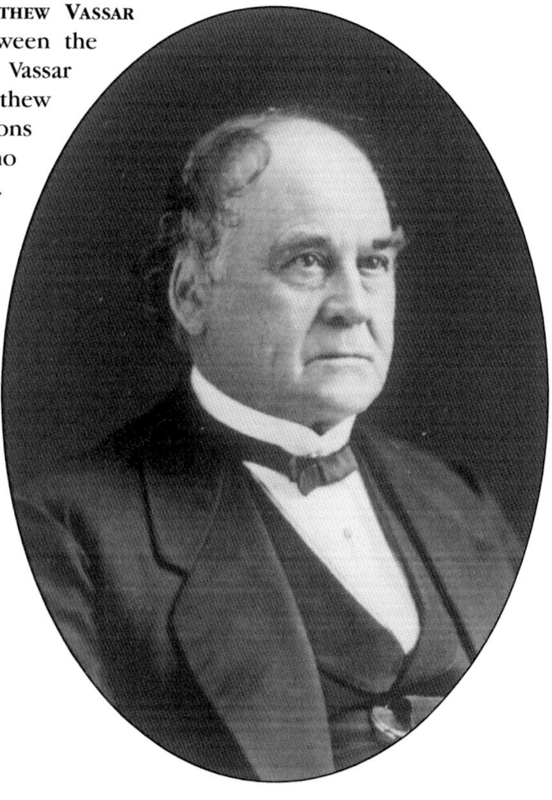

John Guy Vassar Jr. (Above) and Matthew Vassar Jr. (Right). A strong bond existed between the founder and his two nephews, John Guy Vassar Jr. and Matthew Vassar Jr. Childless, Matthew Vassar looked after the interests of the sons of his brother, John Guy Vassar Sr., who perished in a Vassar brewery fire in 1811. Partners in his business, the nephews were also lifetime college trustees. Matthew Jr. served as treasurer of the college from 1861 until his death in 1881. John Guy Jr. joined Samuel F.B. Morse, Benson Lossing, and Rev. Elias Magoon on the Committee on the Vassar College Art Gallery. He died in 1889. Each brother gave generous endowments to the college, but by and large they were both out of sympathy with their uncle's goals and would have preferred that he join them in establishing a hospital. Through bequests in their wills, they endowed chairs at the college.

Charles Swift, Trustee. The college's charter trustees were a mixture of prominent local businessmen, citizens and educators, and Baptist clergymen. Several trustees had served with Matthew Vassar on the board of Rochester University (now called the University of Rochester), including William Kelly (first chair of the Vassar board), Martin B. Anderson (president of Rochester), and John Raymond (the college's second president). Poughkeepsie lawyer Charles Swift was a typical local trustee.

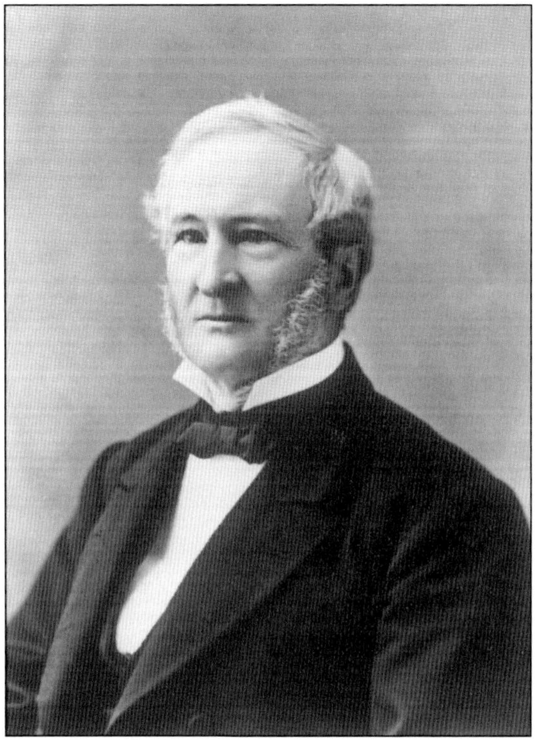

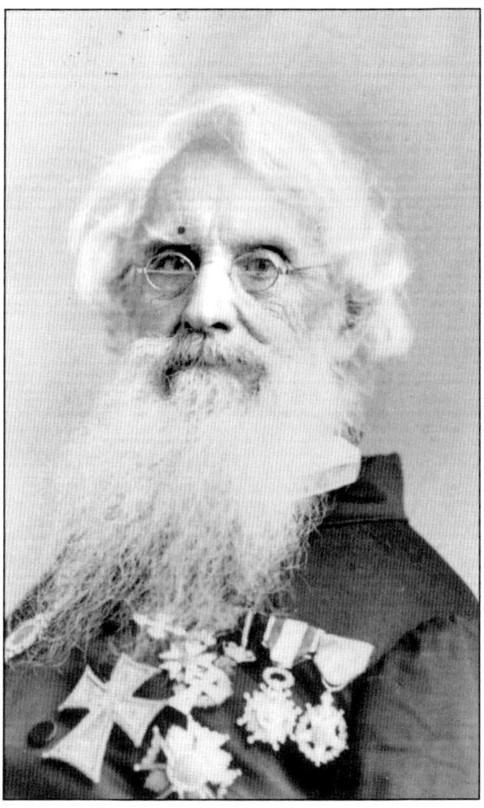

Samuel F.B. Morse, Charter Vassar Trustee. Samuel F.B. Morse, the founder's summer neighbor, was a charter trustee of the college and a member of the Committee on the Vassar College Art Gallery. The committee—composed of Rev. Elias Magoon, John Guy Vassar Jr., Benson Lossing, and Morse—established the gallery on the fifth floor of Main Building as a resource for refining the students' taste and their understanding of art.

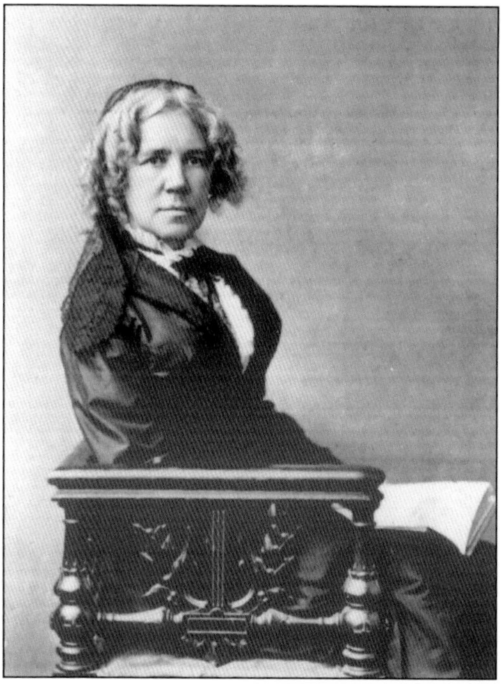

MARIA MITCHELL, PROFESSOR OF ASTRONOMY (1865–1888). In 1862, Matthew Vassar sent a trustee to Lynn, Massachusetts, to invite Maria Mitchell to become the college's professor of astronomy, an offer she accepted. Mitchell was already world famous for having won a gold medal presented by Frederick VII, king of Denmark, to the "first discoverer of a telescopic comet." Mitchell discovered the comet, subsequently named the Maria Mitchell Comet, while she was "sweeping the skies of Nantucket" on October 1, 1847.

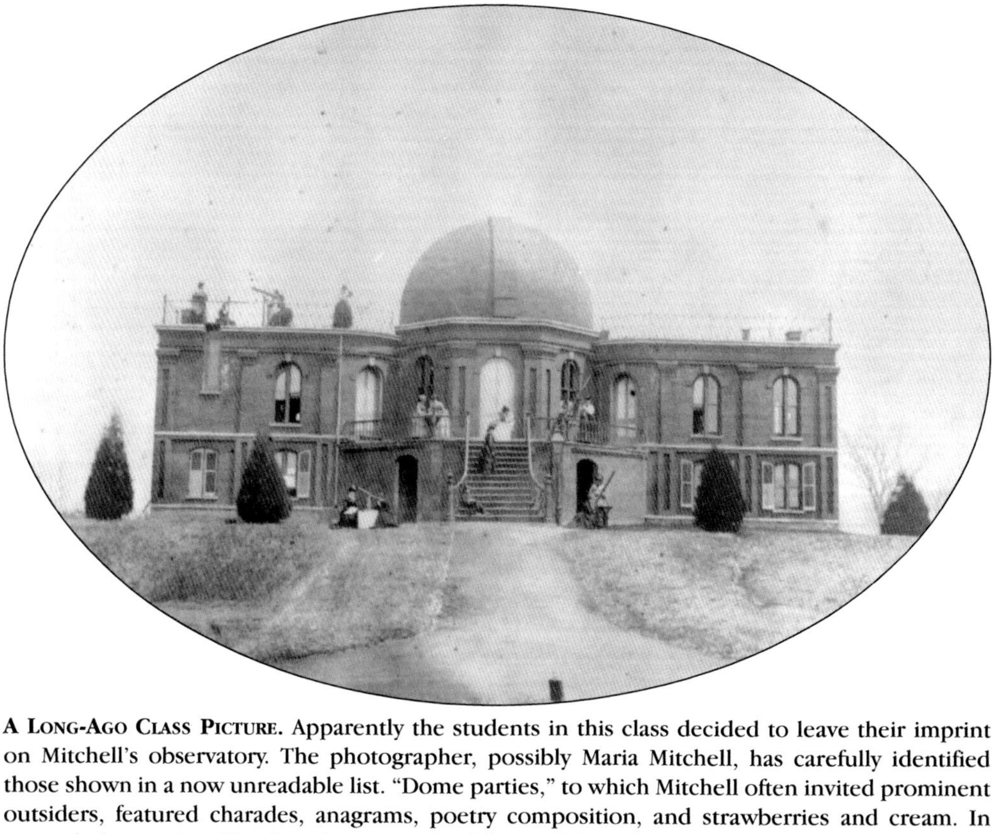

A LONG-AGO CLASS PICTURE. Apparently the students in this class decided to leave their imprint on Mitchell's observatory. The photographer, possibly Maria Mitchell, has carefully identified those shown in a now unreadable list. "Dome parties," to which Mitchell often invited prominent outsiders, featured charades, anagrams, poetry composition, and strawberries and cream. In general, the parties offered students a taste of the world beyond Vassar.

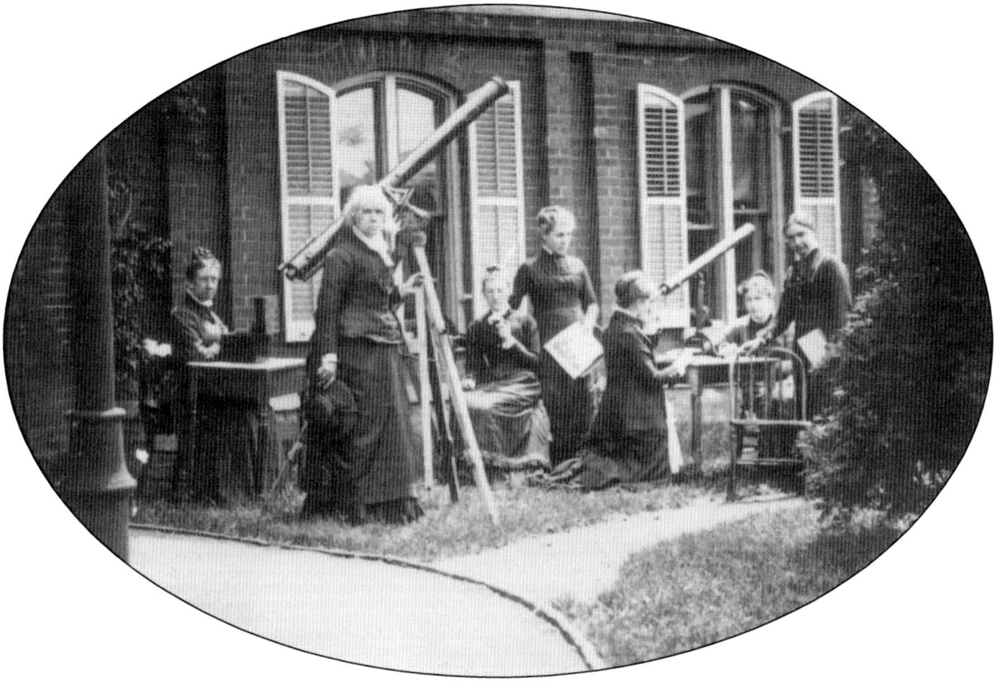

Maria Mitchell in Her Daytime Classroom. Mitchell demanded individual scientific experiments of her students (in this case, members of the Class of 1878). A closet in this observatory recently yielded a series of daily glass plate photographs of sunspots, which were recorded more than 100 years ago and were catalogued in Mitchell's longhand.

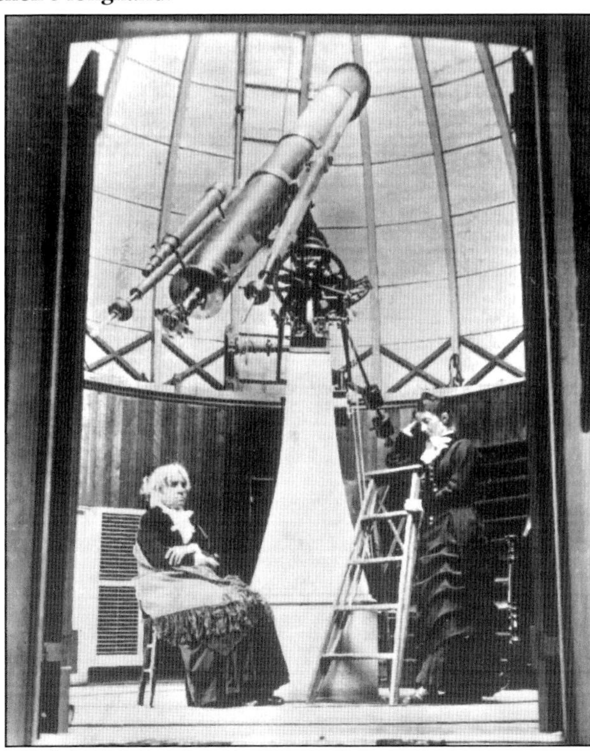

Maria Mitchell in Her Evening Classroom. Mitchell opened her observatory dome to the skies whenever she could. She often sent for her students in the middle of the night when some astronomical phenomenon was taking place. These evening assignments, not compatible with the rules of Main Building, led to a kind of undeclared warfare between Mitchell and Hannah Lyman. Seen in this posed picture are Maria Mitchell (left) and Mary Whitney, her assistant and former student who followed Mitchell as Vassar College astronomer.

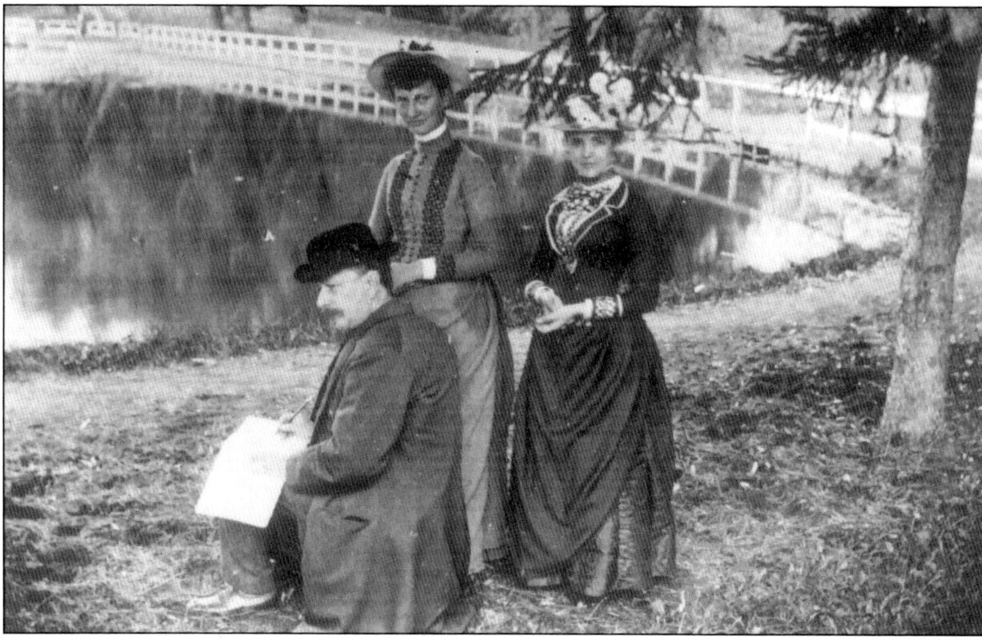

Prof. Henry Van Ingen, Sketching. Adored by his students, Professor Van Ingen was an artist and teacher of the Vassar School of Art from 1866 to 1899. He presided over the Vassar College Art Gallery, which was opened in 1865. The gallery is one of the three predecessors of today's Frances Lehman Loeb Art Center. Besides instructing students in painting and design, Van Ingen gave lectures on the history of art.

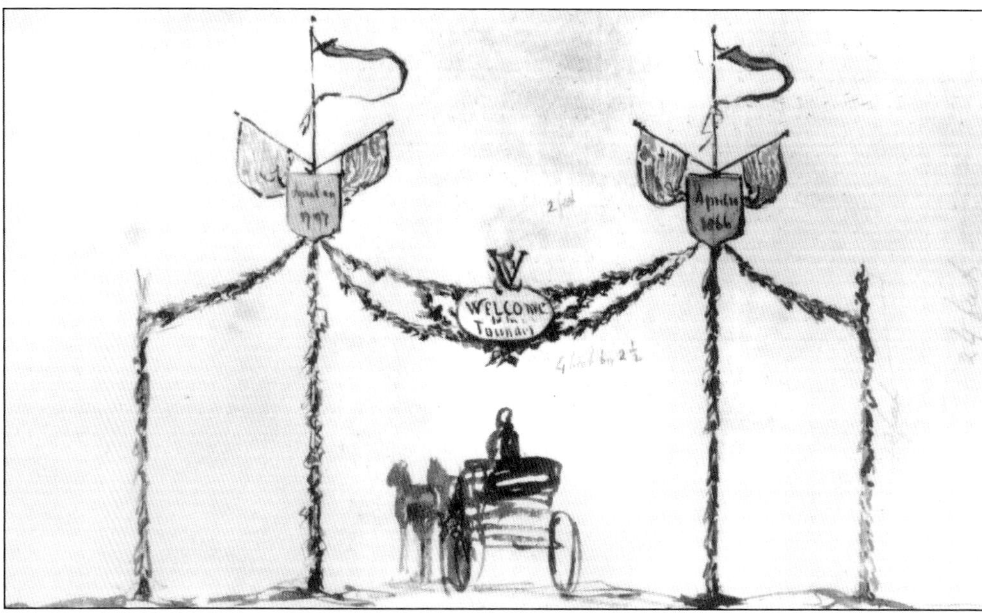

Professor Van Ingen's Arch for Founder's Day, 1866. On April 29, 1866, Matthew Vassar's birthday was celebrated at the college as the first annual Founder's Day. Van Ingen designed an archway of evergreens, and students lined up on the driveway to greet the founder as he passed under the arch. The celebration caused Matthew Vassar to remark, "This one event has repaid me for every cent I have spent for the college."

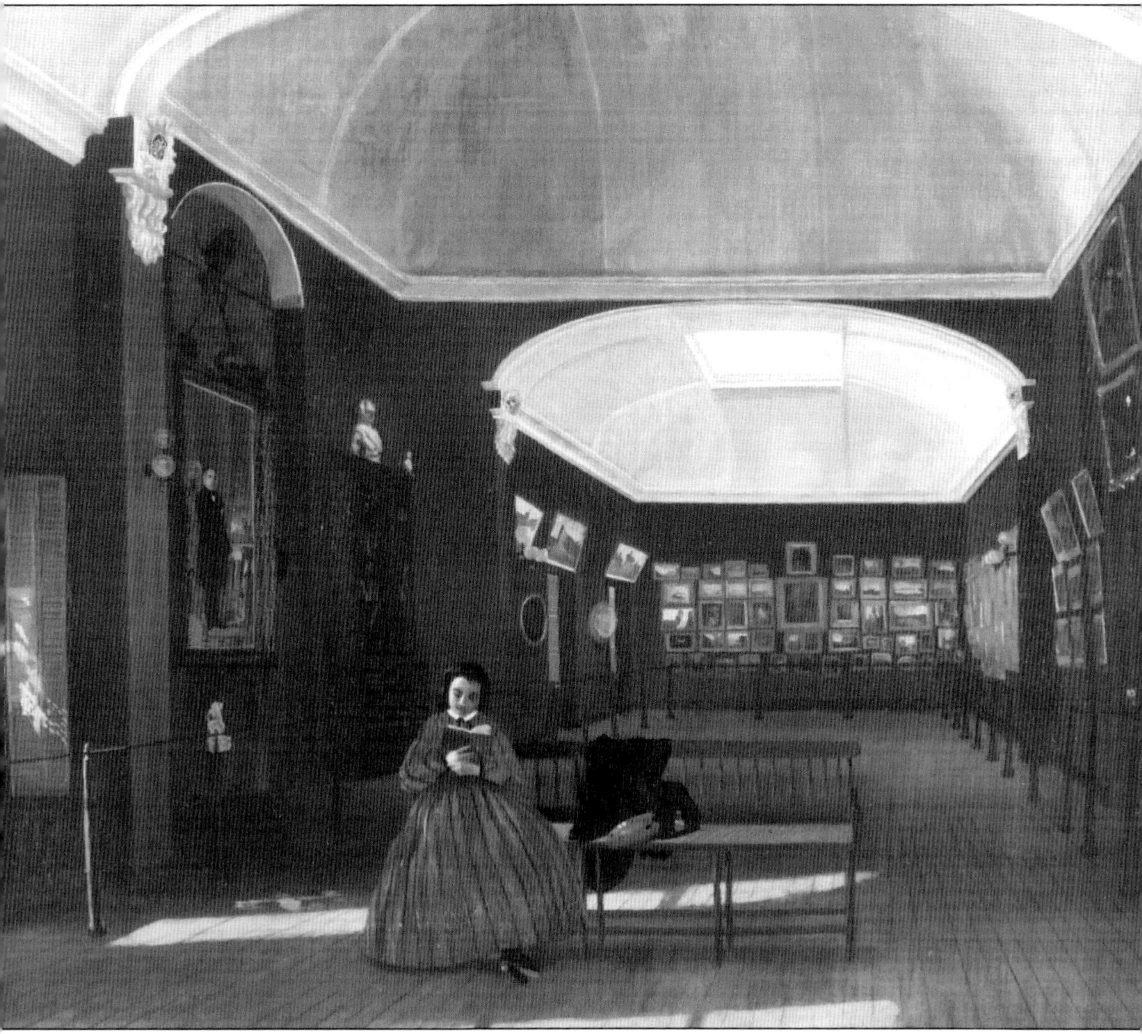

The Apartment of the Art Gallery. This painting by an unknown 19th-century artist depicts the Vassar College Art Gallery, located on the top floor of Main Building. Henry Van Ingen, professor of painting, directed the gallery, which the students used as a studio, sometimes copying the paintings. By 1875, when the gallery's collection had been relocated to the museum (formerly the Riding Academy), students were painting from live models. As the basis for the college's collection of art displayed in the gallery, Matthew Vassar purchased in 1864 the art collection of trustee Elias Lyman Magoon, a noted collector of Hudson River paintings. Magoon, never one to hide his light under a bushel, predicted that the influence of the college's collection would spread "until the Great Cities of our land would send pilgrims thither perpetually." The college has added thousands of works to its art collection, now housed in the Frances Lehman Loeb Art Center, which was designed by Cesar Pelli and opened in 1993. (Photograph by Douglas Baz; courtesy Frances Lehman Loeb Art Center.)

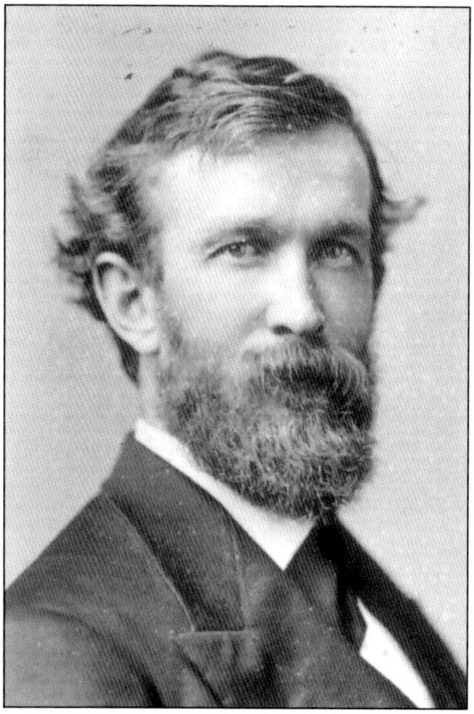

Truman Backus, Professor of Rhetoric, Belles-Lettres, and the English Language. A Rochester graduate, Truman Backus came to Vassar after he organized the first school for freed slaves in Richmond, Virginia. Although he was offered the chair of English at Harvard, he chose to stay at Vassar for many years. He introduced essay writing, the discussion method of teaching, and faculty-student conferences, which have been the hallmark of the department ever since.

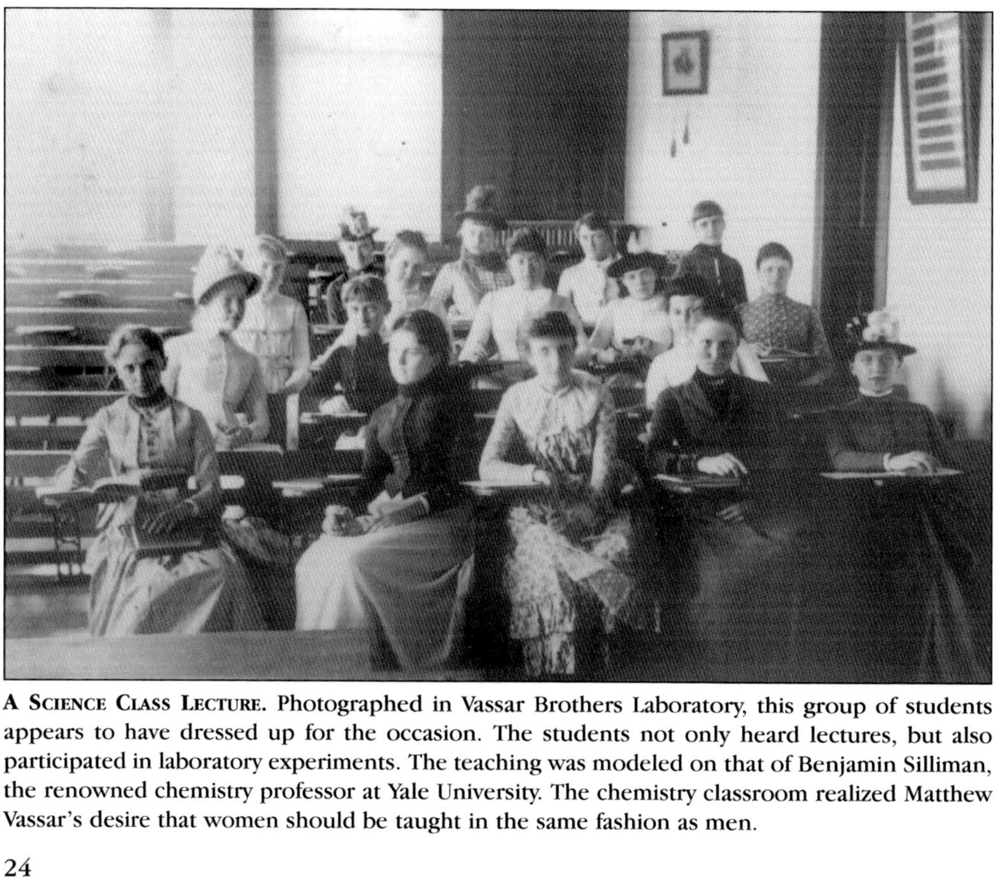

A Science Class Lecture. Photographed in Vassar Brothers Laboratory, this group of students appears to have dressed up for the occasion. The students not only heard lectures, but also participated in laboratory experiments. The teaching was modeled on that of Benjamin Silliman, the renowned chemistry professor at Yale University. The chemistry classroom realized Matthew Vassar's desire that women should be taught in the same fashion as men.

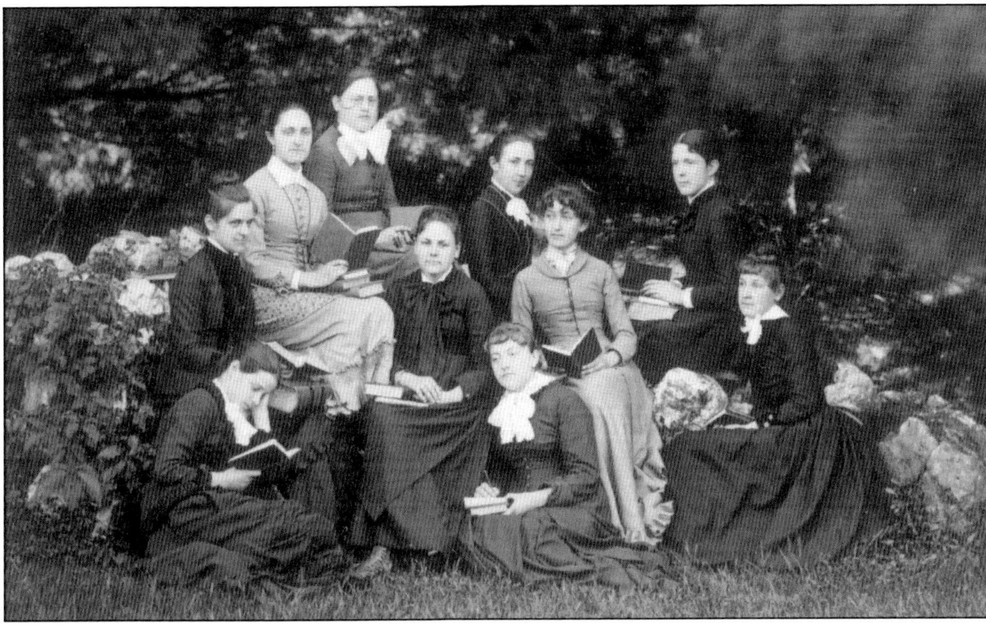

A Class Photographed on the Lawn. Through the years, Vassar students have enjoyed the college's beautiful grounds, and classes have often been held on the lawns in good weather. This photograph is said to show a classics class. Were the students really studying or just taking time out to pose for a picture?

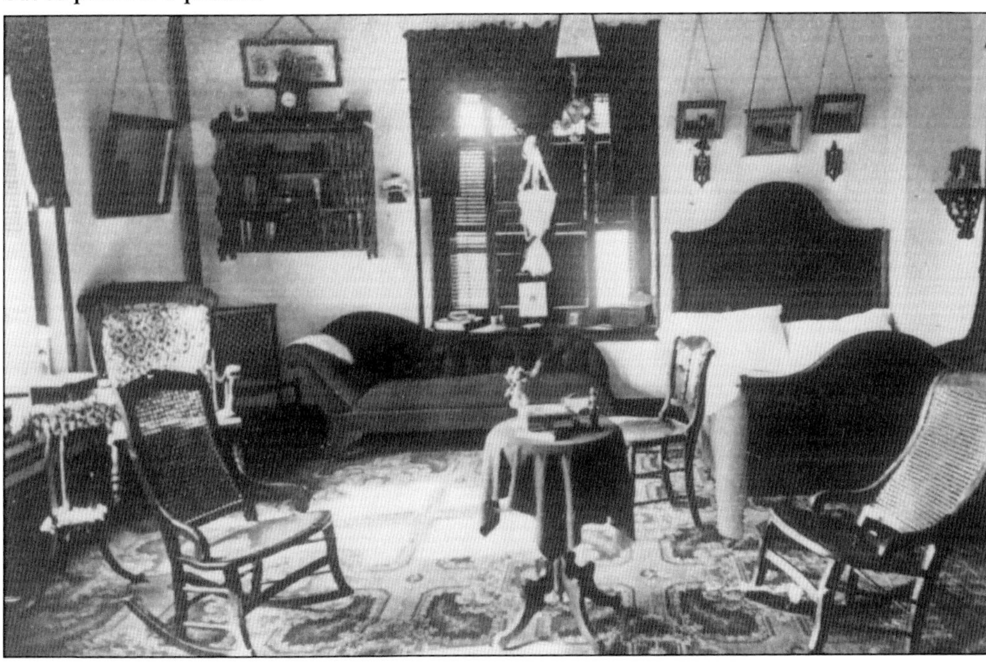

A Student Room, 1877. The Vassar students all lived in Main Building until the 1890s, when there was an exodus to new dormitories. One of the residents of this room was Caroline Swift, who graduated in 1877. In 1900, Caroline Swift (Atwater) gave Swift Infirmary to the college in honor of her father, a charter trustee. A few years earlier, her husband, Edward Atwater, gave a mastodon to the college's museum.

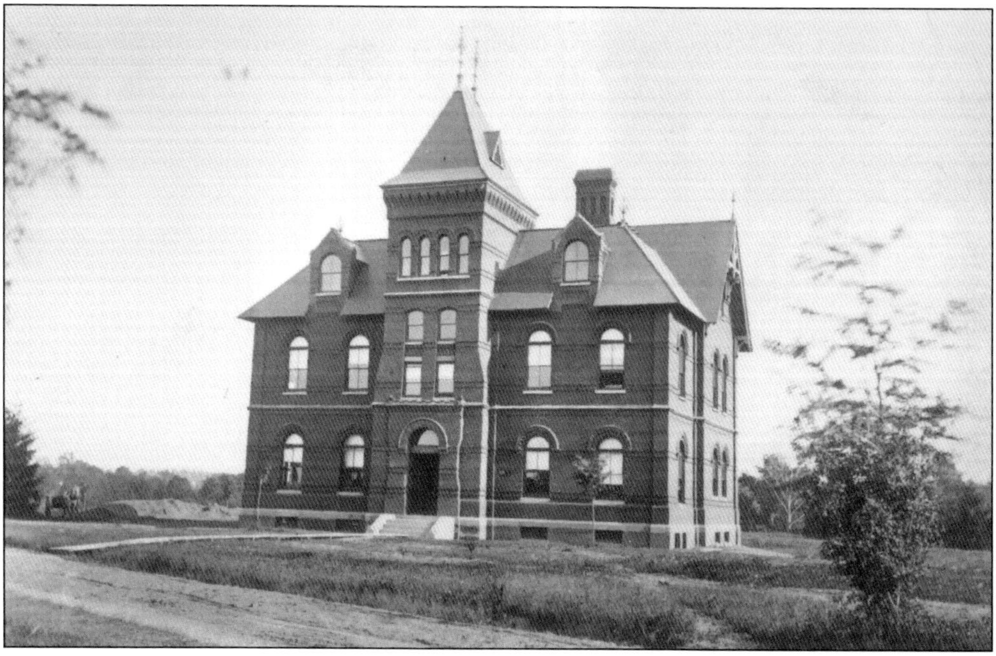

Vassar Brothers Laboratory, 1880. Vassar Brothers Laboratory was the first classroom building (other than the observatory and Main Building) and was the first separate laboratory building at a college for women. It was a relief to the authorities to get the overcrowded science classes with their fumes and burners out of Main Building's dark ground floor. The building housed the psychology and economics departments after it was vacated by chemistry and physics. It was razed in 1938.

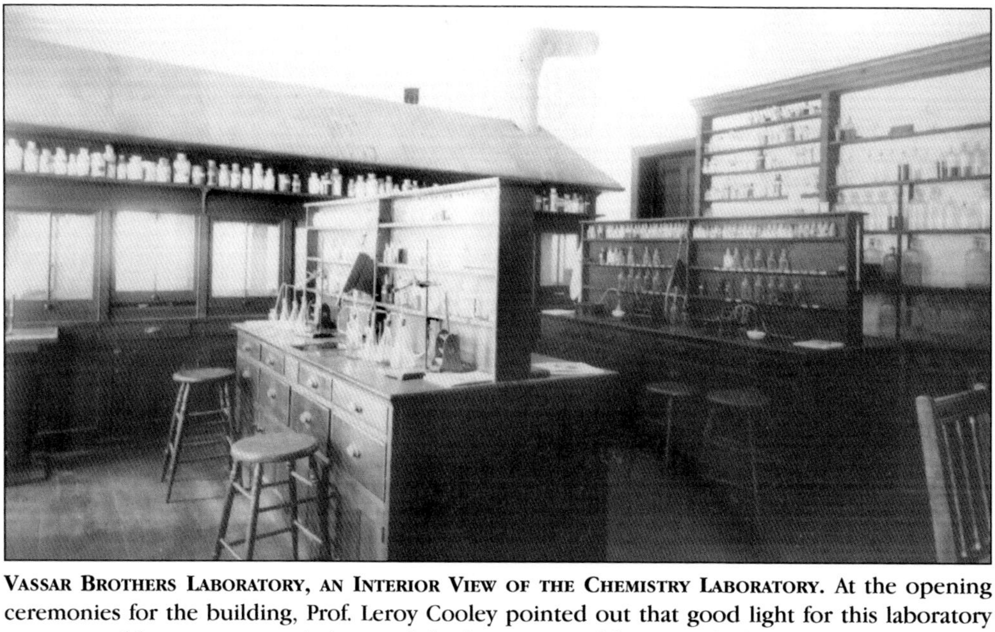

Vassar Brothers Laboratory, an Interior View of the Chemistry Laboratory. At the opening ceremonies for the building, Prof. Leroy Cooley pointed out that good light for this laboratory was secured by numerous windows, while the previous laboratory had used gaslight. He also noted that good air was ensured by a series of flues and ventilating chambers and that 62 working tables were supplied with reagent and specimen bottles.

Florence M. Cushing (Class of 1874). Florence Cushing was retroactively named to Phi Beta Kappa when the Vassar chapter, Mu of New York State, was admitted to national membership in 1898, a trendsetting admission for women's colleges. Cushing also studied at the Massachusetts Institute of Technology and Radcliffe. She was the librarian at Vassar from 1874 to 1876 and was one of Vassar's first alumnae trustees.

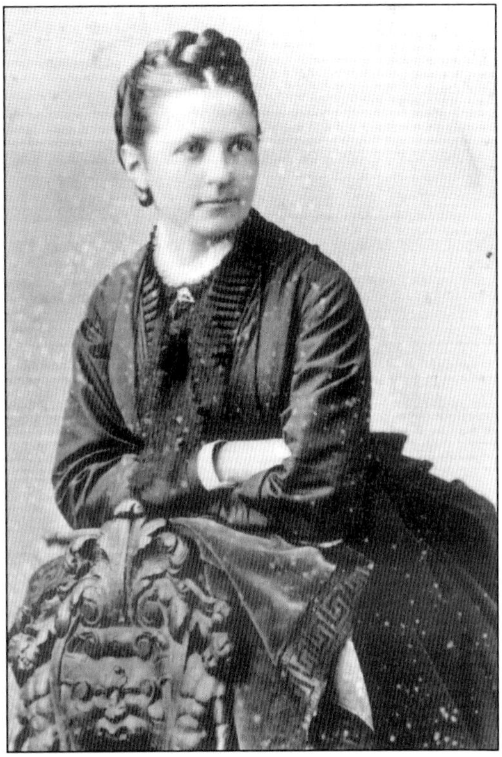

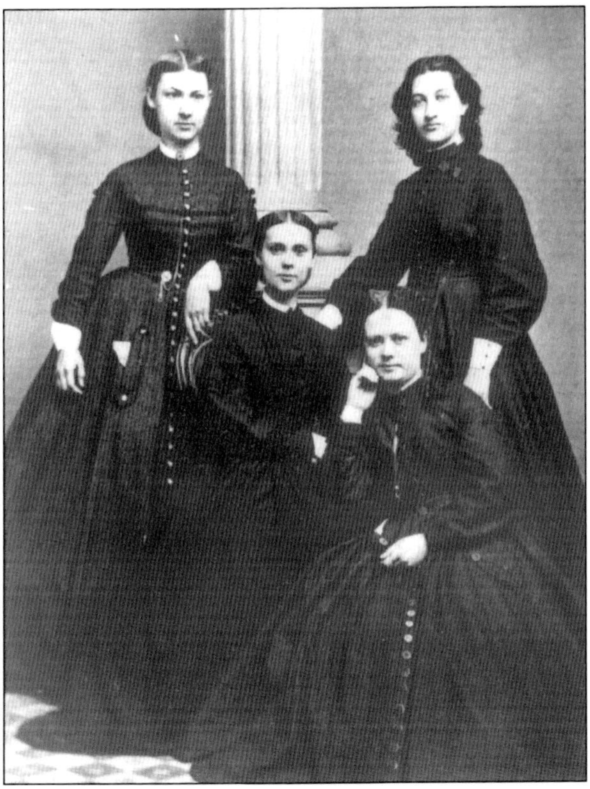

Early Preparatory and Regular Students. Many of the college's early students were not able to pass the entrance exams, which were administered after they arrived. President Raymond said that only about one-third of the earliest students were adequately prepared for college work. Seen here, from left to right, are (seated) Louise Blatchley (Class of 1868) and Ella Stevens (Class of 1865–66); (standing) Sarah Glaser (Class of 1868) and Isabel Treadwell (Class of 1865–66).

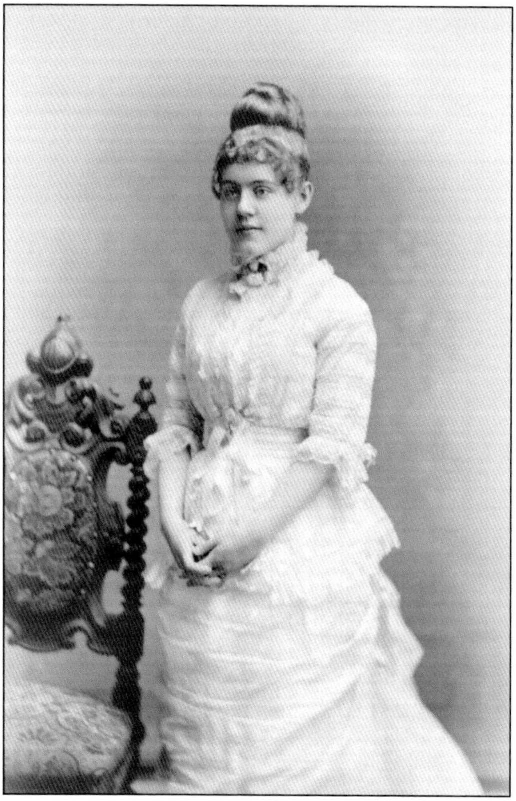

Early Students. The college developed preparatory work for the two-thirds of the student body who did not qualify for regular status. The students moved into the regular college program only after they were able to pass the exams. In 1890, the college was finally able to give up the preparatory division. These photographs demonstrate the attention to fashionable hairstyles and costume often shown when students were dressed up, as on the occasion of having a picture taken. Yet the lady principal's rules encouraged simplicity in everyday dress.

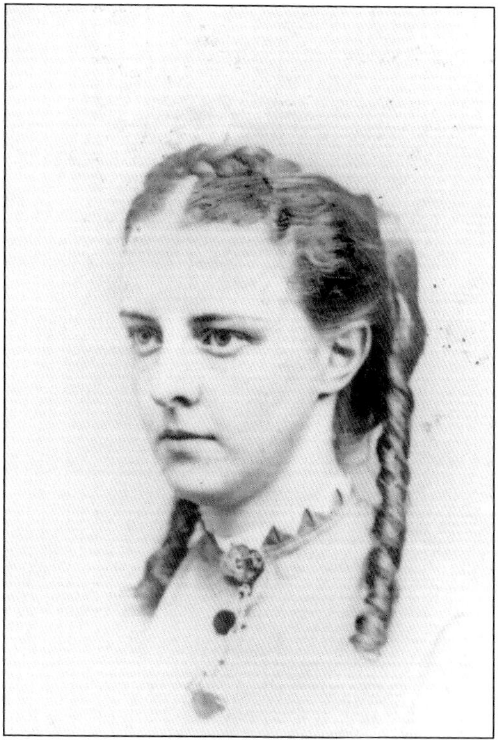

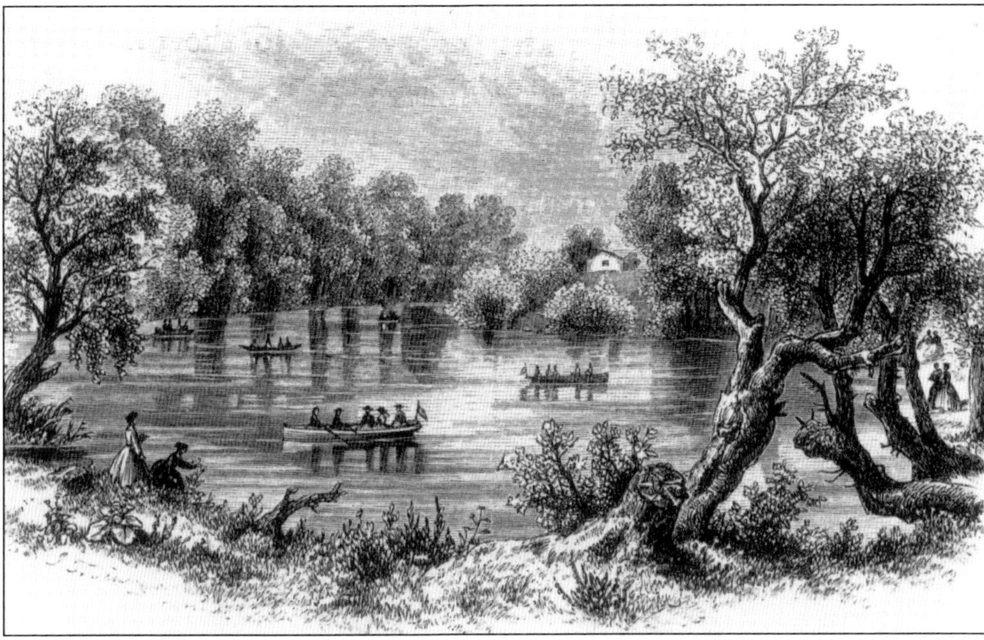

MILL COVE LAKE IN SUMMER. One of the attractions to the site chosen for the college buildings was the proximity to the spring-fed Mill Cove Lake, later called Vassar Lake. The students used the lake for boating in the spring and fall and for skating in the winter. The college's water supply was pumped from the lake to tanks at the top of Main Building, and ice was cut from the lake for domestic refrigeration.

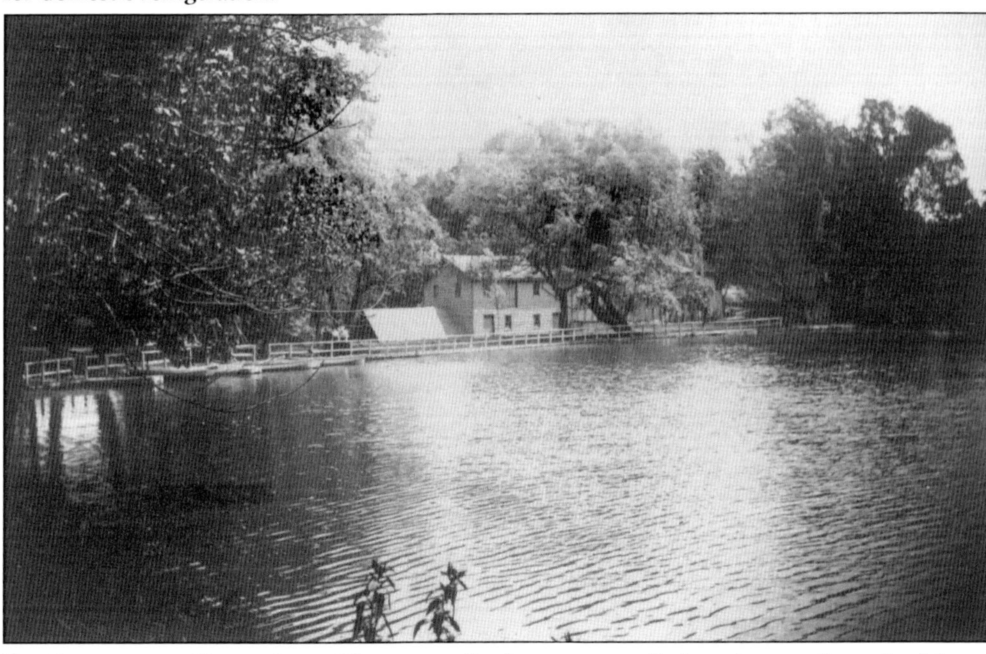

THE ICEHOUSE ON VASSAR LAKE. The steward's department relied on ice cut from the lake to refrigerate the college's food. The ice was stored in this icehouse and then transported to the service area of the steward's department in the cellar of Main Building. Conflicts sometimes arose between the students' interest in smooth skating and the steward's need to have a cold cellar.

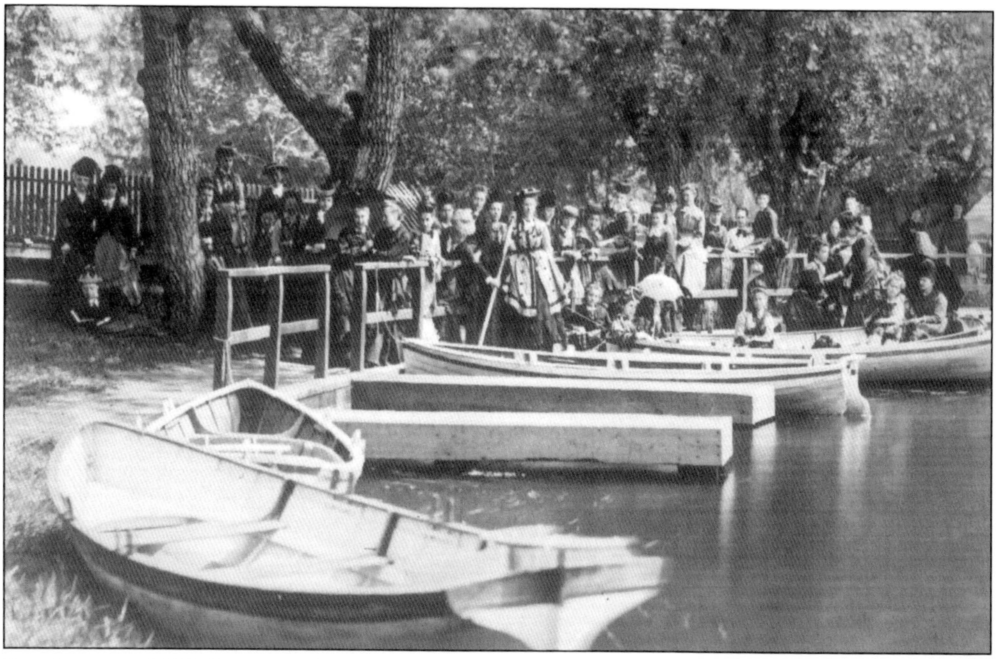

THE CLASS OF 1873 POSED BY BOATS AT VASSAR LAKE. Boating was a preferred activity despite the special charge of 50¢ for using the rowboats. In 1867, boat club members competed in flat-bottomed boats called *Dido, Feather, Juanita, Verdant, Maid of the Mist, Undine, Lady of the Lake, Water Witch,* and *Aureole.*

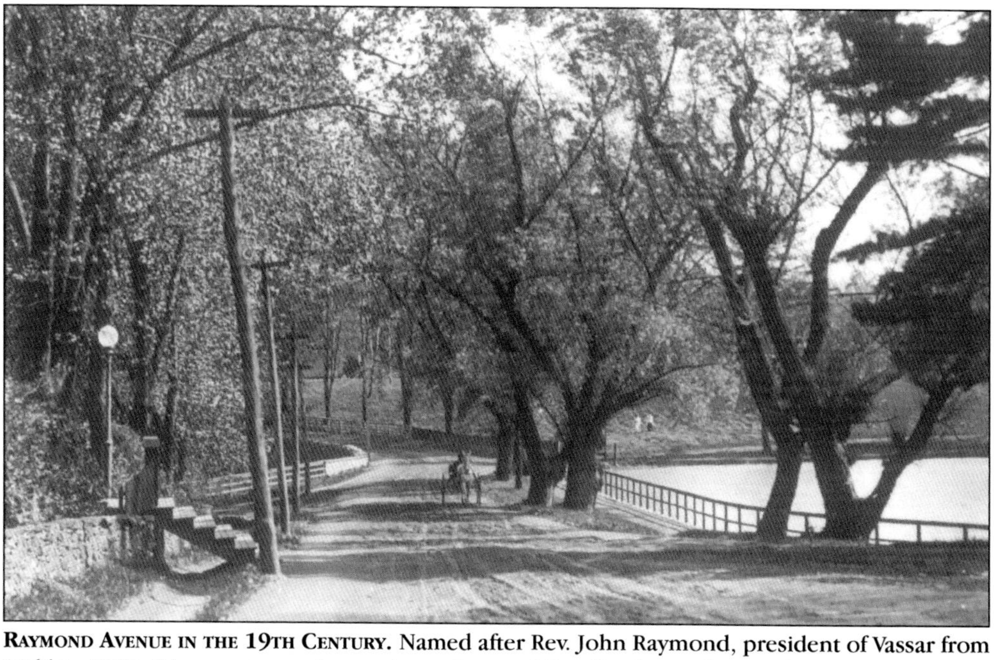

RAYMOND AVENUE IN THE 19TH CENTURY. Named after Rev. John Raymond, president of Vassar from 1864 to 1878, this country road served as a thoroughfare for the student walks that were part of required daily exercise. In later years, it accommodated the trolley cars that transported students from the Gate Lodge to town. It was not exclusively a college road, however, as it also led to Red Oaks Mills, a community to the southeast.

The Resolutes, June 1876. Baseball was introduced to Vassar in the early years. Played by soldiers during the Civil War, the game became popular among women, and Vassar students organized a team right away. Several Vassar baseball clubs existed, among them the Sure-Pops, the Daisy-Clippers, and the Royals. The Resolutes are pictured here in June 1876. They are, from left to right, as follows: (front row) S. Sheppard, Gertie Crane, Mollie Dickey, Maud Gould, and May Bryan; (back row) May Gardner, unidentified, Mollie Woodward, and Ada Thurston.

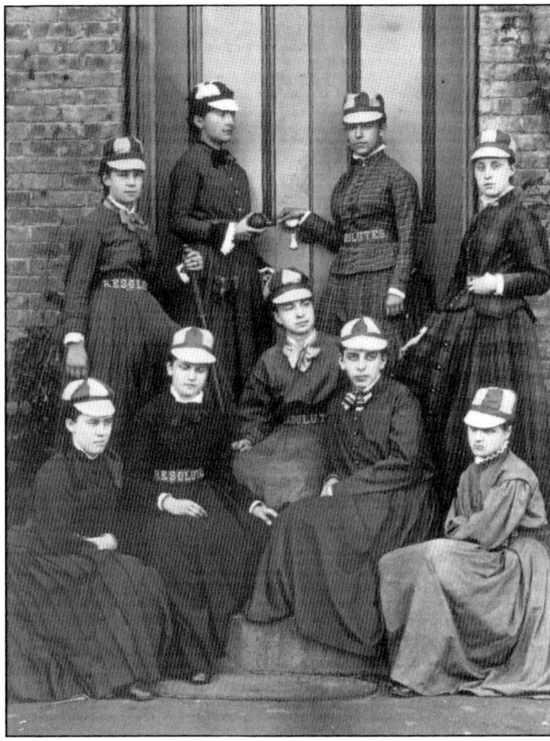

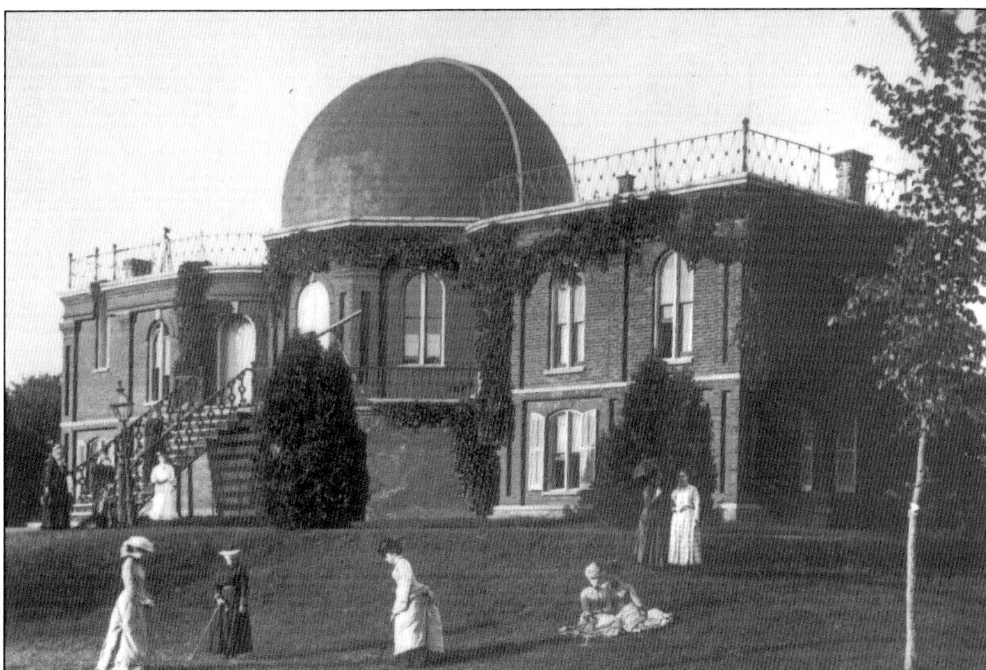

Croquet in Front of the Observatory. Croquet was popular at Vassar College in the 19th century and was often played in front of the observatory. Tennis, which was introduced in 1879, was also in vogue. In 1886, Adeline McKinley (Class of 1888) organized a tennis tournament in the athletic circle, giving gold medals to the winners.

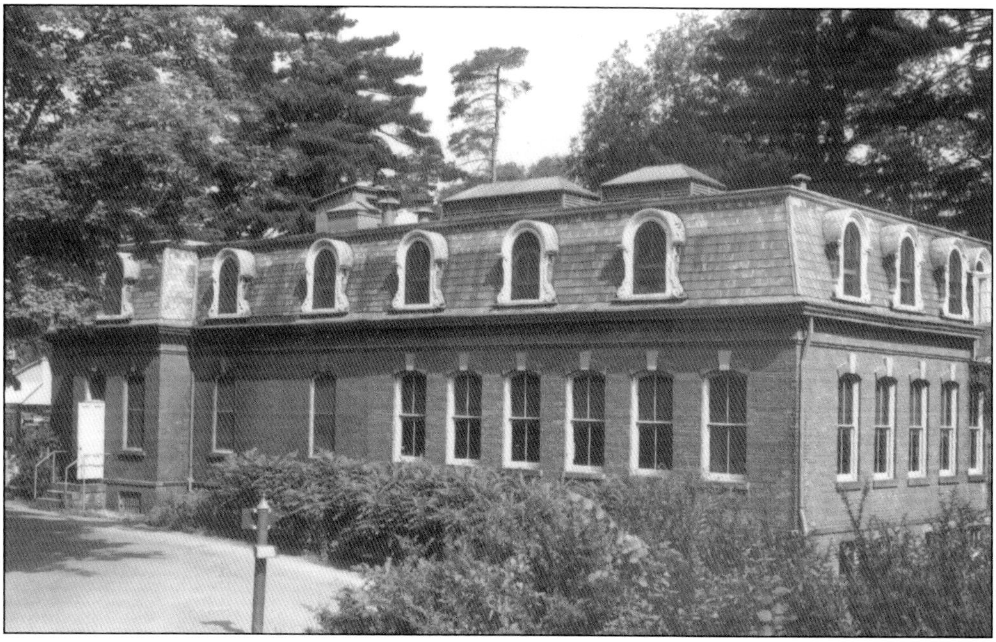

THE LAUNDRY. Completed in 1872, the laundry was added to the college's original buildings out of sheer necessity. At the same time, additions were made to the Main Building kitchen and the dining hall. James Post, who erected the Pardee Block on the corner of Main and Garden Streets in the city of Poughkeepsie, was the architect.

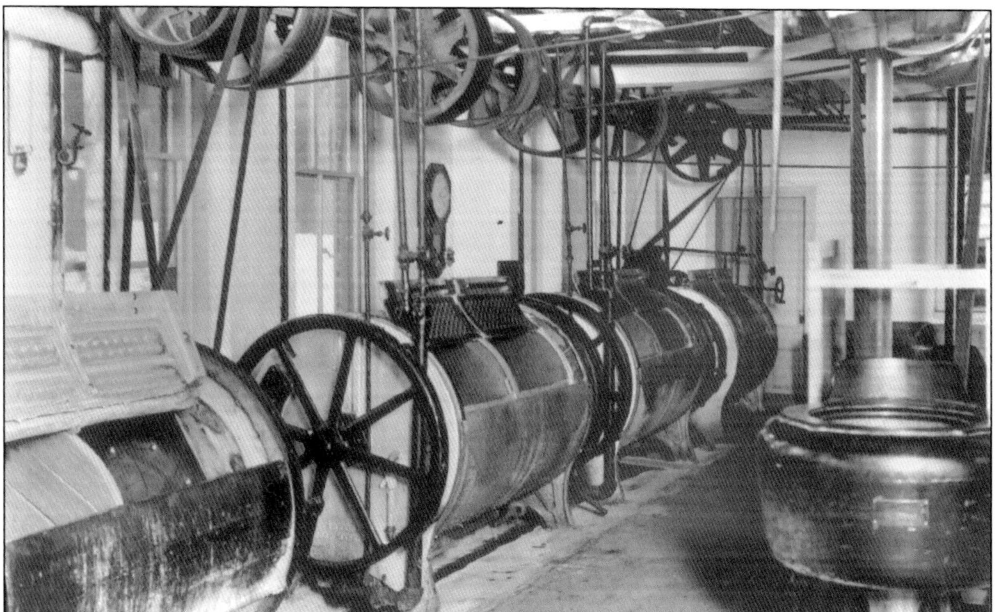

THE INTERIOR OF THE LAUNDRY. The whole college community used the laundry. Until well into the 20th century, many of the dining room servants doubled as clothes bundlers in the laundry, folding the clothes and returning them to their owners. Laundry lists and charge books in the college's archives testify to the intricacies of the operation. The building has been converted for use by the computer science department and the development office in recent years.

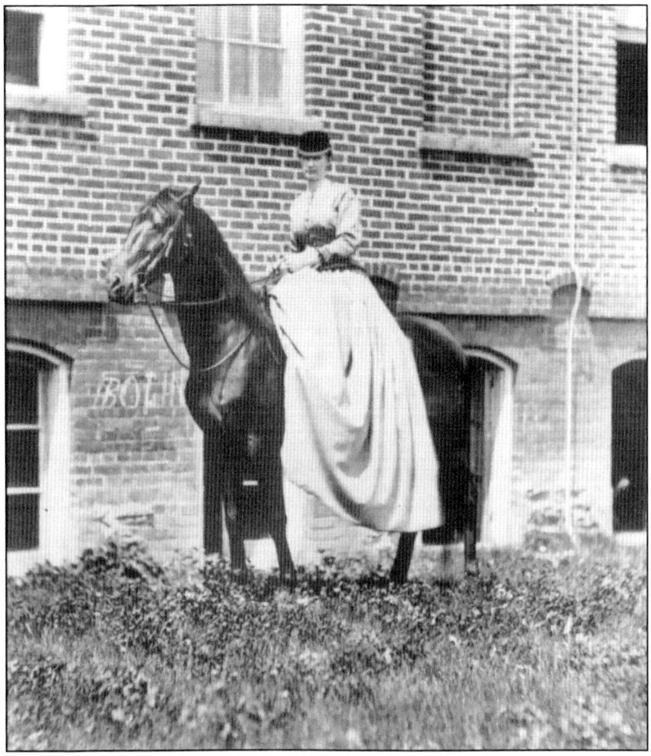

Baroness von Seldeneck, Teacher of Riding. Although she received little mention in history for her labors, Baroness von Seldeneck probably joined her husband in teaching riding in 1866. Unfortunately, we have no picture of Baron Leopold von Seldeneck, who had been a cavalry officer in the Prussian army and had served also in the Civil War. The Riding Academy was closed in 1872 because it proved too expensive. Many of the paths that were originally riding paths have left their traces on the campus.

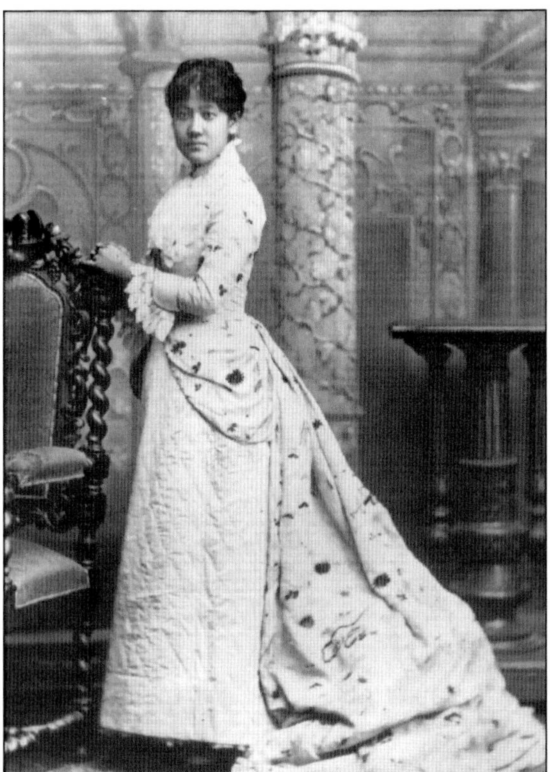

Stematz Yamakawa, Vassar College's First Foreign Graduate, 1882. Stematz Yamakawa came to this country in 1871 as part of a group of five Japanese children sent to the United States at government expense to receive an American education. After living in the household of Rev. Leonard Bacon in New Haven, Connecticut (where she prepared for Vassar and learned English), she came to the college in September 1878. She was elected president of the Class of 1882 and graduated with honors. She later returned to her country, married Prince Oyama, and thereafter led a traditional Japanese life.

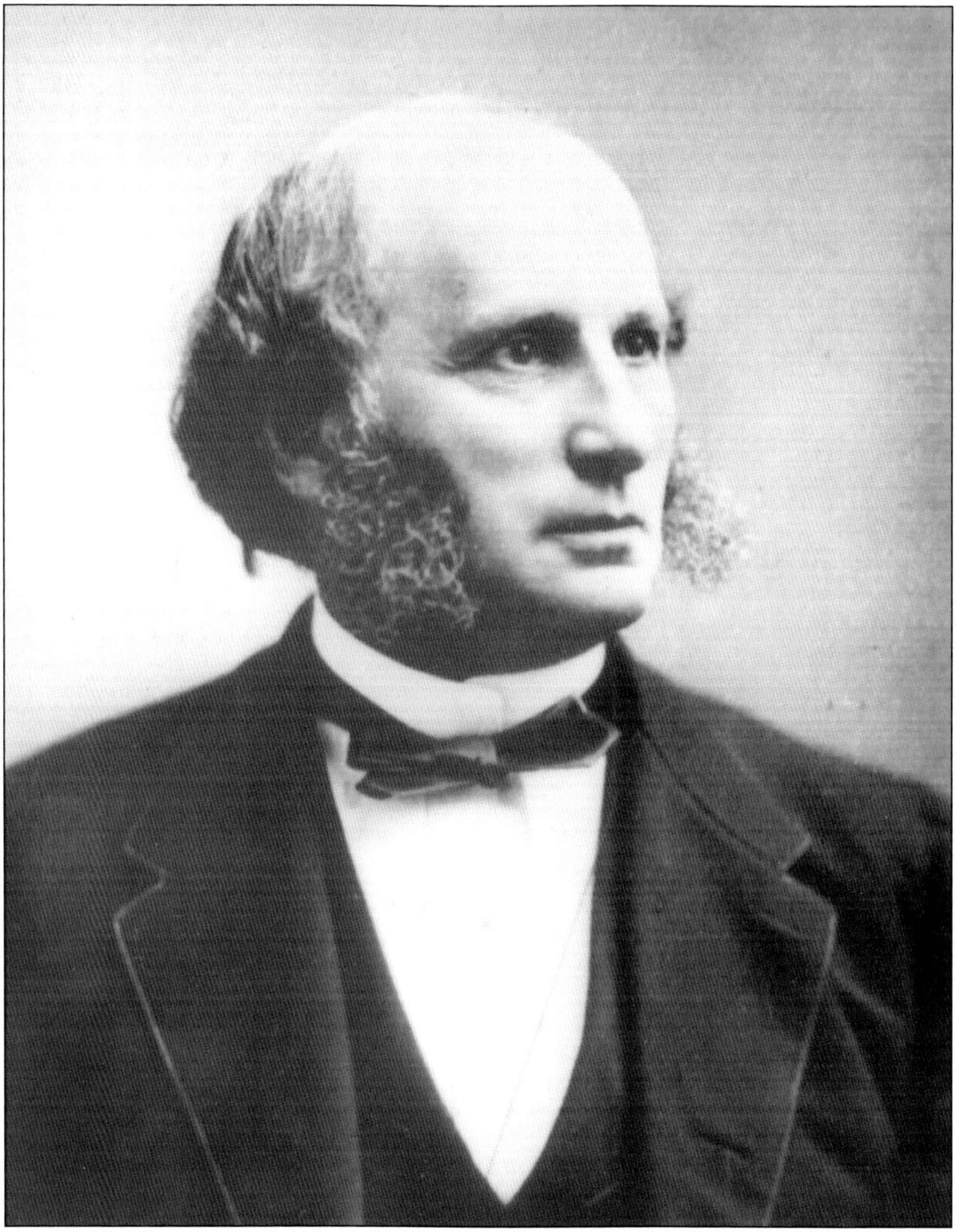

Rev. Samuel L. Caldwell (1878–1885). After President Raymond died in the summer of 1878, the trustees elected one of their members, Samuel Caldwell, as president. At the time of his election, Caldwell was professor of church history at the Newton Theological Seminary. The newly organized Vassar alumnae became increasingly critical of Caldwell's administration. They feared that he was not doing enough to attract qualified students to Vassar in the light of growing competition from other women's colleges, which by the 1880s offered a larger variety of educational opportunities. On June 9, 1885, the trustees accepted Caldwell's resignation and appointed one of their number, James Ryland Kendrick, as acting president while they looked for a new president.

Two

Consolidating and Expanding: 1886–1914

Under the administration of James Monroe Taylor (1886–1914), the college entered upon its first expansive period. By the late 1880s, the college was in need of funds, and President Taylor embarked upon Vassar's first fundraising campaign to increase the endowment. As funds became available, Taylor was able to carry through his plans for modernization.

Taylor's administration was notable for the building expansion on campus. Vassar had opened its doors to 353 students in 1865. By the end of Taylor's long tenure, the enrollment had grown to 1,000. When Main Building could no longer provide adequate space for students and faculty, the trustees agreed to build a new dormitory. Strong House, the first of four residential halls that form the quadrangle, was erected in 1893 and was soon followed by Raymond, Lathrop, and Davison. Between 1895 and 1913, five additional buildings were erected on campus: Rockefeller Hall (a much needed academic building), a home for the president, the library, the chapel, and Students' Building. By the beginning of the 20th century, the college had abandoned the idea that an educational institution for women should be under one roof.

In 1903, a more liberal curriculum was established. The number of elective courses was also increased, and course offerings were enriched. There were many firsts at Vassar during President Taylor's administration: team sports were formalized; the Vassar Student Association was granted limited governing powers; and the first women's field day in the country was celebrated on campus. In 1898, President Taylor's efforts to preserve Vassar's preeminence were rewarded when the Mu chapter of Phi Beta Kappa was chartered at Vassar, the first chapter at a college for women. In 1888, student financial aid was introduced through the generosity of two trustees, thus enabling the college to give employment and loans to needy students.

By 1914, at the end of President Taylor's tenure, Vassar College's place in history in the education of women was well established.

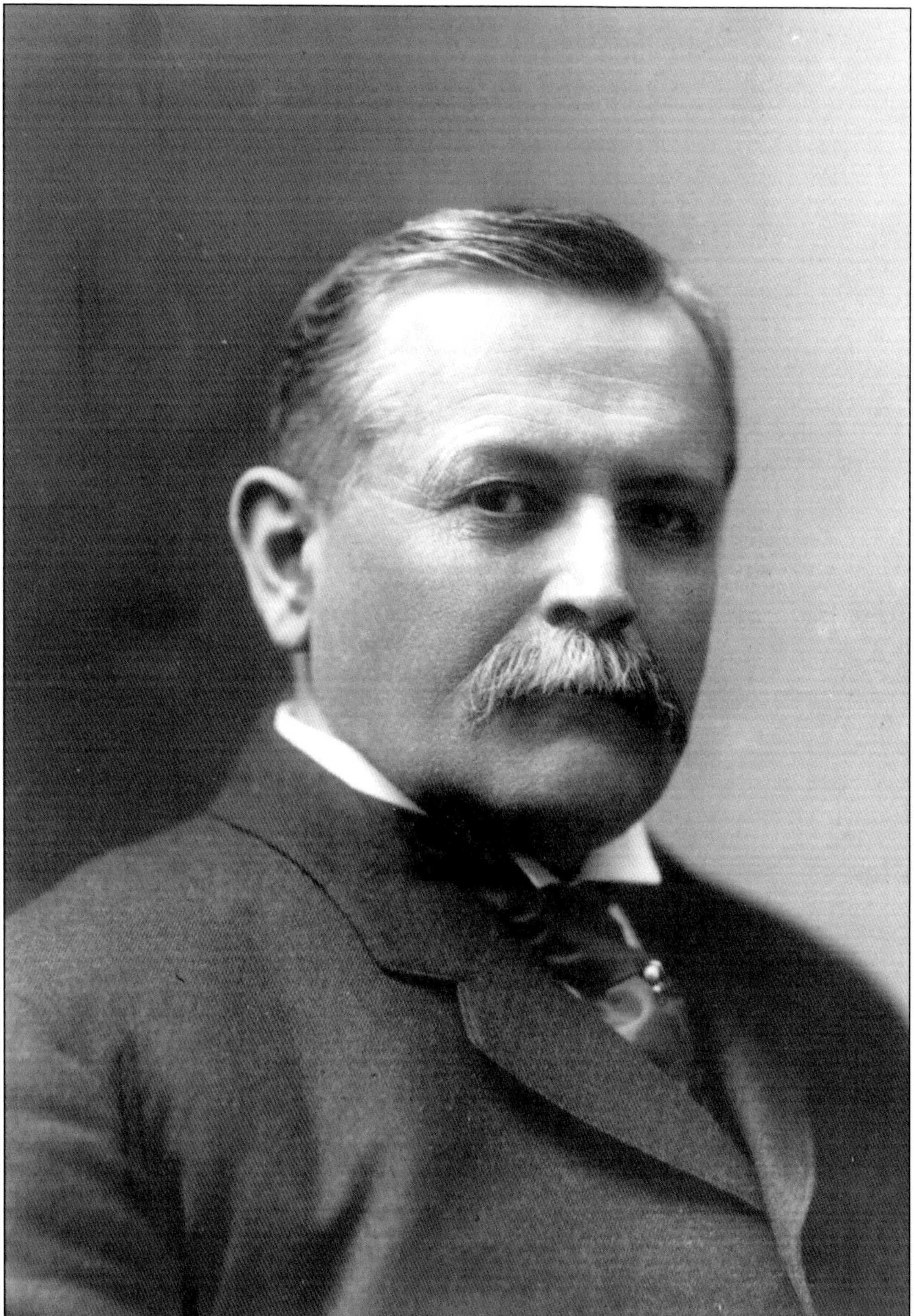

James Monroe Taylor (1886–1914). Dr. Taylor, a graduate of Rochester University, earned his doctor of divinity degree from the Rochester Theological Seminary. He was the pastor of the fourth Baptist church in Providence when he accepted the presidency at Vassar in 1886.

J. Ryland Kendrick, Acting President. Following the resignation of President Caldwell, the Reverend J. Ryland Kendrick (Vassar trustee from 1875 to 1889) became acting president of Vassar in 1885 while the trustees searched for Caldwell's replacement.

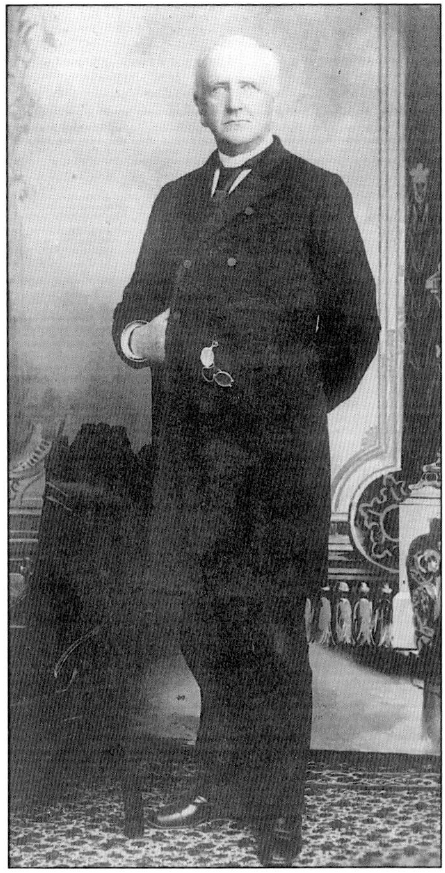

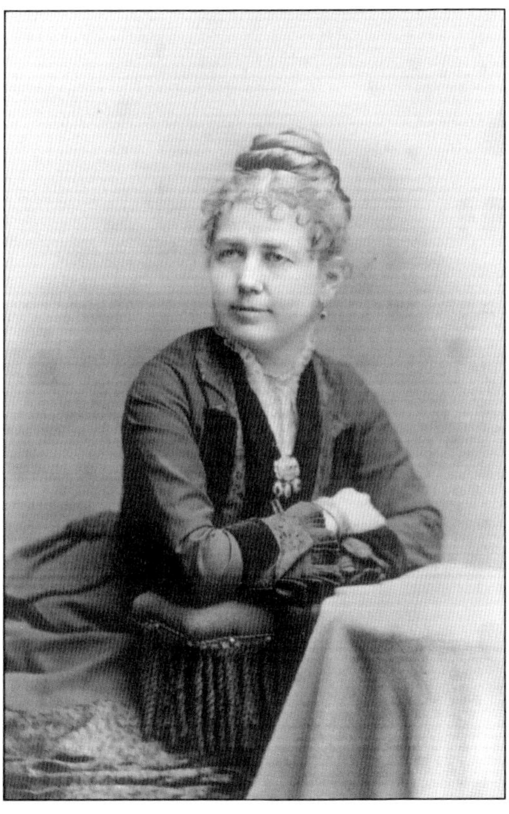

Georgia Avery Kendrick. Georgia Avery Kendrick was lady principal of Vassar from 1891 to 1913. This photograph was taken for her husband, J. Ryland Kendrick, before their marriage. As lady principal, Kendrick was responsible for at least two innovations. Since her voice did not carry well, she placed a bulletin board outside the dining room in Main Building for announcements. Also, since she had neuritis and wrote with her left hand, she had a special typewriter made with the keys slanted backwards. There had not been typewriting machines in the Vassar offices until then. Using a pen name, Kendrick wrote novels on her typewriter.

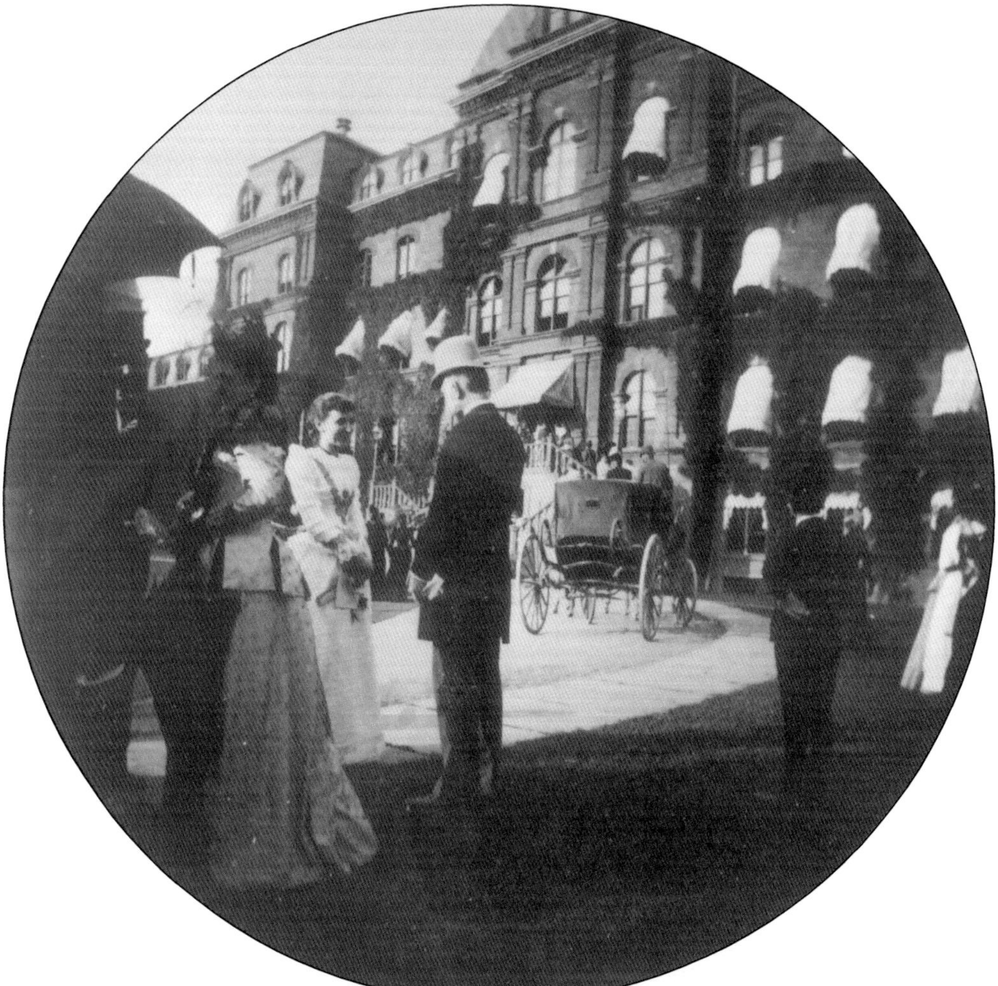

Main Building. With its ivy-covered walls and canopied windows, Main Building is captured in a moment in time on Class Day in 1891. The seniors, dressed in white, held their exercises in the old chapel in Main. The mode of transportation was by carriage, and entrance to the building was via the double-sided staircase. The awnings were on the president's house, which occupied three stories to the right of the portico.

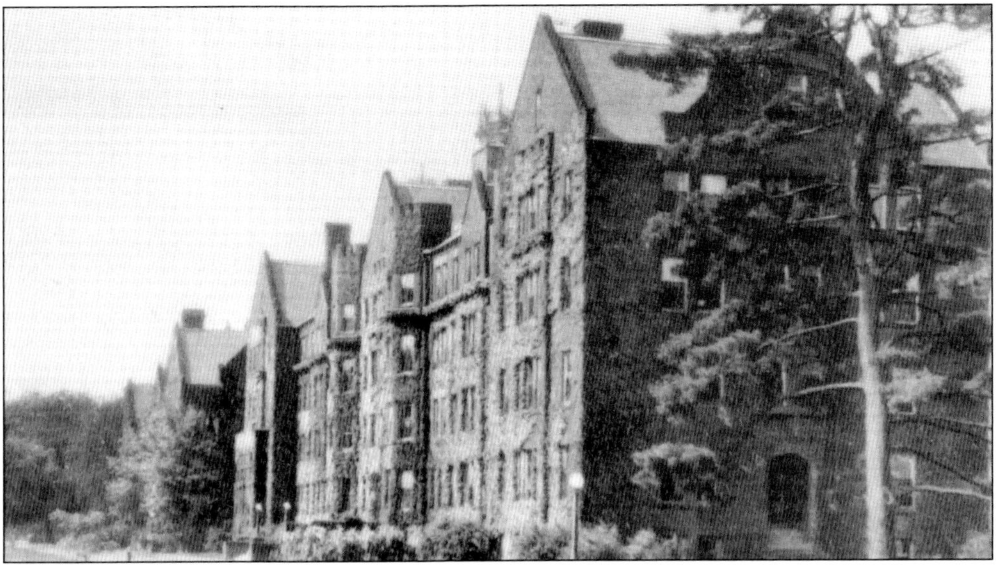

THE DORMITORY QUAD. The four residential halls comprising the quad are Davison House (1902), Raymond House (1897), Lathrop House (1901), and Strong Hall (1893). Strong was the first residence hall and quad house on the Vassar campus. John D. Rockefeller, a trustee at Vassar from 1888 to 1905, helped pay for construction of the building and named the house after his daughter, Bessie Rockefeller Strong. In memory of his mother, he also gave the funds for Eliza Davison House. Raymond House, named in honor of Vassar's second president, Dr. John H. Raymond, was built with college funds and was designed by architect Francis R. Allen. Edward Lathrop House (Allen & Vance, architects) was built with college funds and named in honor of Dr. Lathrop, a charter trustee. Students memorized the names of the buildings by affectionately referring to them as "Dear Robert Louis Stevenson."

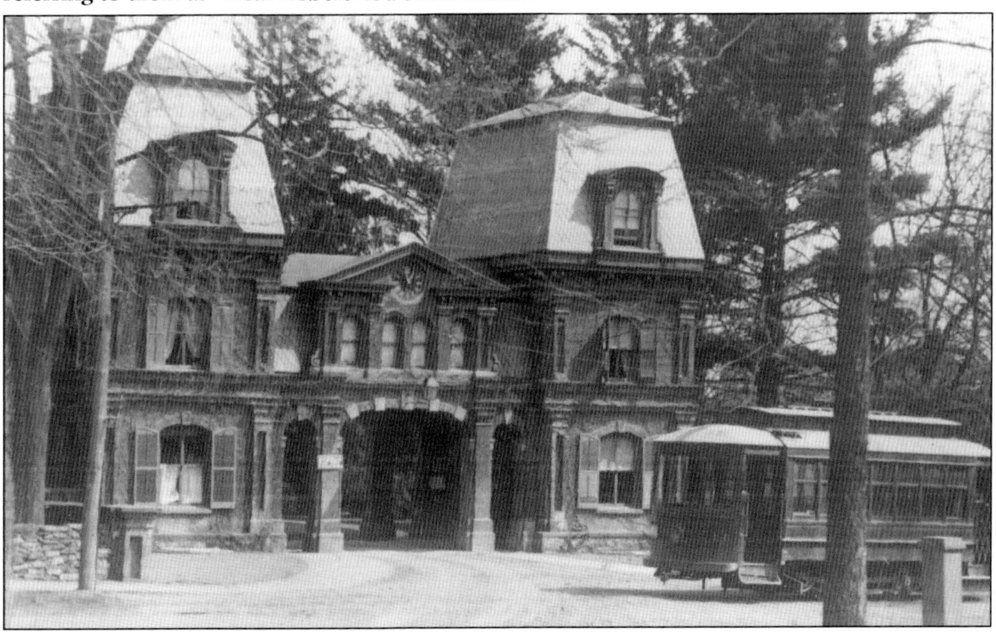

THE ADVENT OF THE TROLLEY CAR. The trolley car appeared on the scene in 1873, making local travel for students easier. Pictured here are the Gate Lodge and trolley as seen from Raymond Avenue.

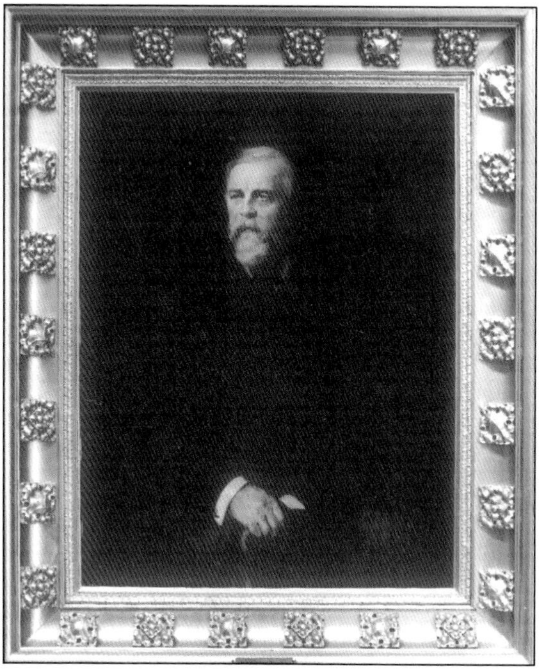

Frederick Ferris Thompson. Serving as a trustee from 1885 to 1899, Frederick Ferris Thompson, affectionately known as "the good times trustee," was a generous benefactor and friend to the college. Vassar's library, built in 1905, was the gift of his widow, Mary Clark Thompson.

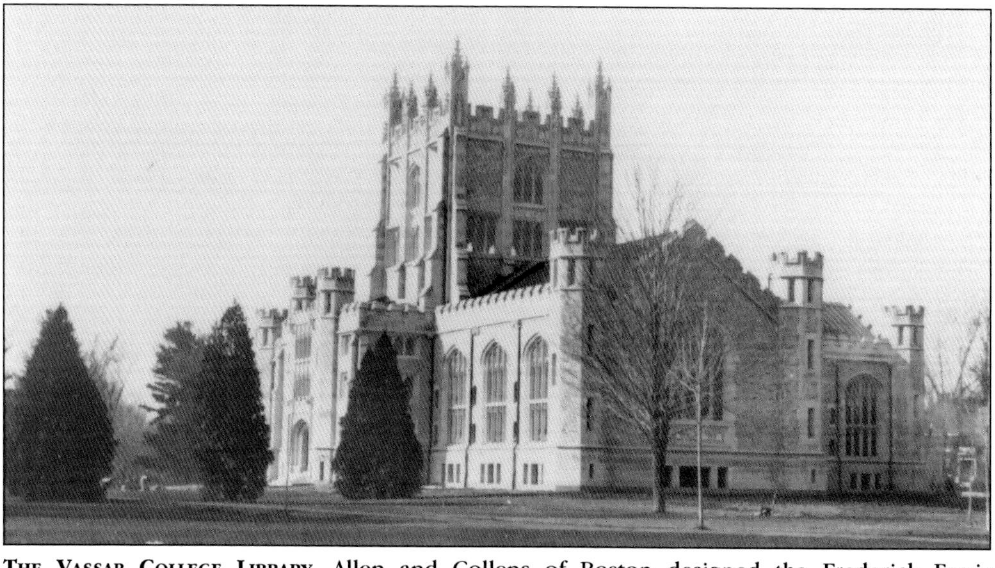

The Vassar College Library. Allen and Collens of Boston designed the Frederick Ferris Thompson Memorial Library in 1905 in a Gothic Perpendicular style. Serving as the centerpiece of Vassar's library system, this building has an exterior of Germantown granite and an interior of Indiana limestone. Mary Clark Thompson also donated five silk-and-wool, 11-foot-high tapestries that were crafted in the early 17th century in Belgium. The tapestries depict scenes from the ancient Greek myth of Psyche. The library's architect, F.R. Allen, purchased them in Paris in 1904 at Thompson's request. The tapestries were recently cleaned at the Textile Conservation Laboratory at the Cathedral of St. John the Divine in New York City. In August 2000, they were rehung in the library lobby. It was realized at that time that the tapestries had been hung according to the availability of wall space and had never corresponded to the sequence of events in the Psyche story.

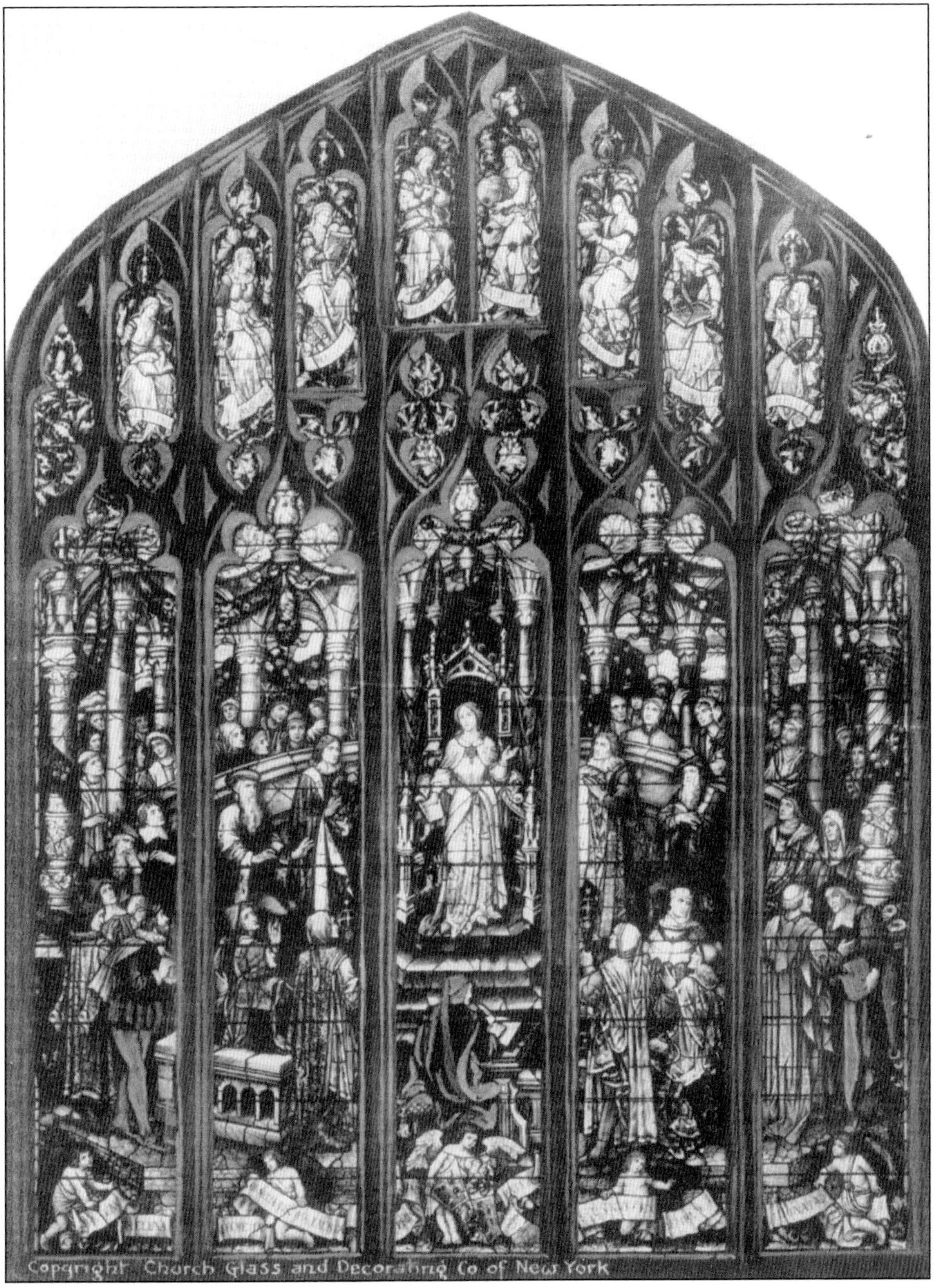

THE CORNARO WINDOW. One of the most notable features of the library is the massive stained-glass window that portrays Elena Lucrezia Cornaro Piscopia receiving her degree from the University of Padua in 1678, the first doctorate awarded to a woman. The window was commissioned by Mary Clark Thompson and installed in 1906. It came from the studios of John Hardman & Company of Birmingham, England, and from the Church Glass Decorating Company of New York. Since Tiffany glass was in vogue in the 1900s and quality Gothic glass was not being produced in the United States, the Church Glass Company placed the order for the Vassar window in England.

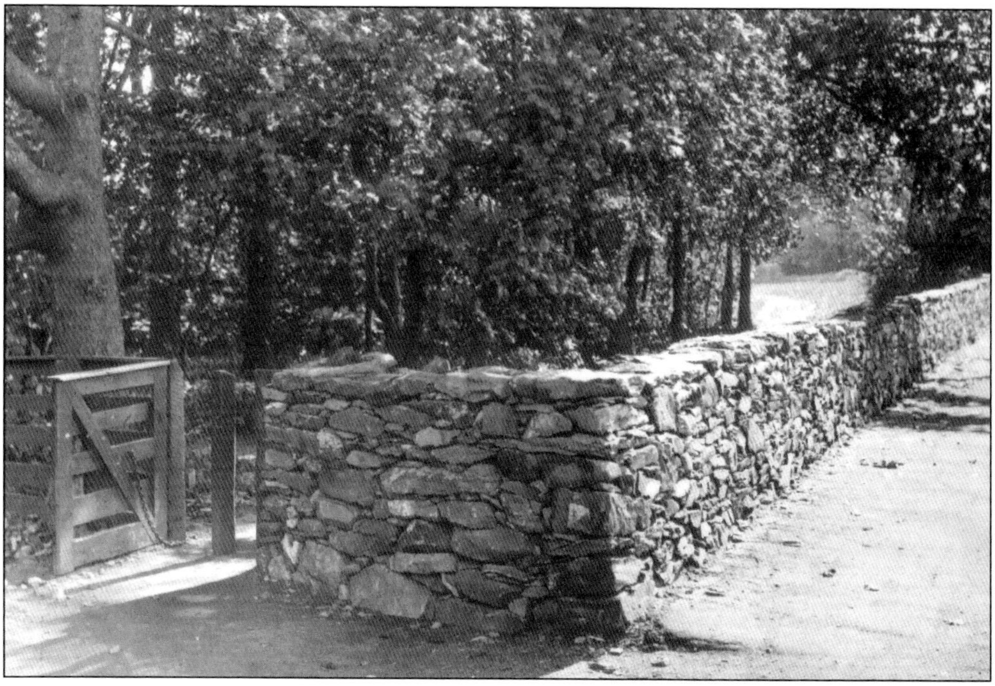

THE STONE GATE. This is the original gate at the corner of Raymond and Collegeview Avenues. It was replaced in June 1931 by a gate honoring Herbert Mills, professor of economics from 1890 to 1931. Professor Mills was director of the Vassar Training Camp for Nurses during World War I.

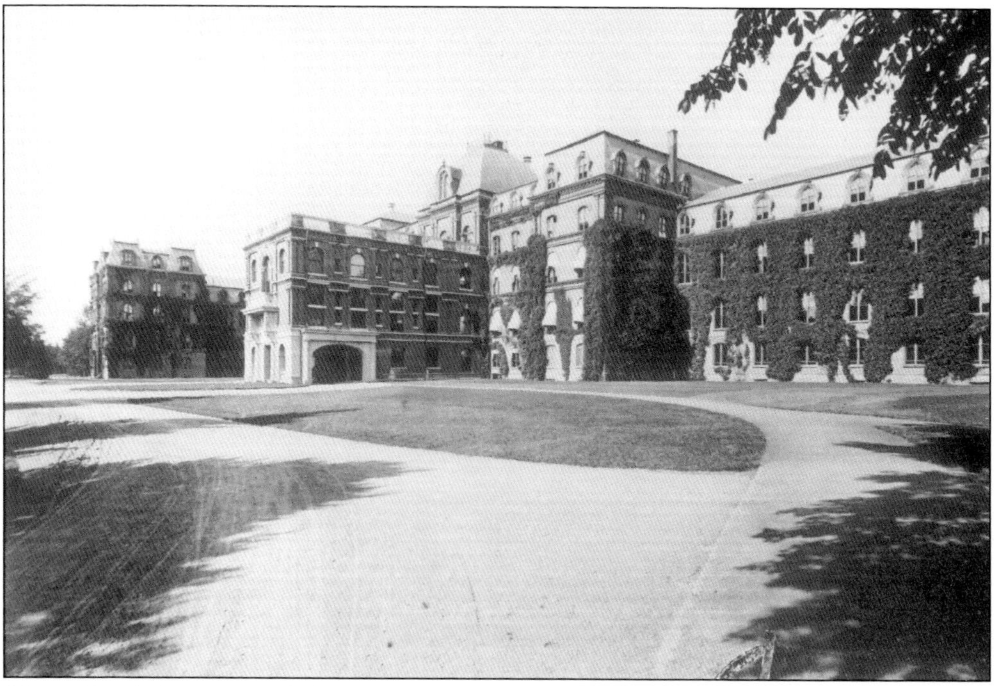

"UNCLE FRED'S NOSE." Popularly known as "Uncle Fred's Nose," the Thompson Annex to Main Building was completed in 1893. The annex, designed by architect Francis R. Allen, was given to the college by trustee Frederick Ferris Thompson to accommodate the expanding library.

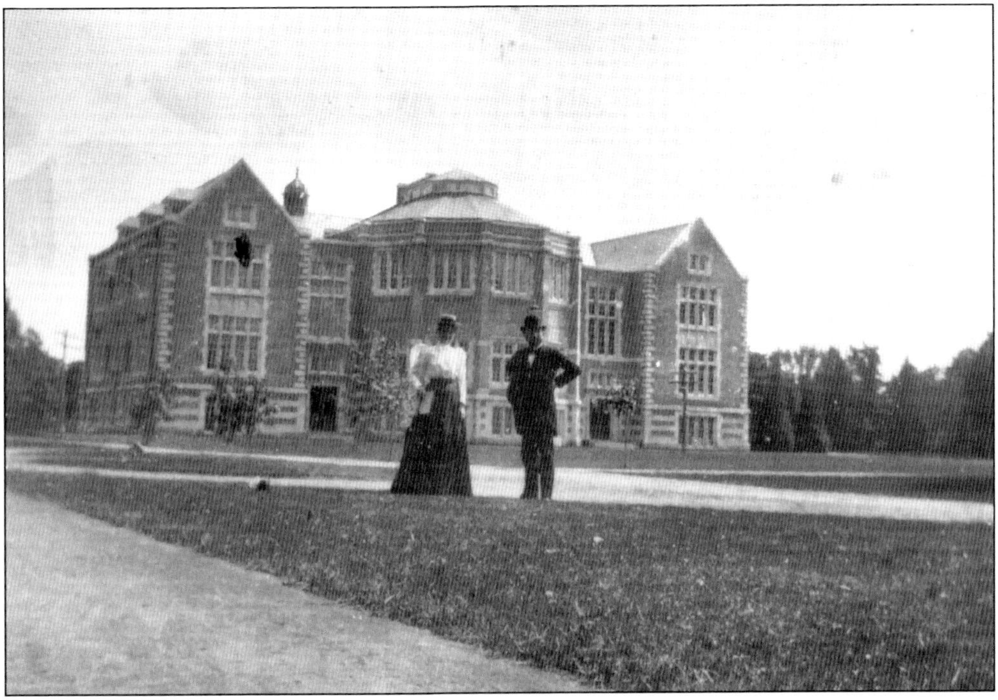

ROCKEFELLER HALL. Rockefeller Hall, dedicated in 1897, was the gift of John D. Rockefeller, who had established a construction goal of $100,000. The story is that the total cost was $99,998.75, thus coming within Rockefeller's limit.

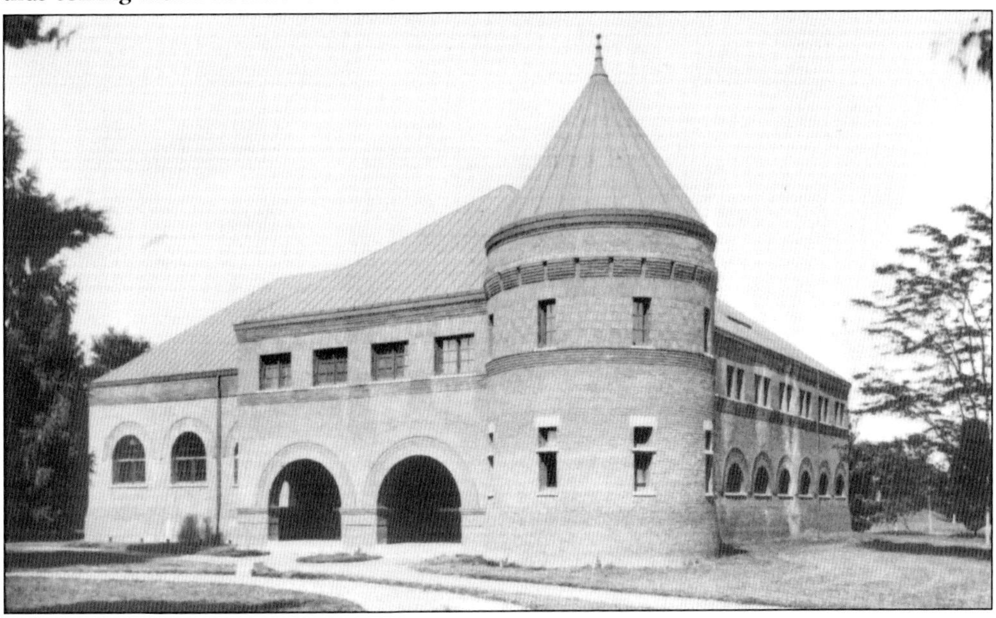

THE ALUMNAE GYMNASIUM. Completed in 1889, the Alumnae Gymnasium was built with funds collected from the alumnae and students under the leadership of Achsah M. Ely (Class of 1868), professor of mathematics from 1887 to 1904. Designed by architect William M. Tubby, the facility included a swimming tank given by trustee Frederick Ferris Thompson. The physical education department was the first regularly recognized department of its kind in an American college.

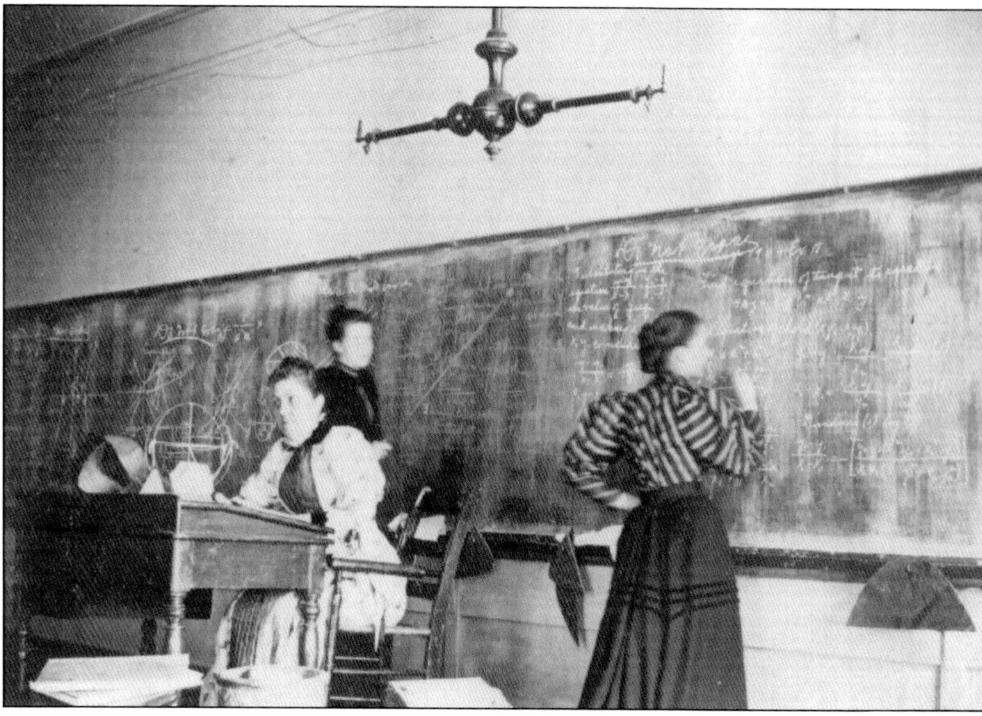

A Mathematics Class, 1895. Mathematics was one of the academic subjects offered when the college began and is listed in the first annual catalogue (1865–66). Achsah M. Ely is pictured here in 1895 instructing her math students.

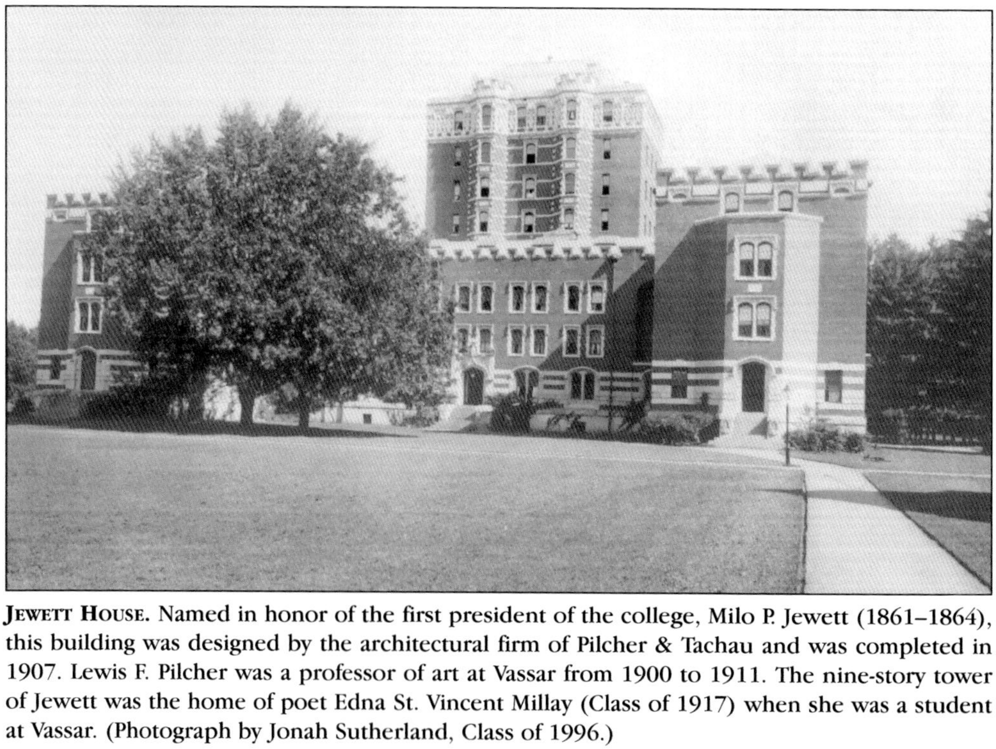

Jewett House. Named in honor of the first president of the college, Milo P. Jewett (1861–1864), this building was designed by the architectural firm of Pilcher & Tachau and was completed in 1907. Lewis F. Pilcher was a professor of art at Vassar from 1900 to 1911. The nine-story tower of Jewett was the home of poet Edna St. Vincent Millay (Class of 1917) when she was a student at Vassar. (Photograph by Jonah Sutherland, Class of 1996.)

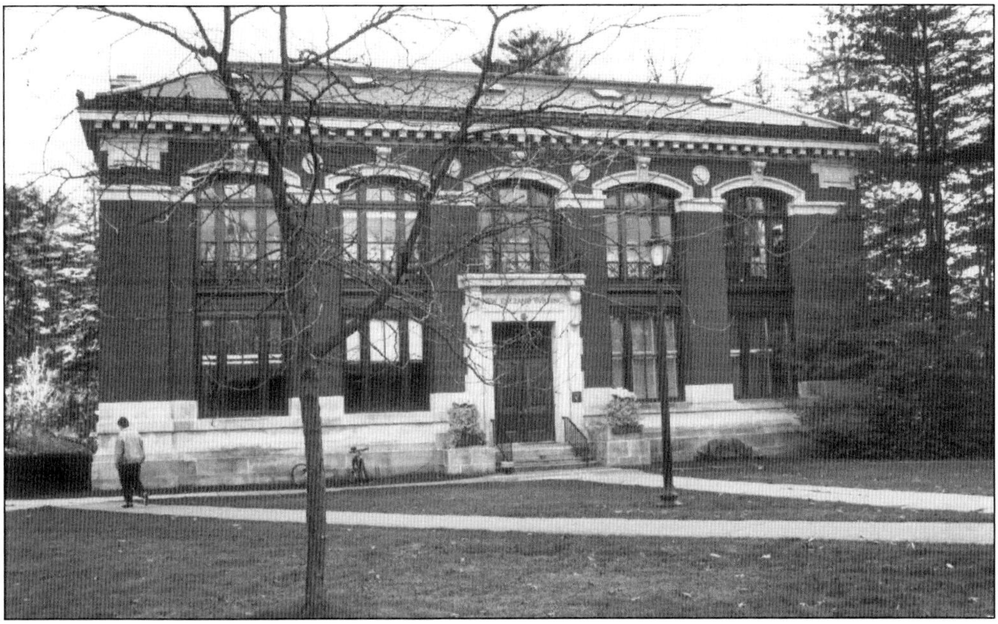

New England Building. New England Building—originally designed for the departments of biology, physiology, geology, and mineralogy—was the gift of the alumnae from New England. Designed by York & Sawyer, it was completed in 1901. A small fragment of Plymouth Rock is embedded in the face of the building above the main door. (Photograph by Diane Zucker.)

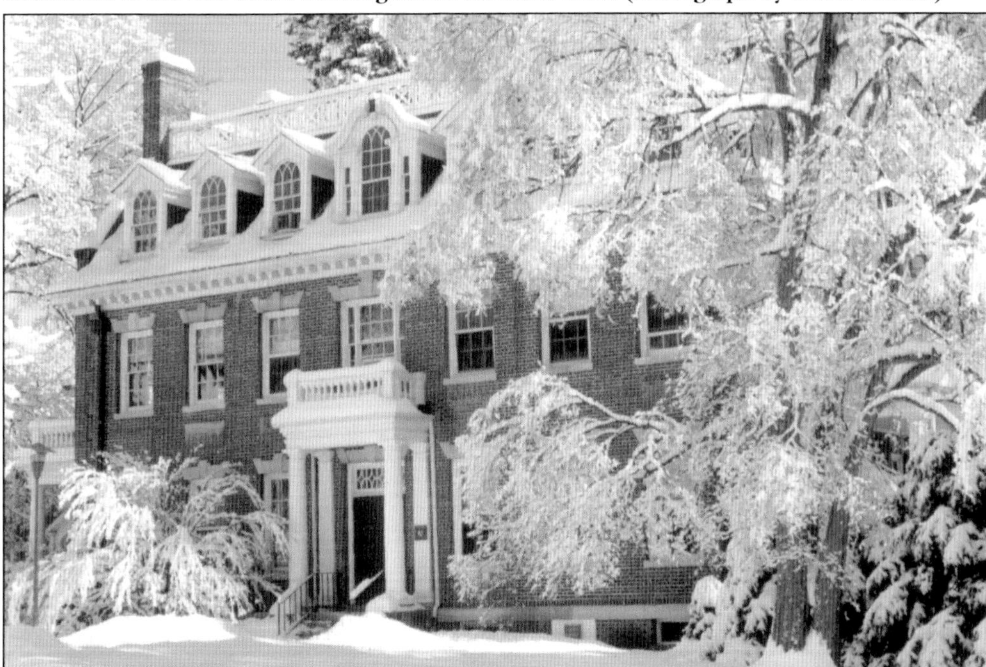

Swift Hall. Originally named Swift Memorial Hall, this building was designed by York & Sawyer and was completed in 1900. Caroline Swift Atwater (Class of 1877) gave it in memory of her father, Charles W. Swift, a charter trustee. The building, originally used as the college infirmary, has been the home of the history department since the 1940s. (Photograph by Sylvia Whitman.)

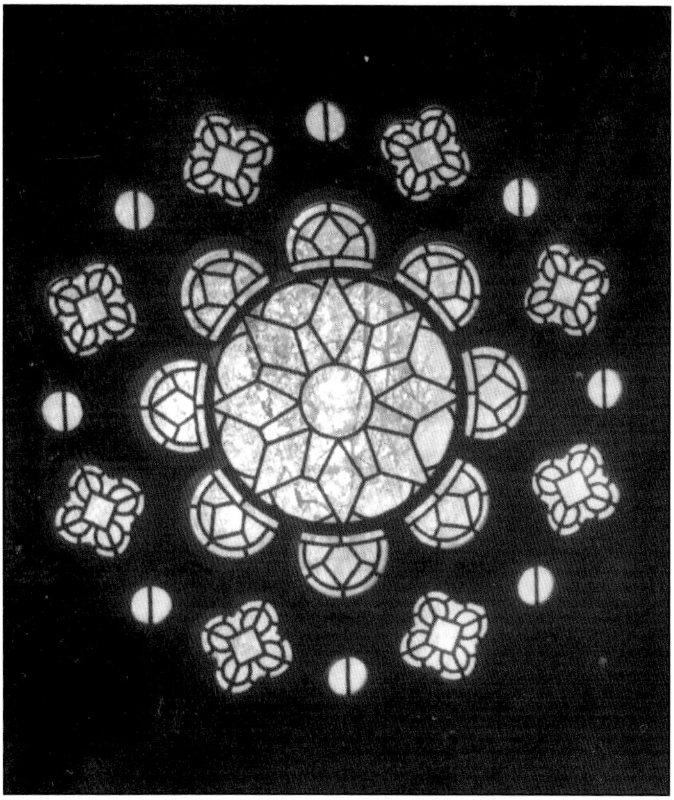

The Rose Window, Tiffany, 1906. Studded with glass jewels, the window (which must be seen *in situ* in the chapel to be appreciated) was a gift from the trustees on the completion of the 20th year of President Taylor's administration (1886–1906). (Courtesy John Lane Studio.)

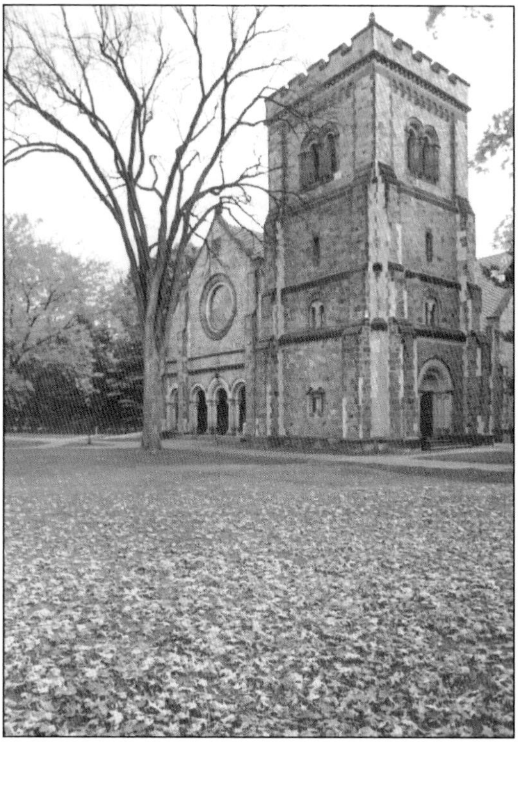

The Vassar College Chapel. The gift of two alumnae, Mary Thaw Thompson (1877) and Mary Morris Pratt (1880), the chapel is the design of architects Shepley, Ruttan, and Coolidge. Dedicated on November 4, 1904, the building is of the Norman style of architecture and is built of seamed Cape Ann granite trimmed with Ohio sandstone. The stained-glass windows are the work of Louis Comfort Tiffany and John La Farge. Also represented is one of their followers, Robert Leftwich Dodge.

The Chapel, Interior. The seating capacity of the pews in the chapel is 1,228, making it ideal for commencement exercises until the college enrollment exceeded that number. Nondenominational in nature and one of the largest gathering places on campus, the chapel is the setting for academic, spiritual, and cultural events. The organ was originally a 3-manual, 49-stop instrument made by Hutchings-Votey of Boston and was dedicated on November 4, 1904. In 1967, the organ was replaced by an instrument built by Gress-Miles of Princeton, New Jersey, based on a design by Prof. Donald Pearson, Vassar organist from 1951 to 1982. This organ consists of 3 manuals and 100 stops. Its case is essentially that of the 1904 instrument.

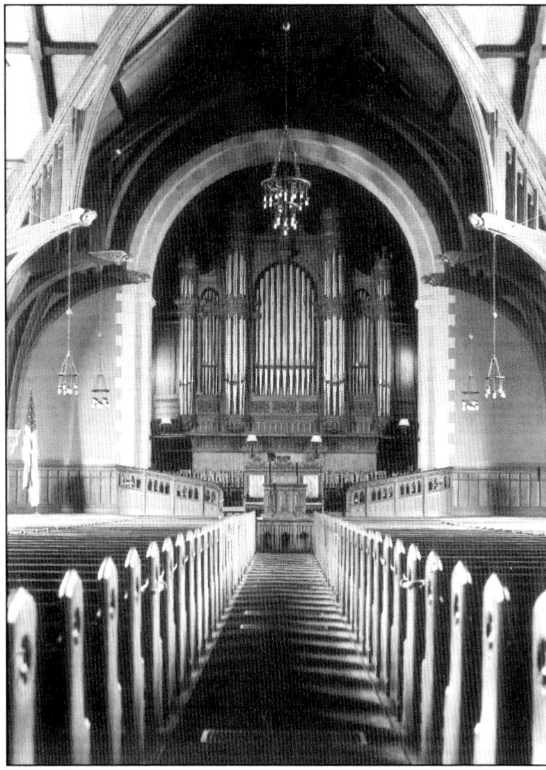

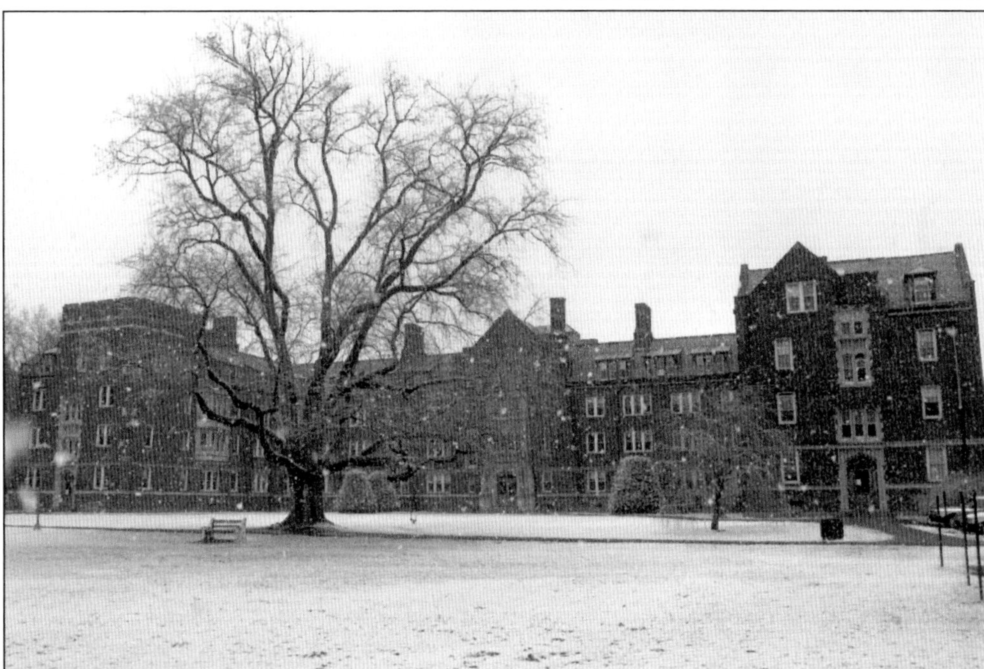

Josselyn House. Olivia Josselyn House, a residence hall, was completed in 1912. Designed by Allen & Collens, it was the gift of Mrs. Russell Sage in honor of her grandmother. (Photograph by Tom Furtwangler, Class of 1992.)

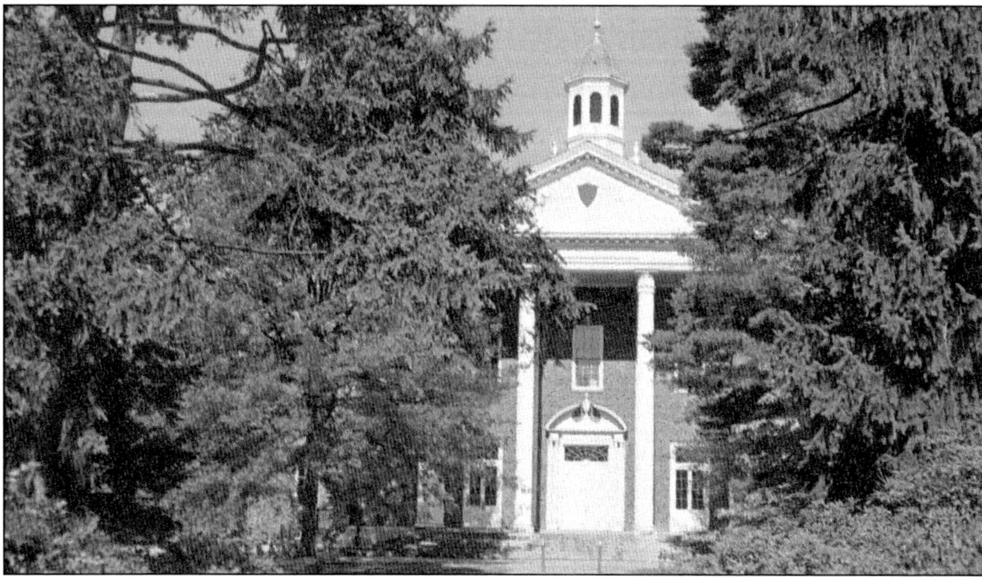

Students' Building. The anonymous gift of a donor for the "exclusive needs and interests of student organizations," Students' Building was completed in 1913. Designed by architects McKim, Mead & White, it was the scene of many student activities for years, including class and faculty plays. Christmas parties were also held there, complete with reindeer (students) pulling a sled and C. Gordon Post, professor of political science, dressed as an imposing Santa Claus. Students' Building was remodeled in 1973 to become the All College Dining Center, thus ending the days of individual dining rooms in each residence hall. (Postcard courtesy of the Honorable Albert M. Rosenblatt.)

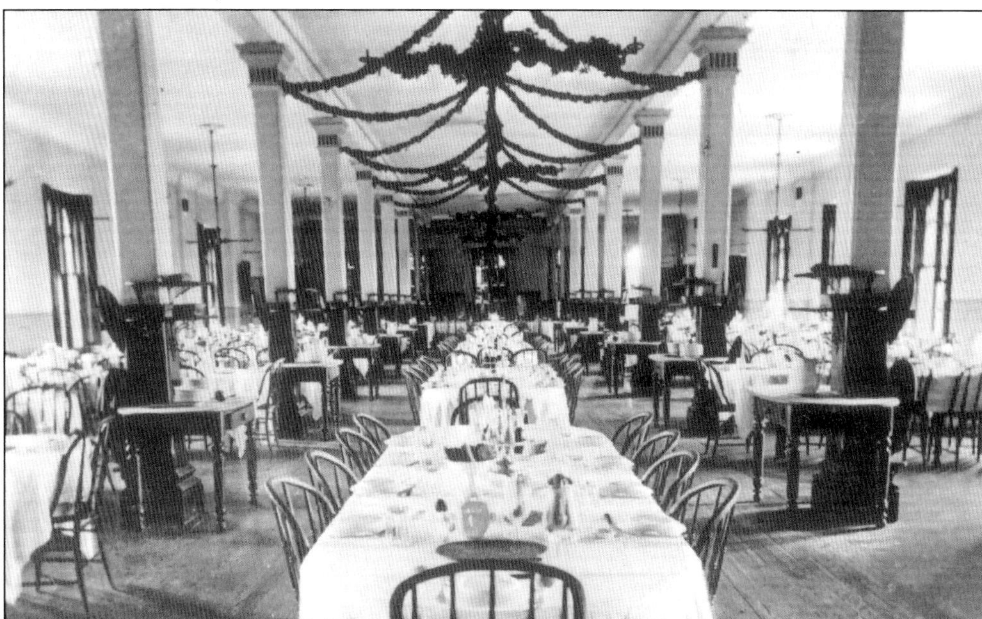

Early Dining. Dining in Main Building during this period was an elegant affair, with cloth napkins and tablecloths, spoon holders, and flowers on every table. The tables seated ten girls, each of whom had a regular place.

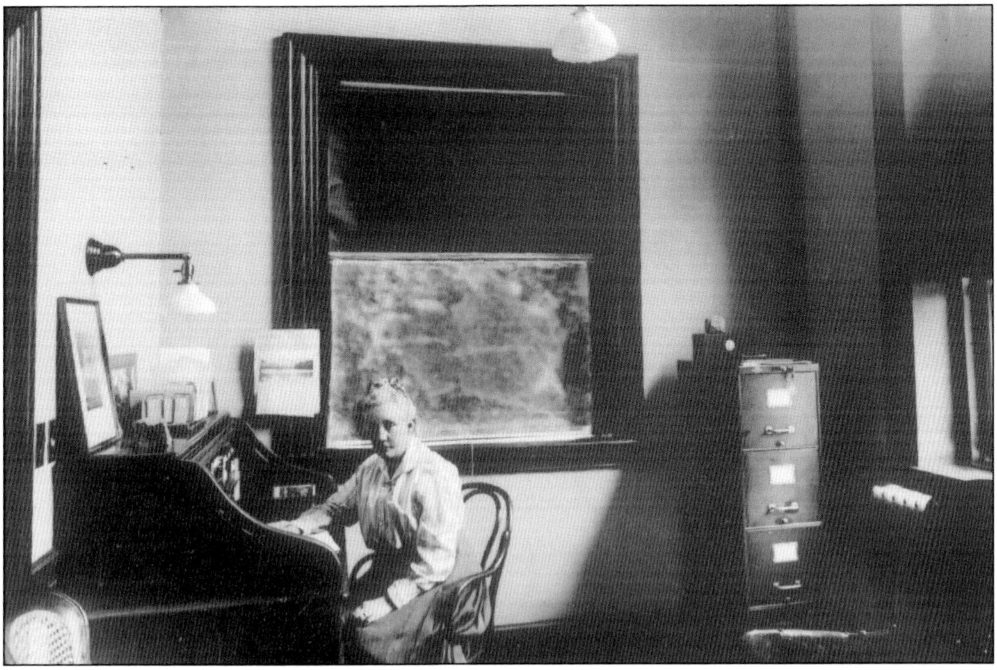

Ella McCaleb (Class of 1878). In recognition of Ella McCaleb's devotion to the college, alumnae and friends gave the dwelling at 71 Raymond Avenue as a faculty house. McCaleb held the position of dean from 1913 to 1923. For 20 years before that, she had served as secretary to the college.

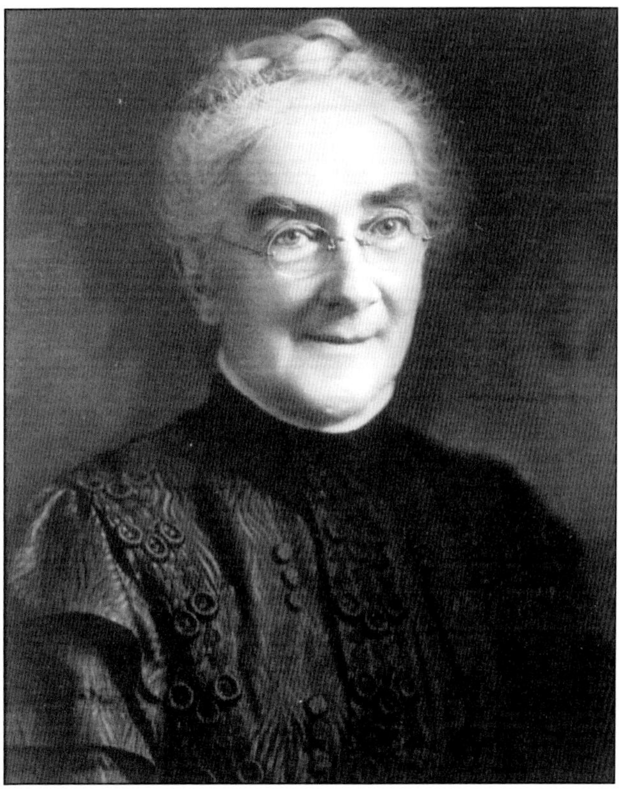

Ellen Swallow Richards. An environmental planner, Ellen Swallow Richards (Class of 1870) became the first woman to study and teach at the Massachusetts Institute of Technology. She was a chemist and home economist and an alumna trustee of Vassar. The author of *Euthenics,* she came to campus in 1889 to give a lecture entitled "The Education and Occupations of the Twentieth Century Woman."

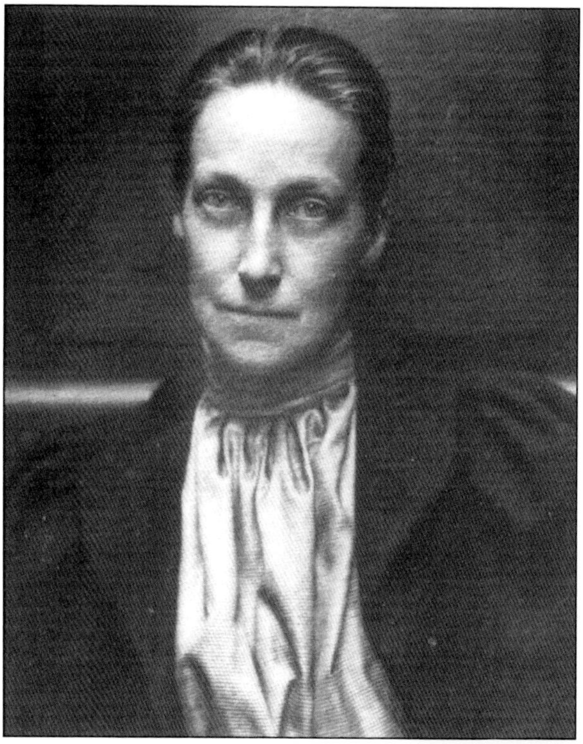

Lucy Maynard Salmon. The history department began at Vassar when Lucy Maynard Salmon was appointed associate professor in 1887. Coming to Vassar from the University of Michigan, she initiated the practice of teaching history from primary sources rather than depending too heavily on secondary "authorities." Her approach has been the hallmark of the college's teaching philosophy from 1887 to the present. Her students would send source materials back to the library after graduation.

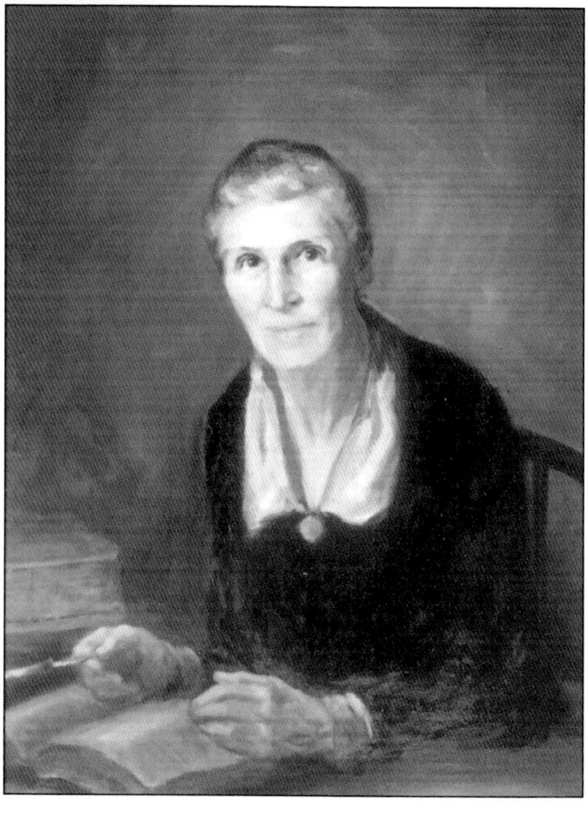

Laura Johnson Wylie (Class of 1877). Author and teacher at Vassar from 1894 to 1924, Laura Johnson Wylie was the first woman to receive a Ph.D. from Yale University in English. She presided over Vassar's English department beginning in 1894 and joined historian Lucy Maynard Salmon in requiring students to rely on their own observations in both writing and reading. She lived in downtown Poughkeepsie—entertaining townsfolk, Vassar students, and friends in her home—and presided over the County Club, an intellectual and political club for women.

ANITA HEMMINGS LOVE (CLASS OF 1897). Anita Hemmings Love was the first African American woman to receive a degree at Vassar College.

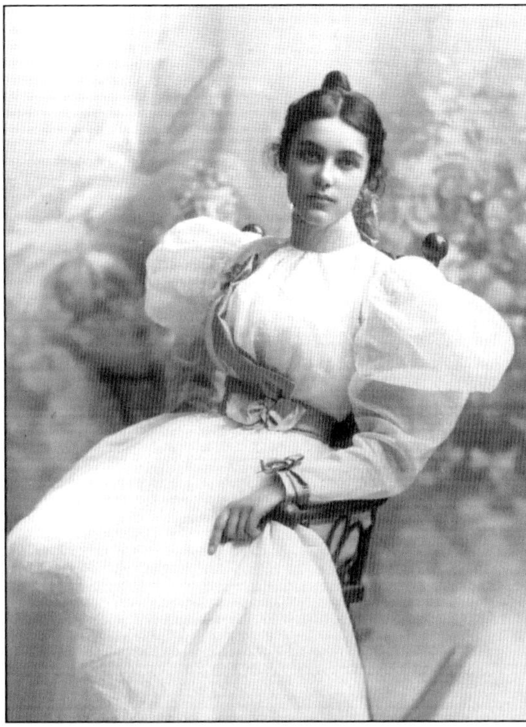

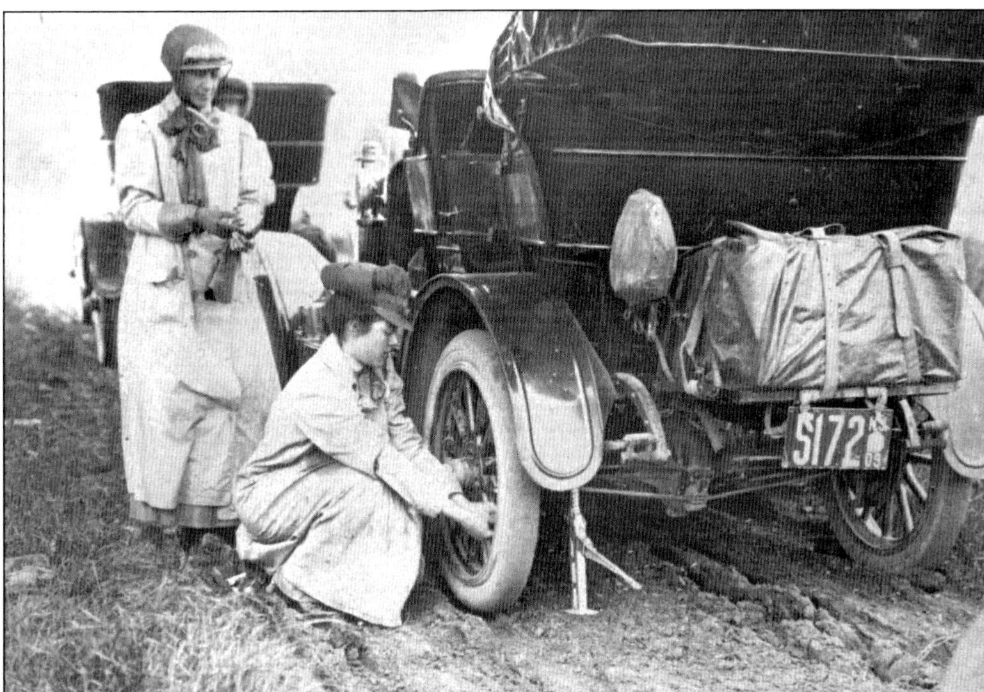

ALICE HUYLER RAMSEY. The first woman to cross the continent in an automobile was Alice Huyler Ramsey (Class of 1907), who made the trip from New York to San Francisco in a Maxwell 30. Her journey of 3,800 miles took 41 days and 11 spare tires.

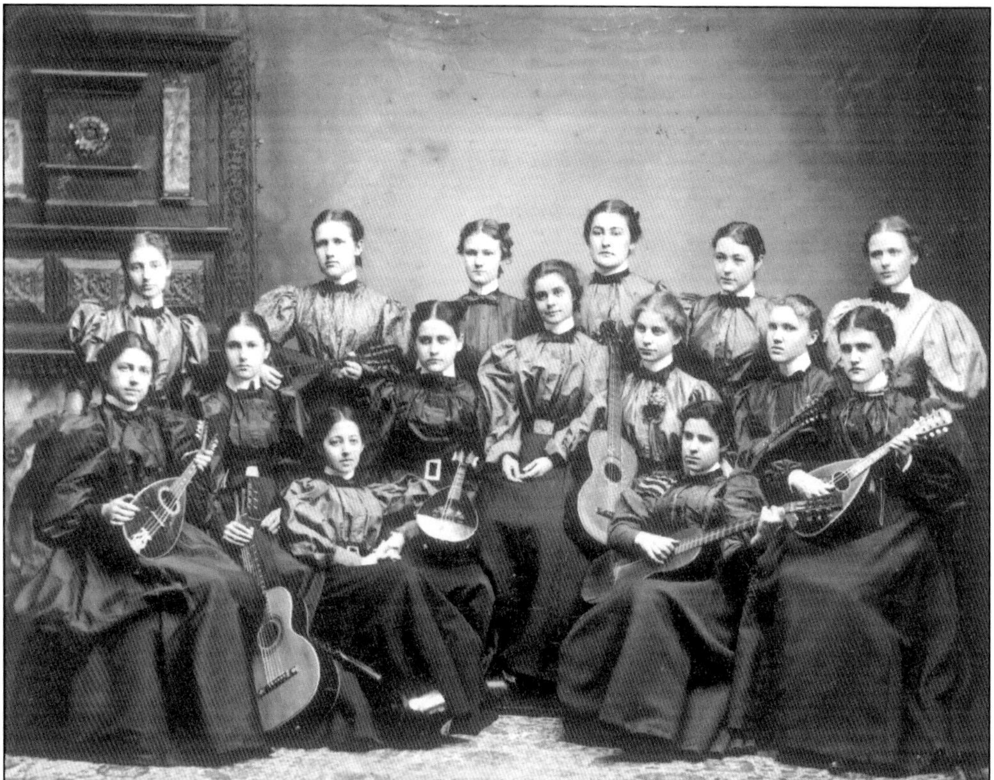

The Guitar and Mandolin Club, 1899. Music was a vital part of student social life. Vassar students participated in many cultural activities, among them musical groups such as the Guitar and Mandolin Club.

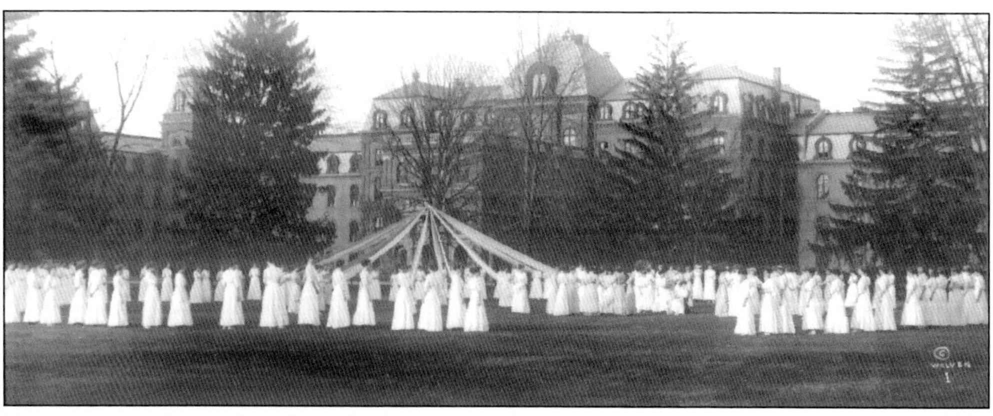

The Maypole (1912). The Class of 1889 instituted May Day customs with a maypole and groups of students paying homage to a queen. Pictured in 1912, students dressed in white dance around the maypole in front of Main Building.

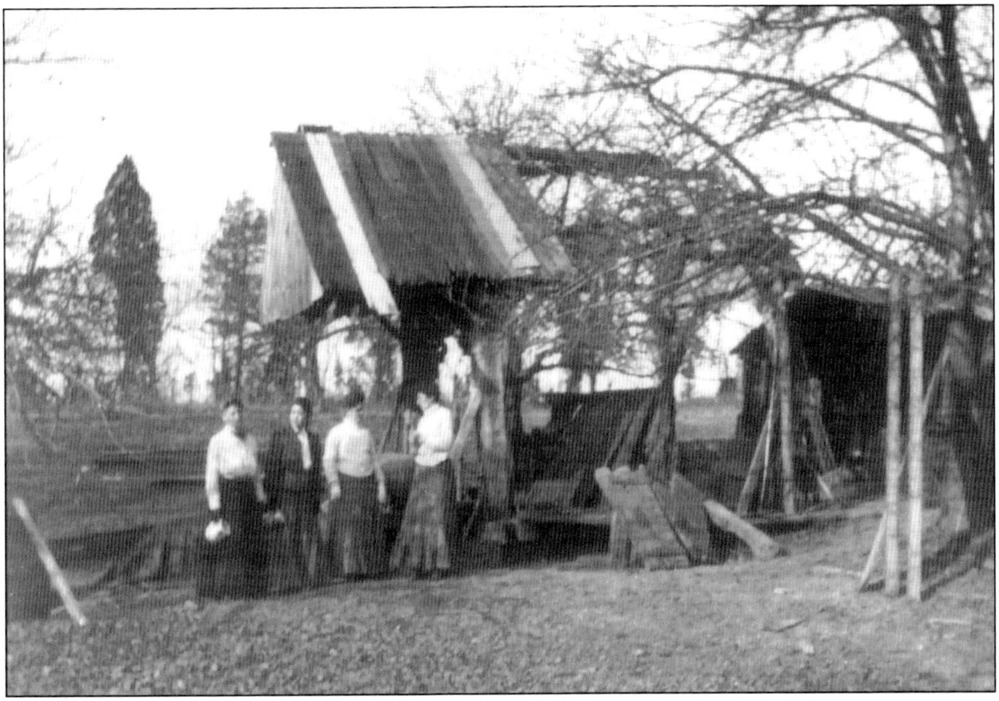

The Cider Mill Press. Kimlin's Cider Mill, located on Cedar Avenue in the Town of Poughkeepsie, was once a popular spot with Vassar students who would gather for cider and doughnuts in front of the mill's stone fireplace.

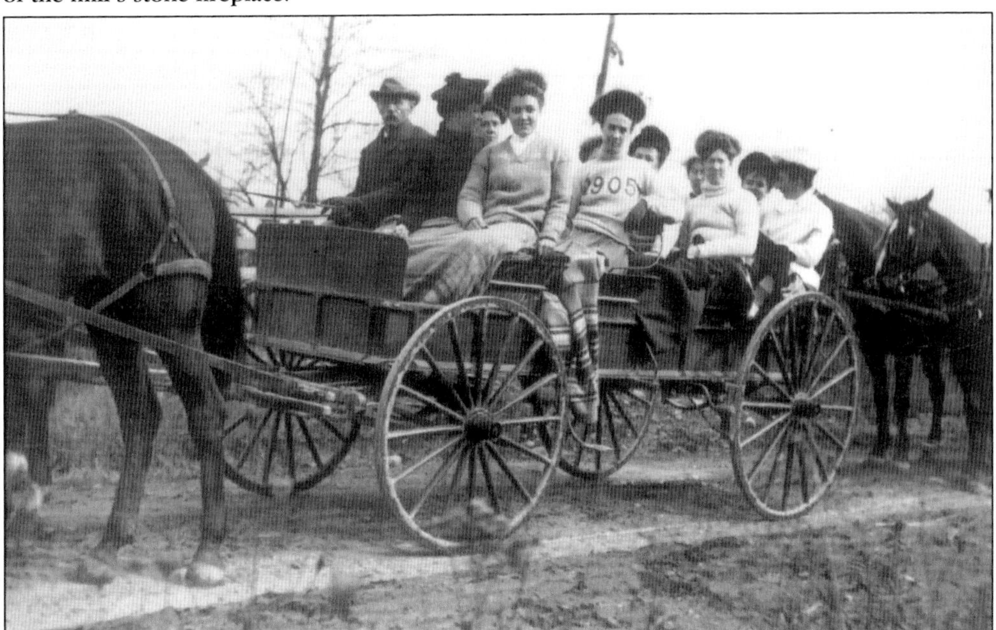

The Annual Trip to Lake Mohonk. The students' annual trip to Lake Mohonk was inaugurated in 1889 by trustee Frederick Ferris Thompson, who invited the entire college to attend as his guests. As the college grew larger, only certain classes could be invited and the trip was eventually discontinued.

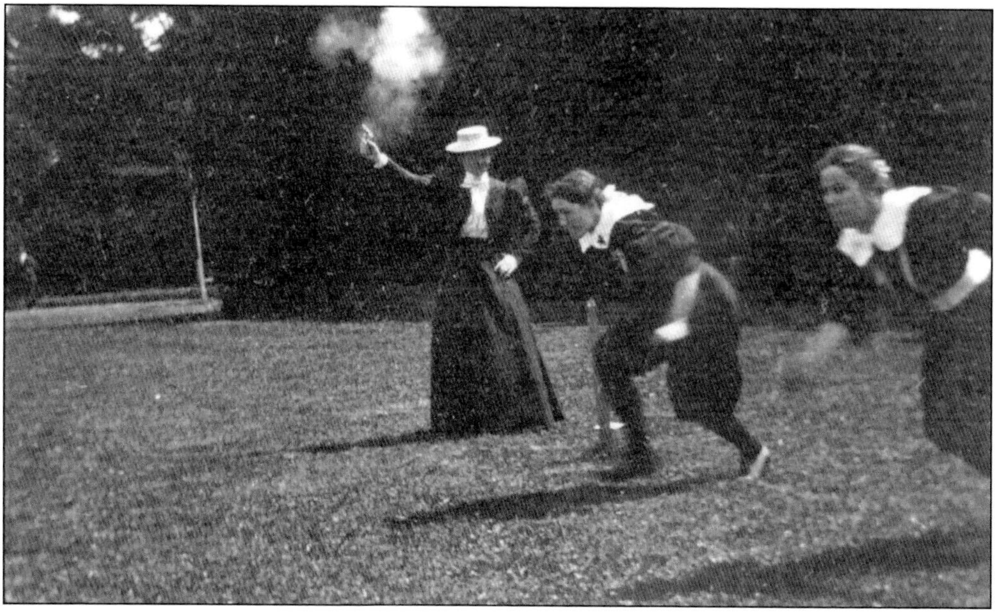

The First Women's Field Day in America. The first women's field day in America was held on November 9, 1895, in what is now known as Noyes Circle, the expanse of lawn in front of the Emma Hartman Noyes residence hall and Students' Building. Track events included the 100-yard dash, the running broad jump, the running high jump, and the 220-yard dash. The event was held despite inclement weather, but eventually even the cartridges in the starter gun grew so damp that they would not go off. In 1995, Vassar celebrated the 100th anniversary of field day with athletic events and a commemorative plaque in the garden surrounding Noyes Circle.

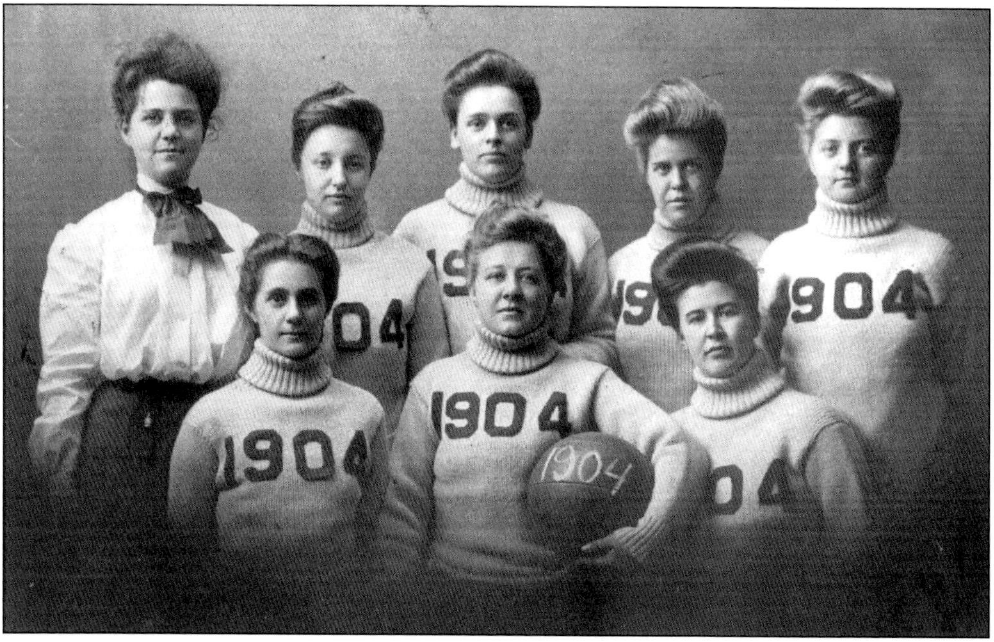

Basketball. The members of the 1904 varsity basketball team and their coach pose for a formal photograph. The turtleneck sweater was almost a requirement of the sports outfit and was popular in the early 20th century, along with the pompadour hairstyle.

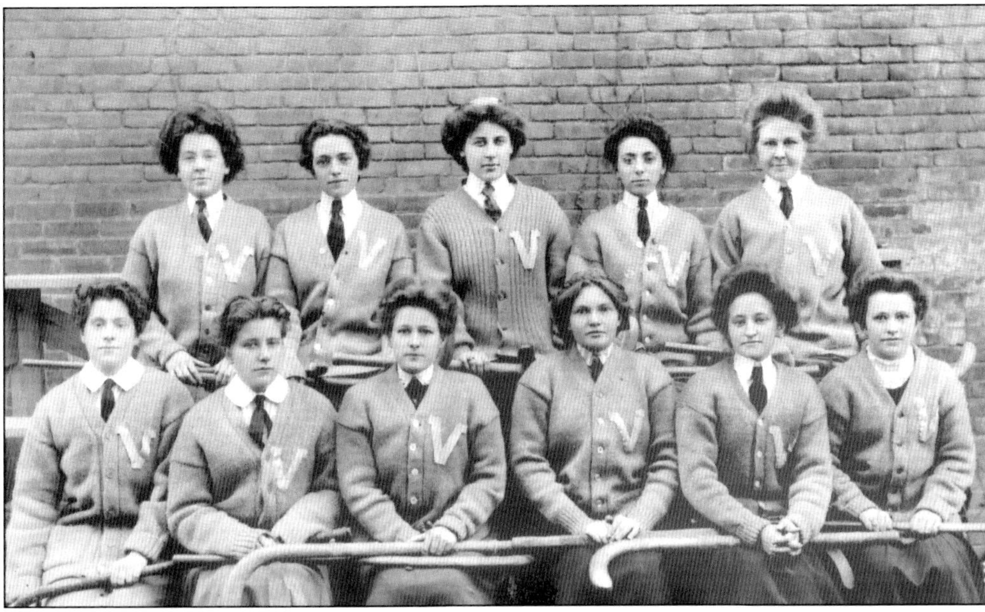

Sports at Vassar. Women at Vassar played an active role in sports, as depicted here in a team photograph that appeared in the 1909 *Vassarion.* Constance M.J. Applebee of England spent a week at Vassar and gave expert instruction in field hockey. Vassar was the first college to employ her. The *Miscellany News* of October 1915 noted, "The founding of the Athletic Association in 1895 marked a period in which athletic sports became an organized organization!"

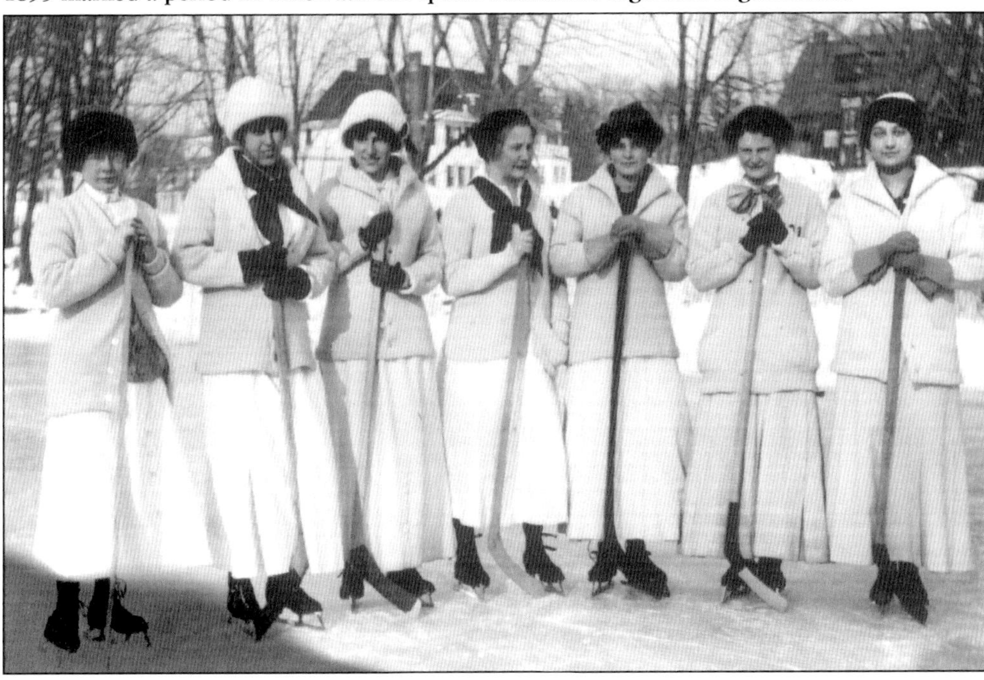

Ice-Skating at Vassar. There is a long history of skating at Vassar on both Sunset and Vassar Lakes in addition to a rink behind Kenyon Hall. With assistance from funds provided by John D. Rockefeller, Sunset Lake was created in 1912 for the purpose of skating. Pres. James Monroe Taylor would frequently join the students on the ice. Students are pictured here on Vassar Lake.

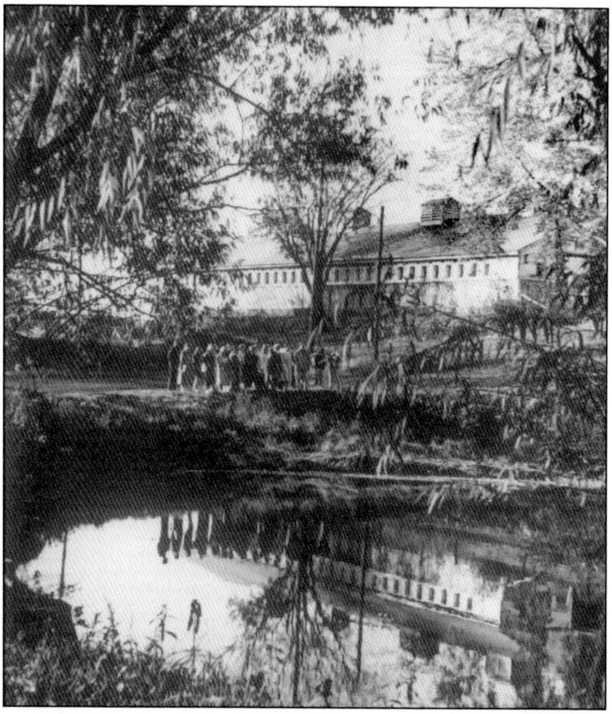

The Vassar Farm. Students are pictured here on Vassar's farm, which fed the college with its produce of eggs, vegetables, and milk. The cow barn can be seen in the background.

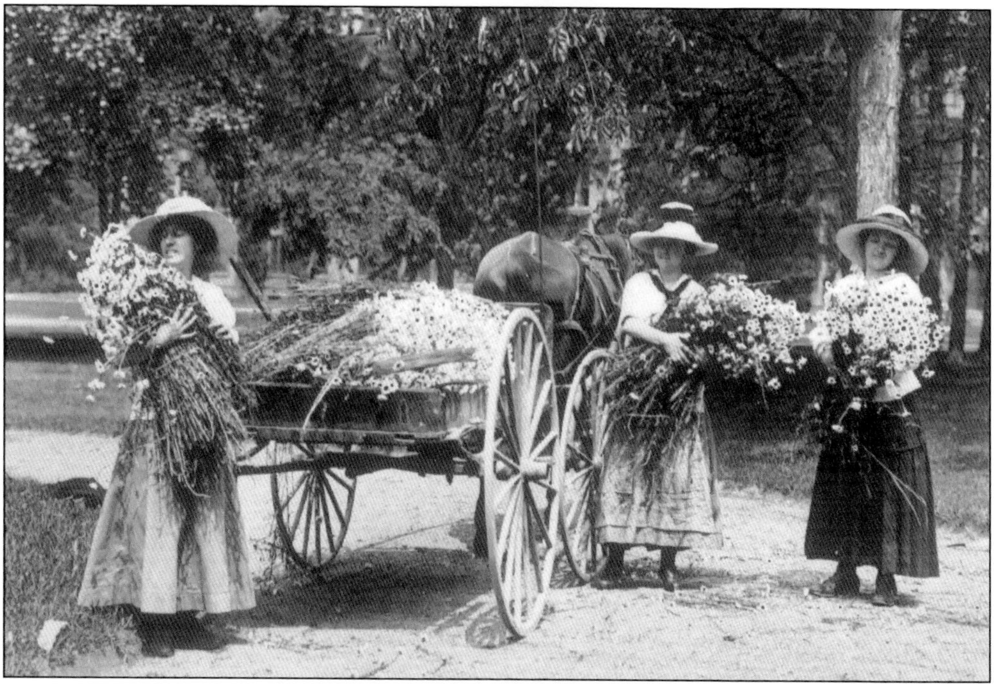

Daisy Picking, 1912. The sophomore pickers of 1912 were delighted with the abundance and quality of the daisies available for that year's daisy chain (see p. 64). Later, when the annual graduation schedule was moved from June to May, daisies had to be flown in from other places. The chain was then made by Saltford Florists and subsequently by Bock Florist, both located in Poughkeepsie.

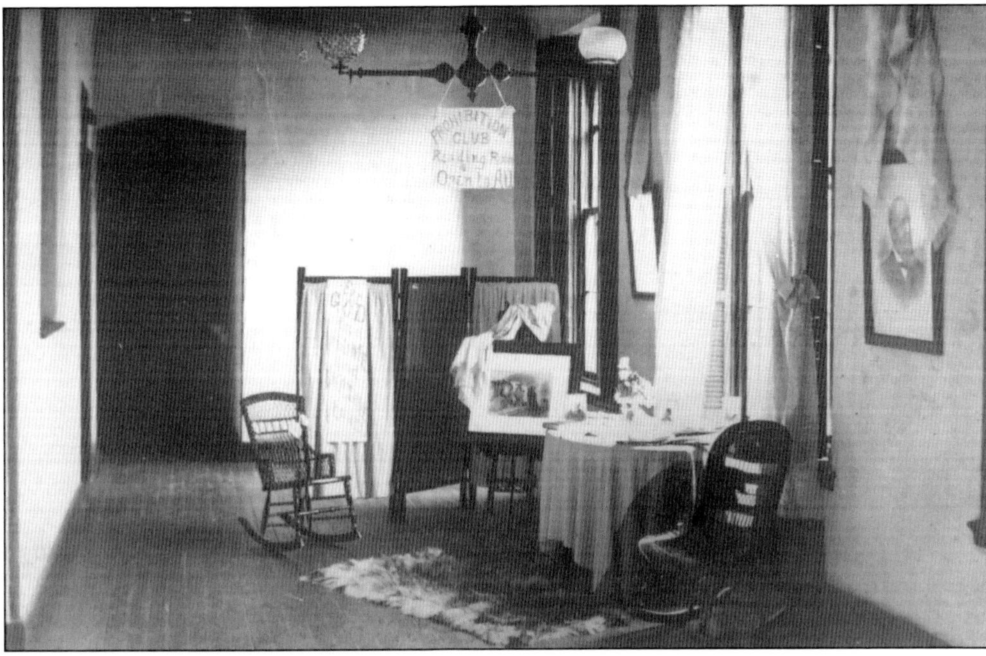

THE READING ROOM. The hanging banner proclaims this room in Main Building as a "Prohibition Club Reading Room Open to All."

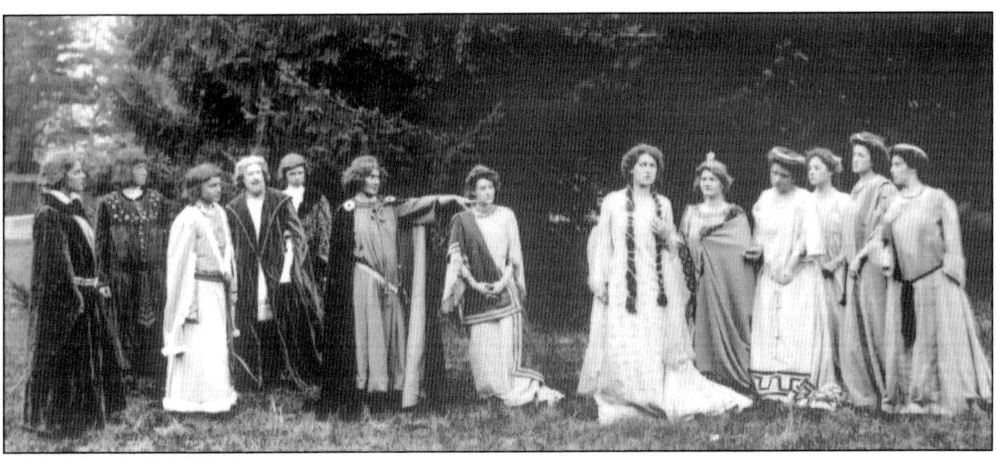

EARLY DRAMA. In 1909, *Much Ado about Nothing* was presented by students as a Third Hall play. Hall plays were directed by students and sponsored by Philaletheis, a student organization. They were put on three times a year: in the fall, the middle of winter, and at the time of Class Day in what is now the outdoor amphitheater.

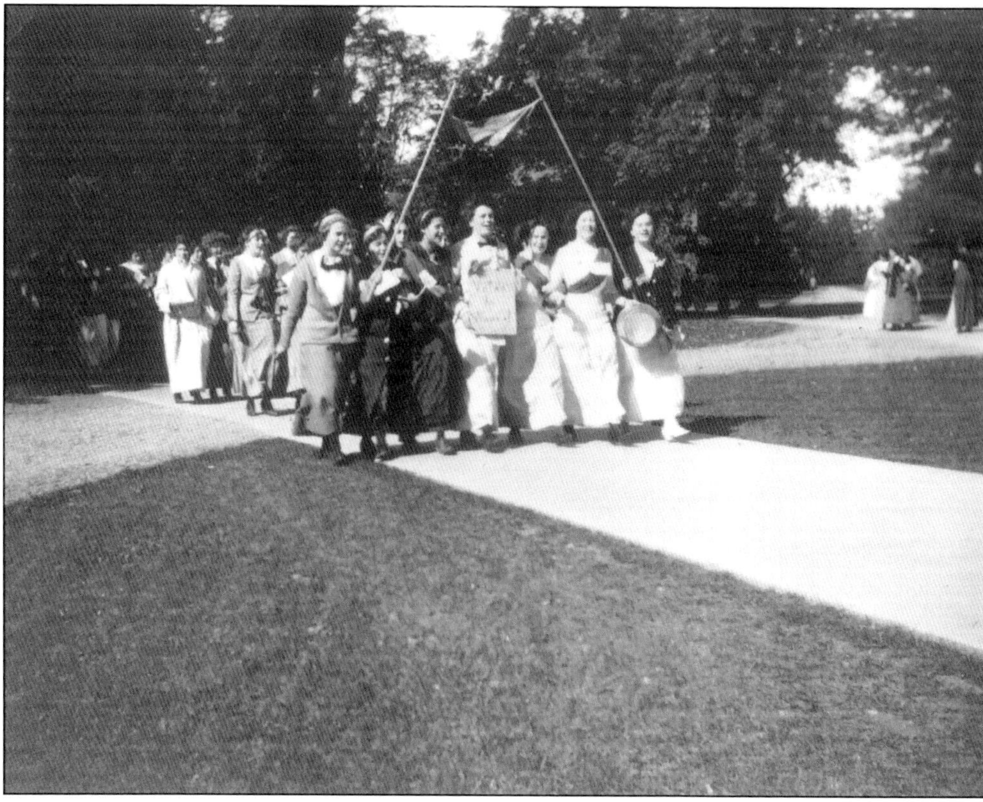

A Student Suffrage Parade, 1912. Inez Milholland (Class of 1909) held a suffrage meeting in 1908 in a small cemetery adjacent to the college, as President Taylor had forbidden suffrage meetings to be held on campus. In response to a student petition of the Class of 1912, however, President Taylor granted permission for a meeting on campus, pictured here.

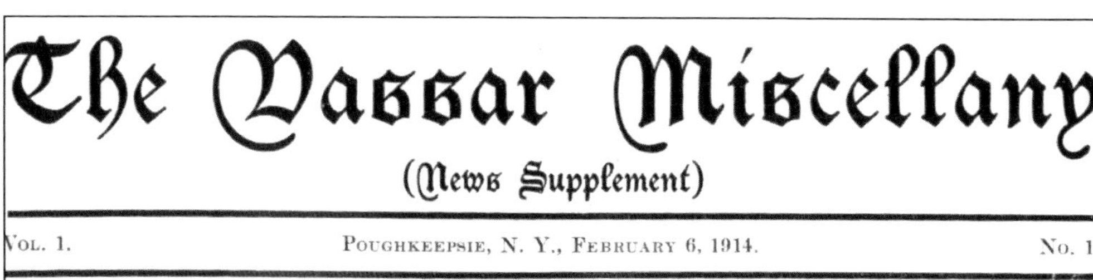

The Vassar Miscellany

(News Supplement)

Vol. 1. Poughkeepsie, N. Y., February 6, 1914. No. 1.

The *Vassar Miscellany News*. The first issue of the *Vassar Miscellany* (the first student newspaper) was published in 1914. After February 9, 1917, it was continued as the *Vassar Miscellany News*.

Three

Reaching out to the World: 1915–1946

The presidency of Henry Noble MacCracken (1915–1946) drew Vassar College broadside into the 20th century. Under MacCracken, the Vassar education enlarged its compass and made new approaches to teaching and learning. These changes were influenced by the advent of women's suffrage in New York and the nation as well as the growing need for modernizing the teaching profession, the incipient student movement, the changing mores of the Jazz Age, and the crisis of the Great Depression. Both by example and precept, internationalist MacCracken, the college's first non-clergyman president, drew the campus into the affairs of a larger and fast-changing world facing issues of totalitarianism and war. Traditions of excellent scholarship continued, but students were confronted with an enhanced context that emphasized contributions to society. For 34 years until the end of World War II, MacCracken presided over the college, making life at Vassar a 24-hours-a-day affair. MacCracken stimulated new ventures while cherishing familiar ones that were part of the college's tradition.

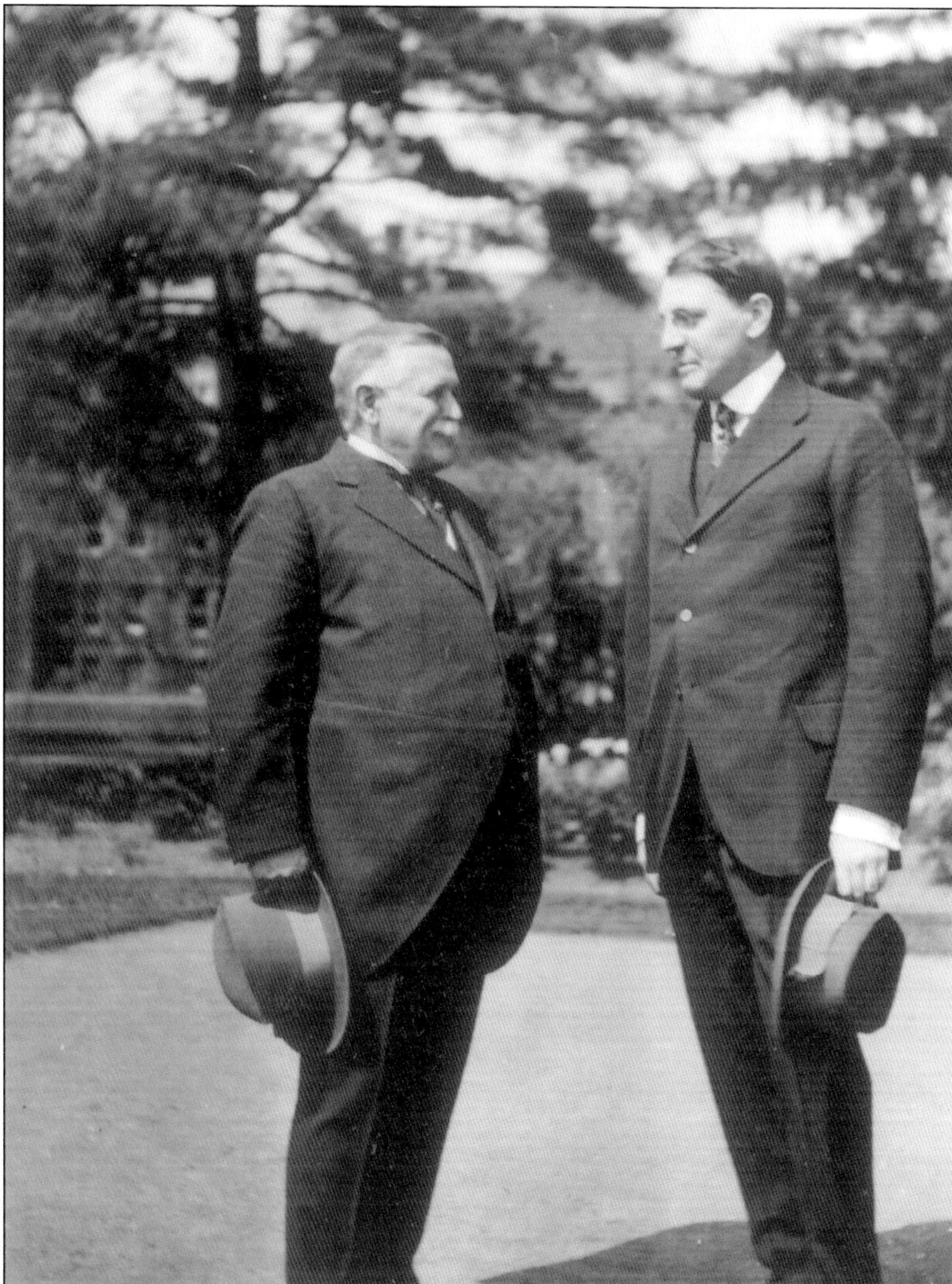

The Changing of the Guard in 1915. President Taylor (left) retired in February 1914, and MacCracken (right) succeeded him. They are shown here having a word with each other at the October 1915 inauguration of MacCracken. Taylor passed on to MacCracken a thriving college of high academic standards that had some 1,000 students, several dormitories, a classroom building, laboratories, a chapel, a library of 80,000 volumes, and a modest endowment.

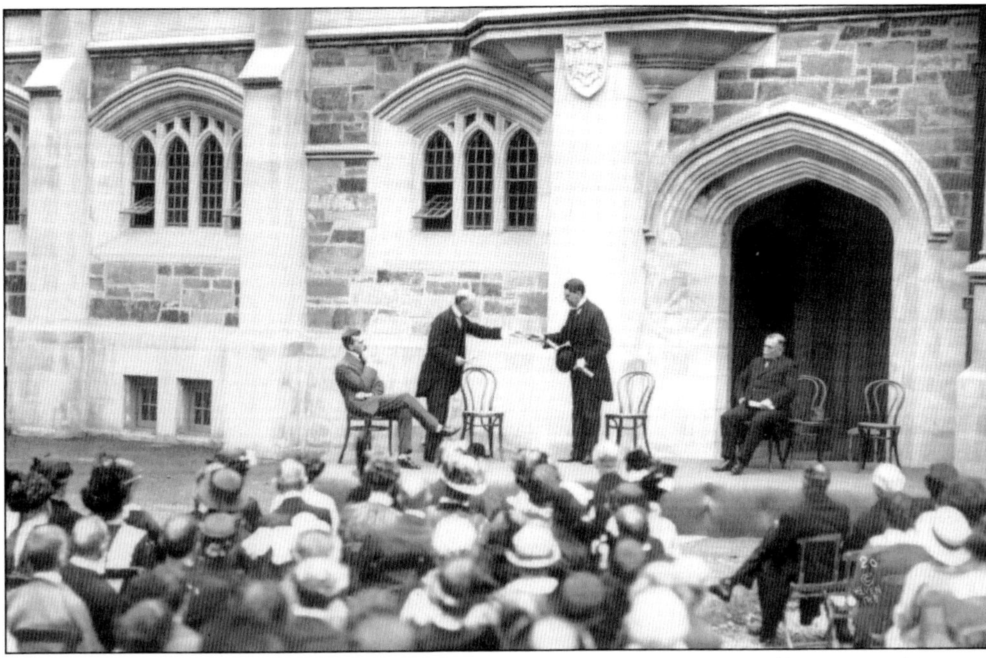

The Opening of Taylor Hall, May 7, 1915. The Gate Lodge, built in 1866, was razed in 1913 because its entryway was too narrow for automobiles. In its place, Taylor Hall was given by Mr. and Mrs. Charles M. Pratt to honor James Monroe Taylor, president from 1886 to 1914. The Vassar College art collection was then moved to Taylor Hall from the museum (Avery), where it had been housed since 1875.

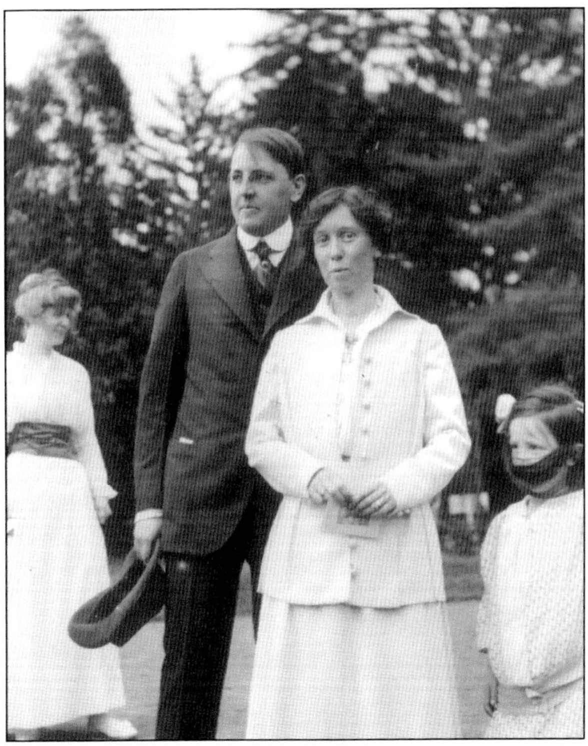

"Prexy" and Marjorie MacCracken and Their Daughter Maisry in the Circle. The MacCrackens and their children had an easy friendly relationship with members of the college community. They are shown here at a gathering in the informal outdoor athletic circle and gathering place designed by Matthew Vassar.

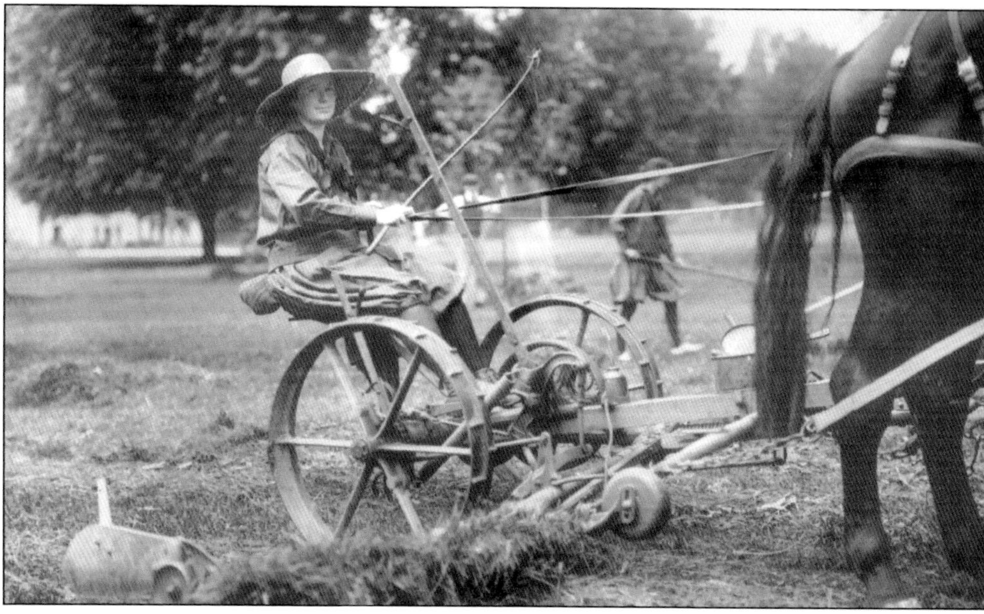

Wartime Activity, World War I. In the summer of 1918, the trustees authorized 12 Vassar students to work eight hours a day on the college farm. For the first time ever, Vassar College had a summer academic program, which was financed by the American Red Cross. This Training Camp for Nurses offered nursing instruction to college graduates. Four hundred and thirty-five students attended, led by Prof. Herbert Mills, dean.

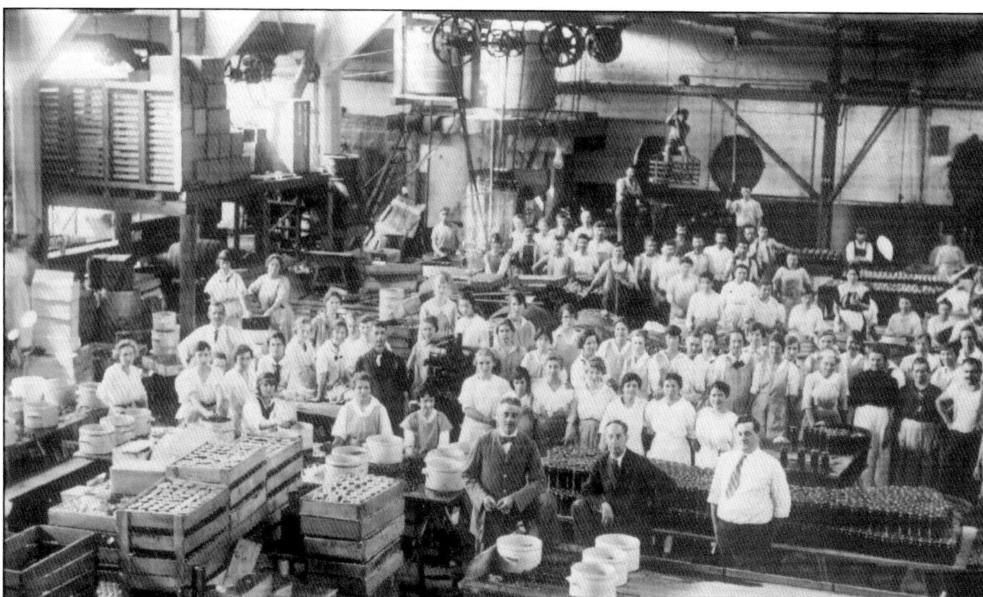

The Delapenha Canning Factory during World War I. A number of Vassar students in the summer of 1918 worked in the Delapenha Canning Factory canning tomatoes for the war effort. Some of the students can be seen in this photograph. The Delapenha parcel of land, located near the Hudson River south of Poughkeepsie, was subsequently sold to a munitions manufacturer that merged with IBM in 1942. A large IBM manufacturing plant and accompanying buildings occupy the property now.

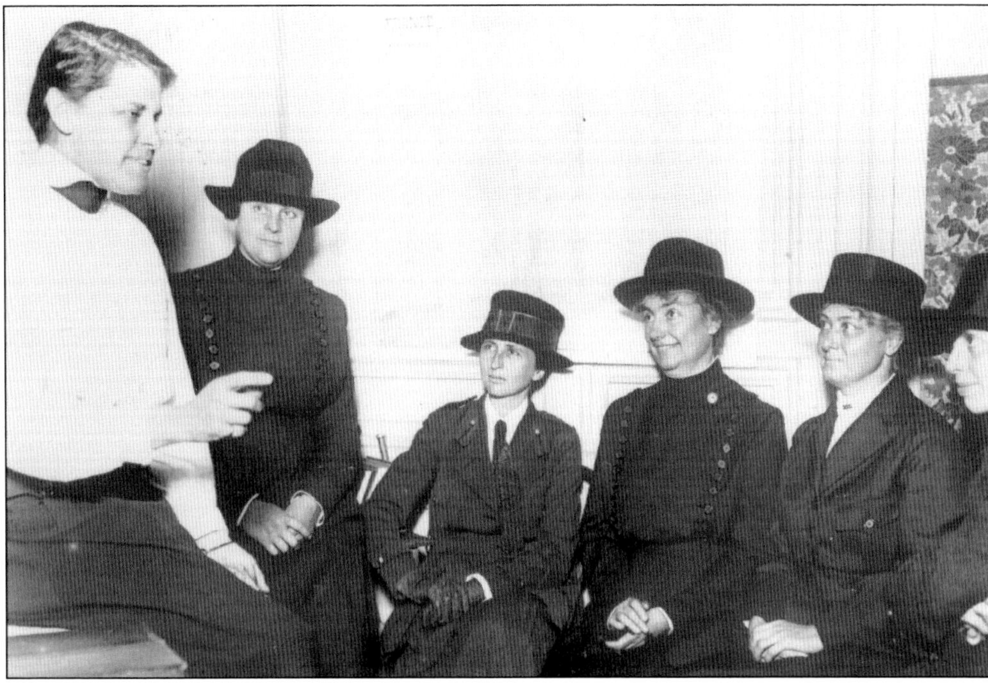

The Vassar Relief Unit Abroad, 1918. The Vassar alumnae sent a Vassar Relief Unit abroad in 1918 to care for convalescent soldiers in Savenay, France. Here, some members of the unit are gathered with a French administrator. In March 1919, *La Goutte de Lait,* a milk station for babies under Relief Unit auspices, was established in Verdun and continued after the armistice.

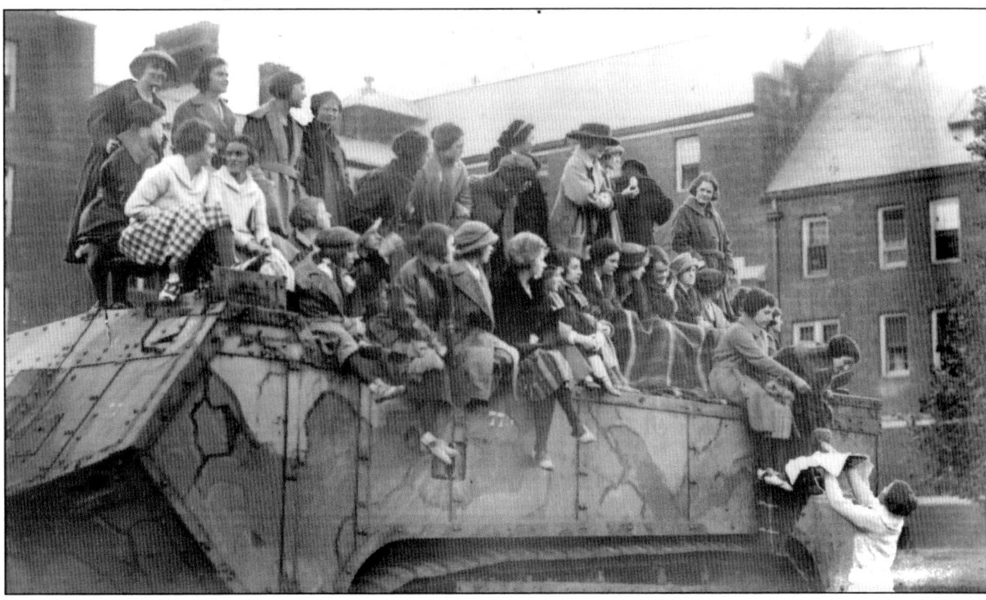

The French Tank. In 1920, the French government sent a gift of an army tank to Vassar to serve as a memento of the Vassar students' war service. The tank was shipped to the campus by transatlantic steamship, riverboat, and flatbed car and was deposited on the grounds of Vassar near Josselyn House. President MacCracken had some tales to tell about its use as a bootlegging drop during Prohibition. The tank eventually rusted and was removed.

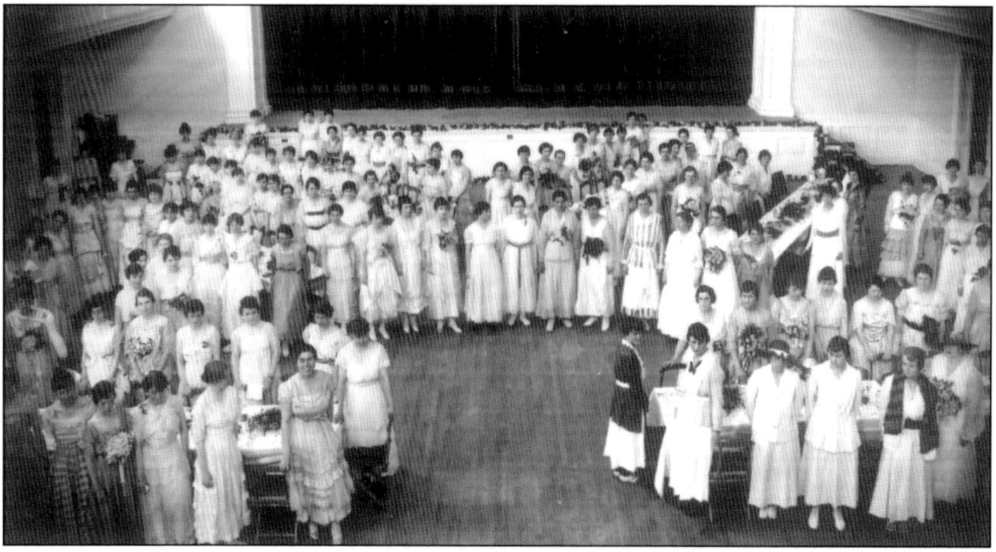

The Class of 1916 Class Dinner. Throughout Vassar College's history, the graduating classes have engaged in many valedictory activities the week before commencement. Here, the class is gathered for the last time before graduation. Commencement took place on the auditorium floor of Students' Building, which had been given to the college in 1913 for student activities.

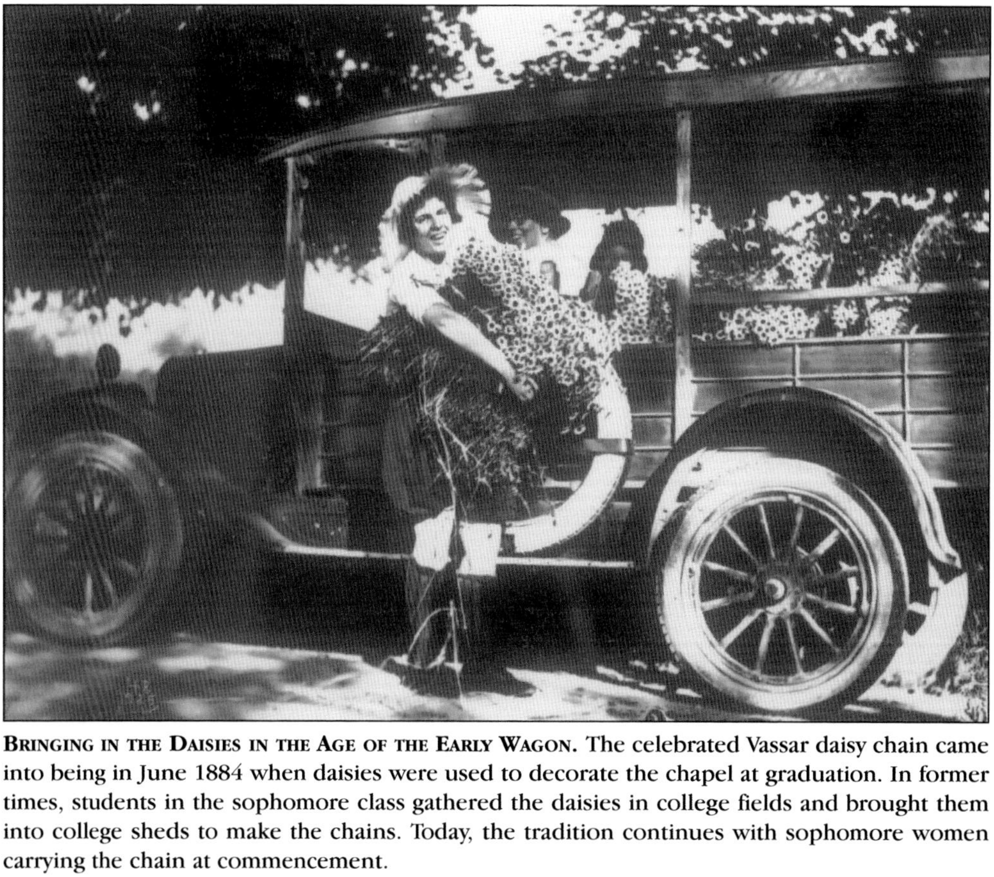

Bringing in the Daisies in the Age of the Early Wagon. The celebrated Vassar daisy chain came into being in June 1884 when daisies were used to decorate the chapel at graduation. In former times, students in the sophomore class gathered the daisies in college fields and brought them into college sheds to make the chains. Today, the tradition continues with sophomore women carrying the chain at commencement.

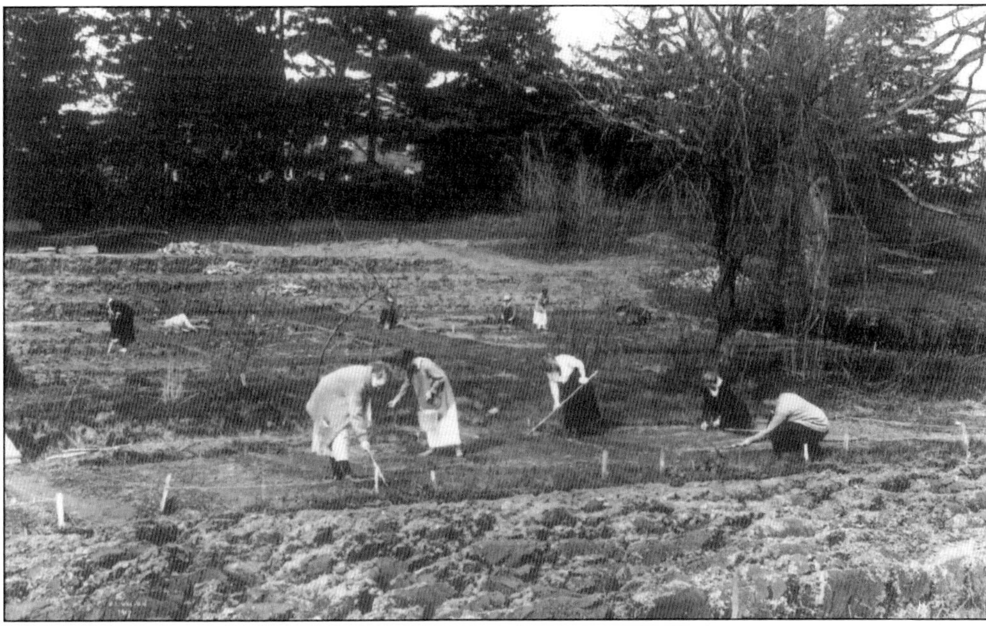

THE SHAKESPEARE GARDEN, APRIL 24, 1916. President MacCracken and Prof. Winifred Smith, his colleague in the English department, encouraged their Shakespeare students to identify trees, flowers, and bushes mentioned in the dramatist's work in order that the college might have a Shakespeare garden. Members of a botany class, pictured here, designed and planted the terraced Shakespeare garden near the Fonteynkill stream running through the campus glen.

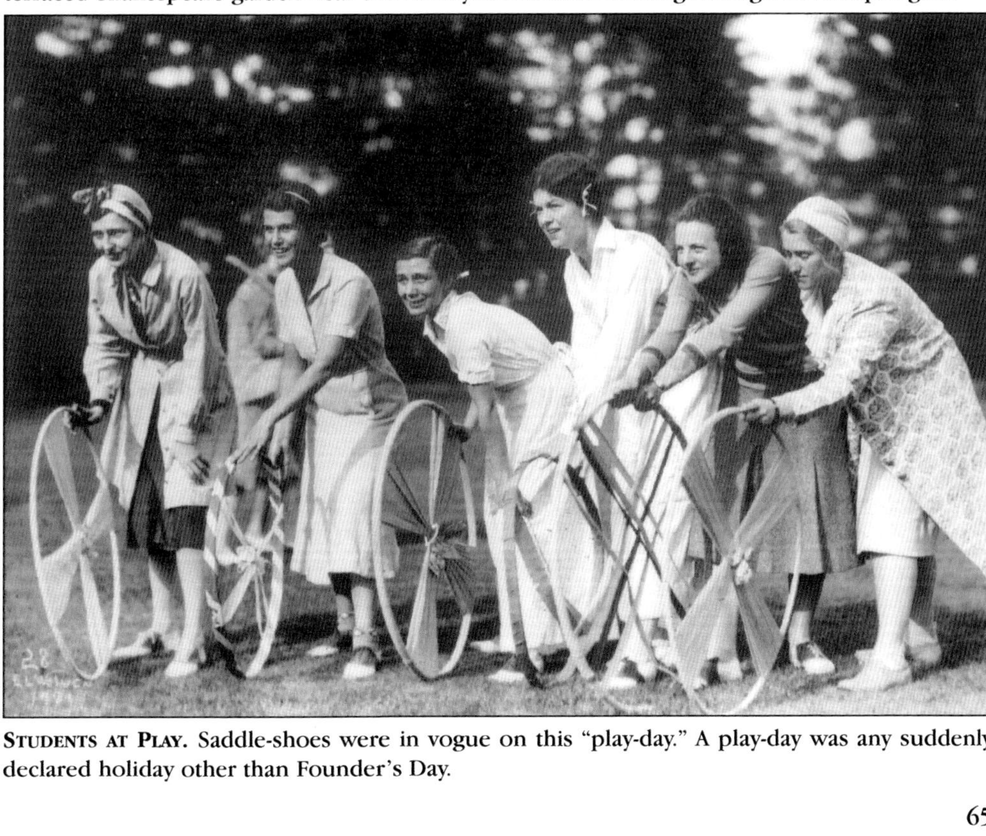

STUDENTS AT PLAY. Saddle-shoes were in vogue on this "play-day." A play-day was any suddenly declared holiday other than Founder's Day.

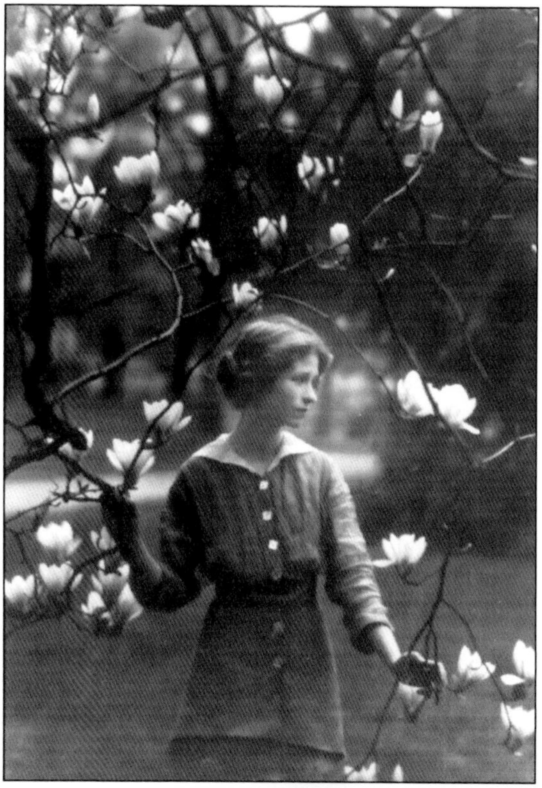

Edna St. Vincent Millay (Class of 1917). Edna St. Vincent Millay was already a recognized poet when she entered Vassar. Fostered by President MacCracken, she contributed her talents to college festivities on almost every occasion. She wrote class plays and performed during the 50th anniversary celebration in 1915. She almost missed her own graduation, owing to her inability to observe regulations, but she was saved through the clemency of her presidential admirer.

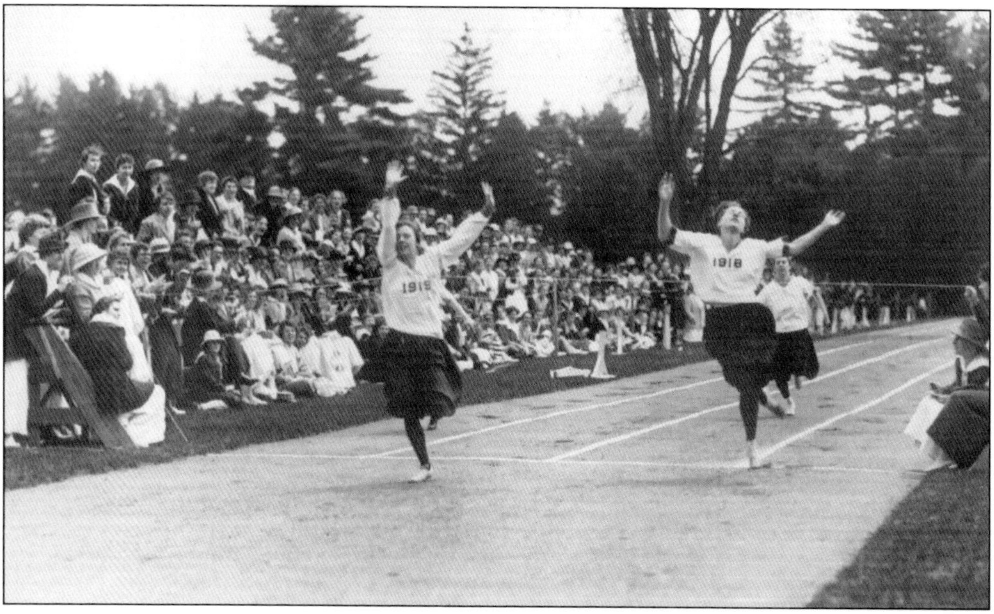

Field Day, 1918. The Vassar Athletic Association was founded on March 27, 1895. On November 9 that year, the first women's field day in America was held in the athletic circle on the campus. The field day—which included the running broad jump, running high jump, 220-yard dash, and, in the afternoon, a basketball game—became an annual spring event for the college community. Men were not welcome.

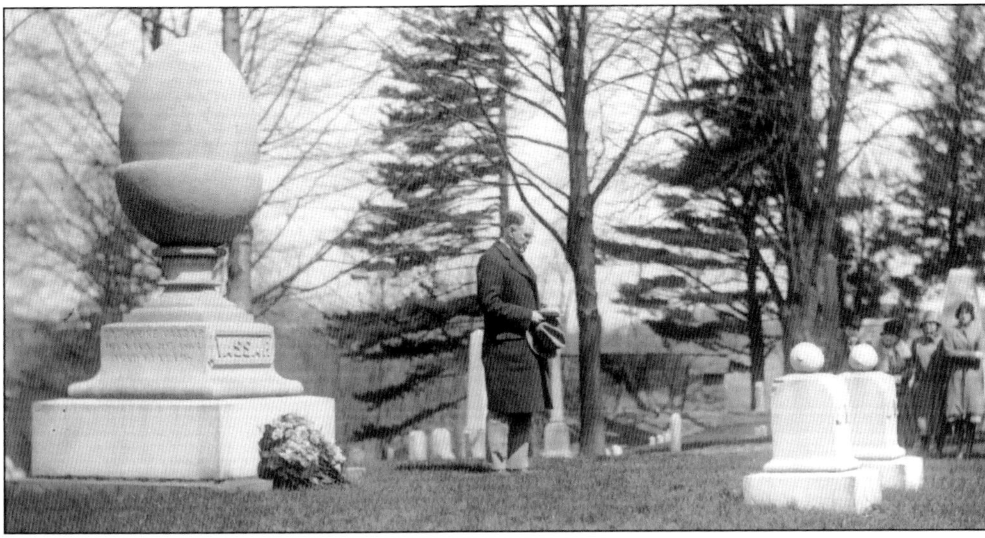

MATTHEW VASSAR'S ACORN TOMBSTONE. Matthew Vassar designed his own tombstone as a comment on founding the college from small beginnings. "Big oaks from little acorns grow. You get the point," he wrote in a note. Some students always made a pilgrimage to the Poughkeepsie Rural Cemetery on Founder's Day with MacCracken. The custom of "sporting the oak" on doors of students' rooms was instituted during this period.

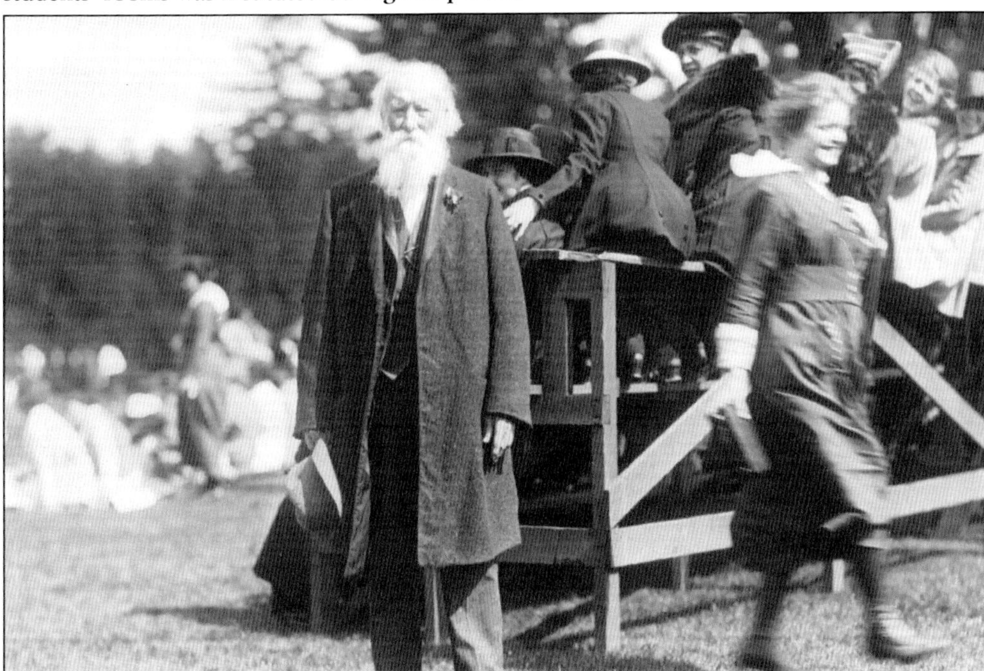

JOHN BURROUGHS AT VASSAR, MAY 2, 1919. John Burroughs, a good friend of the college, often came from his home, Slabsides across the Hudson River in Ulster County, to visit the campus. He was present at the Founder's Day on May 2, 1919, which celebrated the centenary of the birth of Walt Whitman. After a speech by Edgar Lee Masters, Burroughs spoke informally about Whitman, whom he had introduced to the campus in 1878. There was a baseball game that day between faculty (including MacCracken) and students.

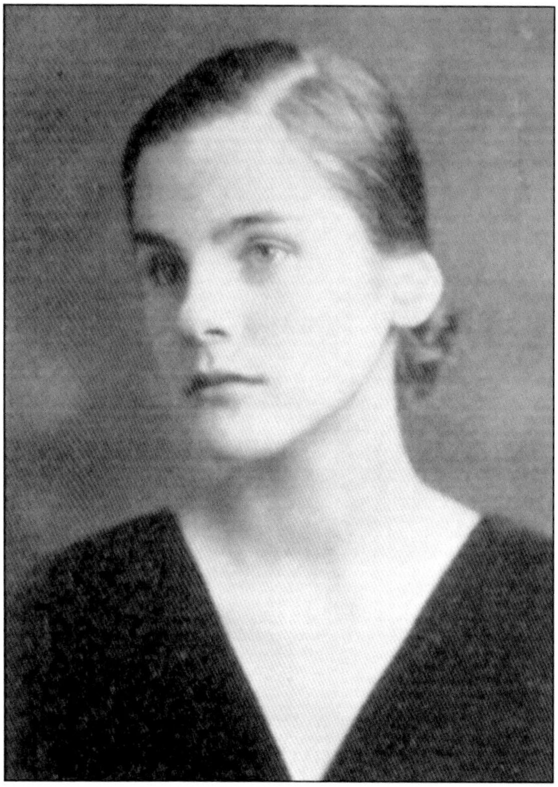

Mary McCarthy. One of many distinguished alumnae, Mary McCarthy graduated from Vassar in 1933, a witty writer even then. Her book *The Group* was based on her experience at Vassar. Its characters depicted her version of the intellectual and social currents of campus life. Her papers were later acquired by the Vassar College Libraries Special Collections, where they now reside along with the papers of Elizabeth Bishop (Class of 1934) and many other writers. (Photograph from the 1933 *Vassarion.*)

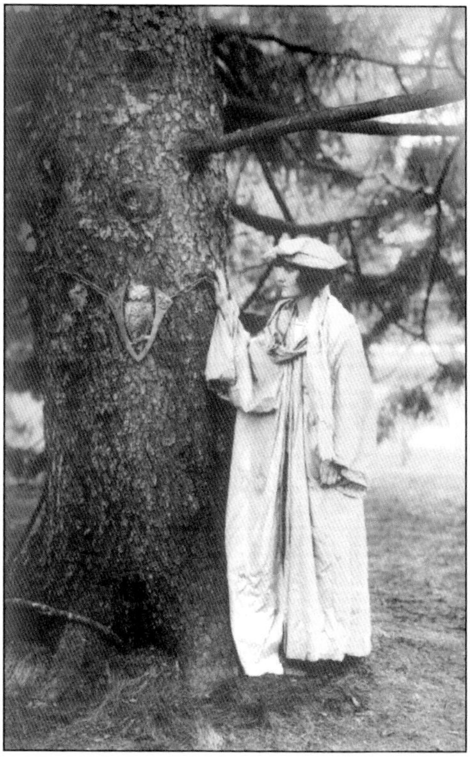

The Class Tree. A strangely costumed class officer dedicates a tree in this picture taken during the MacCracken years. Class trees have been part of the Vassar College tradition since 1867, when the graduating class planted ivy on Main Building. The following year, the Class of 1868 planted a white swamp oak. The owl emblem on the tree signifies an even-year class. Odd-year classes would display a torch.

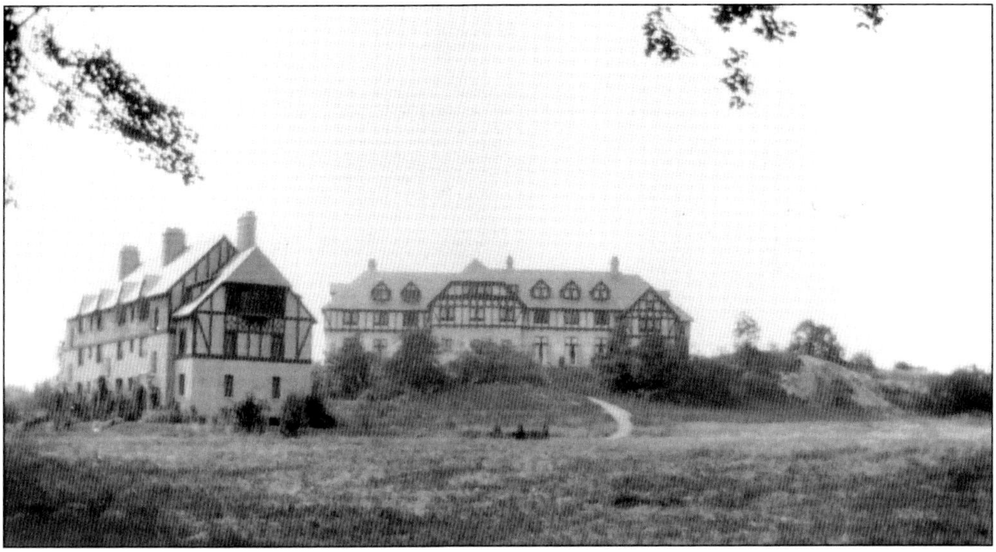

Williams House (Left) and Vassar College Alumnae House (Right). Standing together on the Rock Lot across Raymond Avenue from the main campus, these buildings were completed by 1924. Planned by the women faculty members who were to live in it, Williams House was the gift of Harriet Trumbull Williams (Class of 1870). The Alumnae House was given to the college by Blanche Ferry Hooker (Class of 1894) and Queene Ferry Coonley (Class of 1896). Dedicated on June 8, 1924, the house has always been heavily used by alumnae, alumni, and the resident college community.

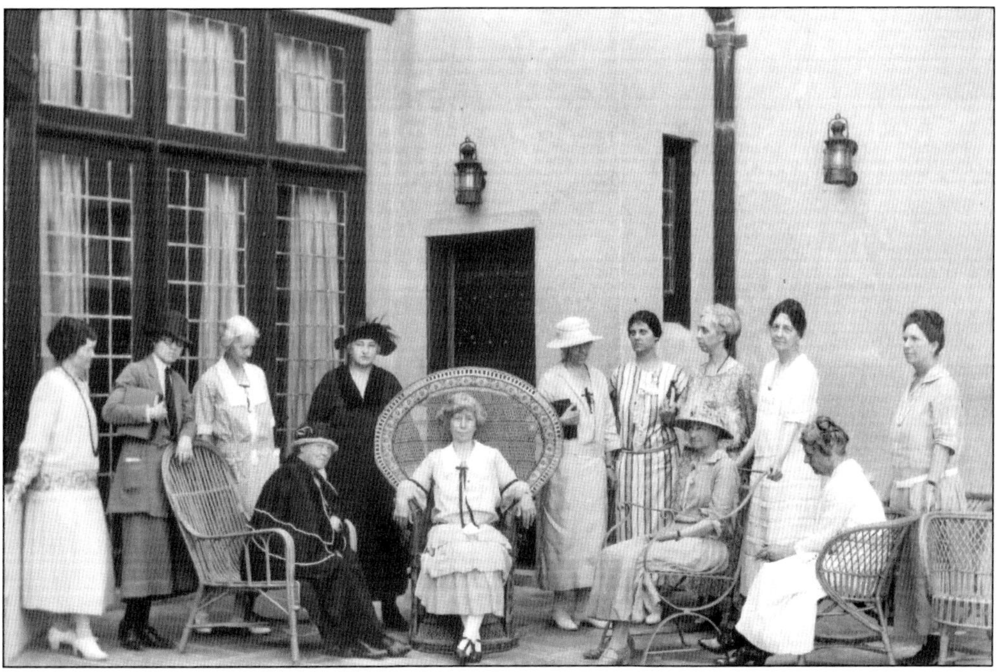

Perhaps a Party for Prof. Margaret Washburn (Class of 1891), Seated Center. Faculty members and alumnae are gathered on the back terrace of the Alumnae House soon after it was built in 1924. The terrace has been a gathering place for hundreds of alumnae and faculty members since that time.

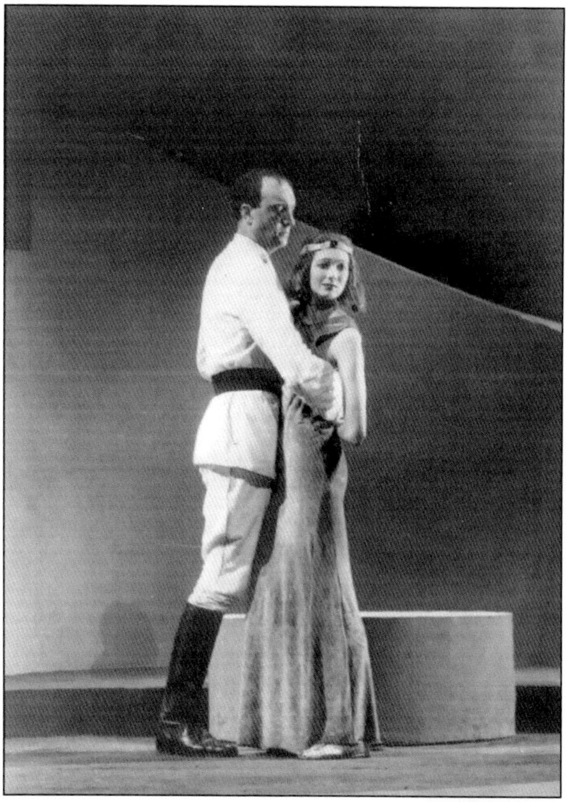

A Scene from *Antony and Cleopatra* in 1935, the Vassar Experimental Theatre. Prof. C. Gordon Post, an actor in the classroom and out, took part in many Vassar Experimental Theatre offerings. He starred with senior Kalita Humphreys (Class of 1935) in this performance, which included President MacCracken as Enobarbus. Other than faculty members and President MacCracken, men from Poughkeepsie also took part in the plays.

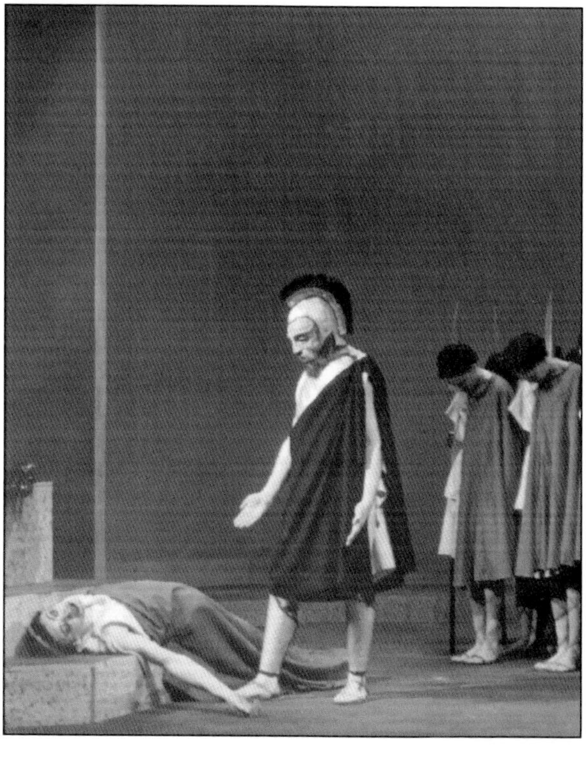

A Scene from *The Hippolytus*. The Vassar Experimental Theatre presented *The Hippolytus* of Euripides in Greek with the cooperation of the departments of music, art, English, and classics in 1931. It was said to be the first presentation of the play in Greek in modern times. President MacCracken, acting in the role of Theseus, missed his lines at a certain point and instead ad-libbed Hamlet's "to be or not to be." Only Grace Macurdy, professor of classics, knew the difference.

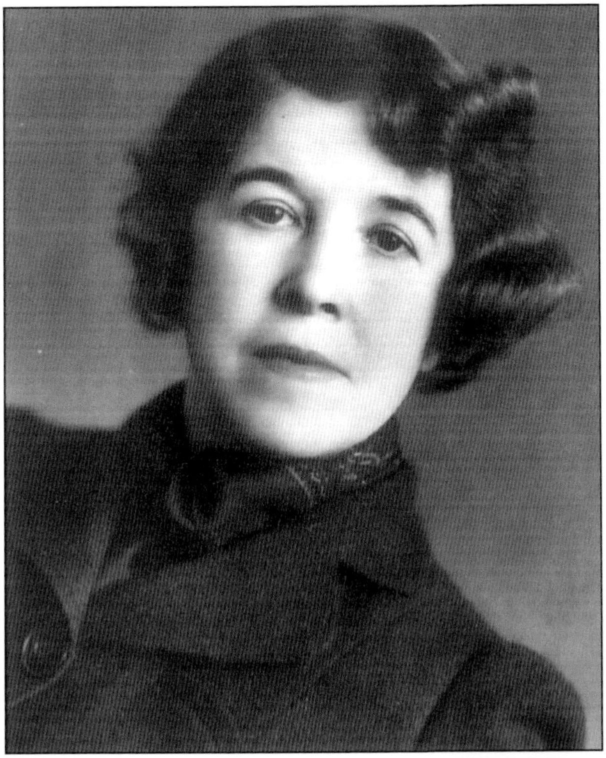

Hallie Flanagan, Director of the Vassar Experimental Theatre. MacCracken hired Hallie Flanagan in 1925 to develop the Vassar Experimental Theatre. Flanagan created a multidisciplinary theatre program, DP (Dramatic Production), a descendant of which continues in today's drama major. Franklin D. Roosevelt, who was a Vassar trustee from 1924 until his death in 1945, appointed Hallie Flanagan to be head of the Federal Theatre Program in 1935 at the suggestion of Harry Hopkins and with the support of Eleanor Roosevelt.

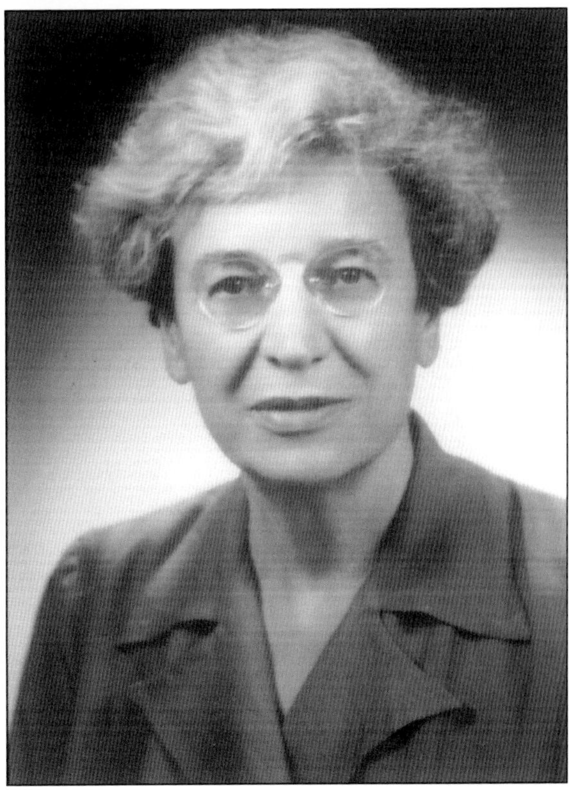

Helen Drusilla Lockwood (Class of 1912). Students composed a song about themselves and certain members of the "funny, funny faculty." One verse observed, "They've gone out from Lockwood's English, far out in the wide / wide world!" Beginning in 1926, Prof. Helen Lockwood's formidable classes, the Contemporary Press and Public Discussion, provoked generations of students to examine their basic assumptions and to think for themselves on issues of the day without falling into stereotypes.

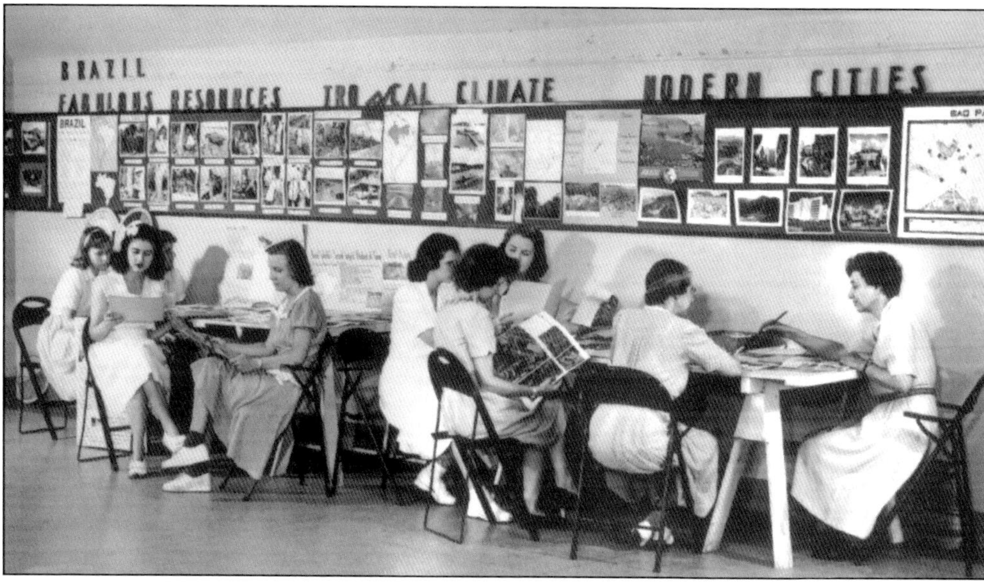

The Social Museum. The Social Museum in Blodgett Hall was first opened with an exhibition entitled "The Development of Housing in New York City." At the exhibition, Eleanor Roosevelt spoke on women and housing in connection with a Conference on Housing held on November 5 and 6, 1937. Seated on the far right is Helen D. Lockwood, professor of English. The students in Lockwood's Public Discussion class helped mount many of the museum's exhibits. To Lockwood's left is her collaborator, Genevieve Lamson, professor of geography.

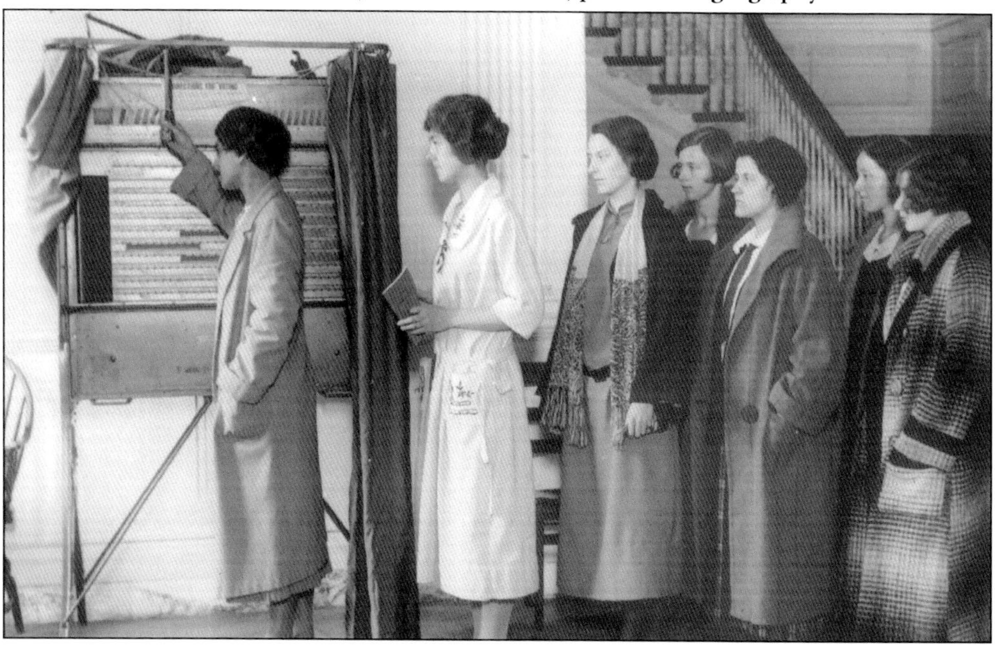

Mock Voting. After the Political Association was chartered in 1921, it often sponsored mock elections for presidential candidates. In the 1920s, a voting booth was set up in Students' Building (now All College Dining Center) and students lined up to cast their votes. In the mock election held for students, faculty, and staff on November 3, 1960, the Democrats won over the Republicans by a margin of five votes.

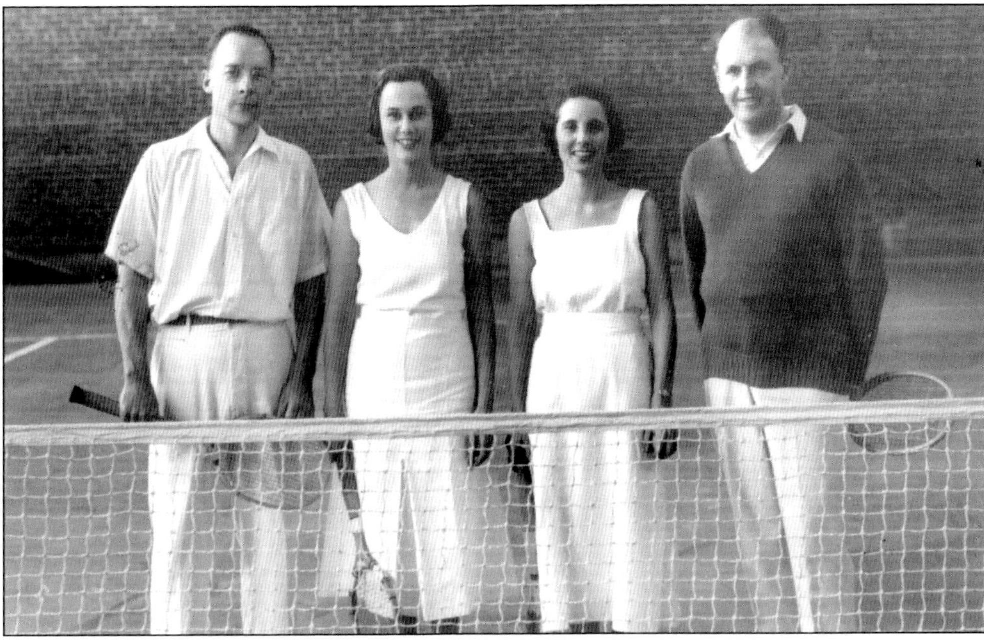

The Indoor Clay Court. Kenyon Hall, the college's third gymnasium (built in 1933), had an indoor clay court. It was initiated by physics Prof. Paul Northrop, President MacCracken (who was a first-class player), and two top-notch student players. Tennis was introduced at Vassar soon after it arrived in the United States from England. The first tennis courts were located in the grassy athletic circle and were graced by players in long-skirted tennis attire.

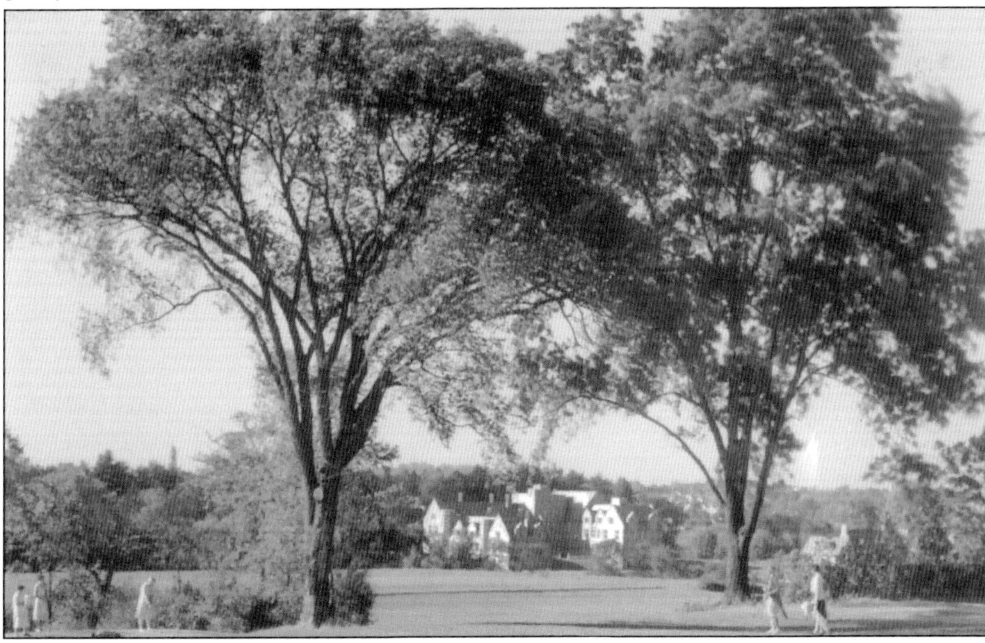

The Golf Course on Sunset Hill. Students and faculty members laid out a nine-hole golf course together after Vassar College acquired property known as the Wing Farm. A golf tournament was held on opening day, September 27, 1930. The course is still in use, now available to the public at large. In the background of this early picture is Blodgett Hall, completed in 1928.

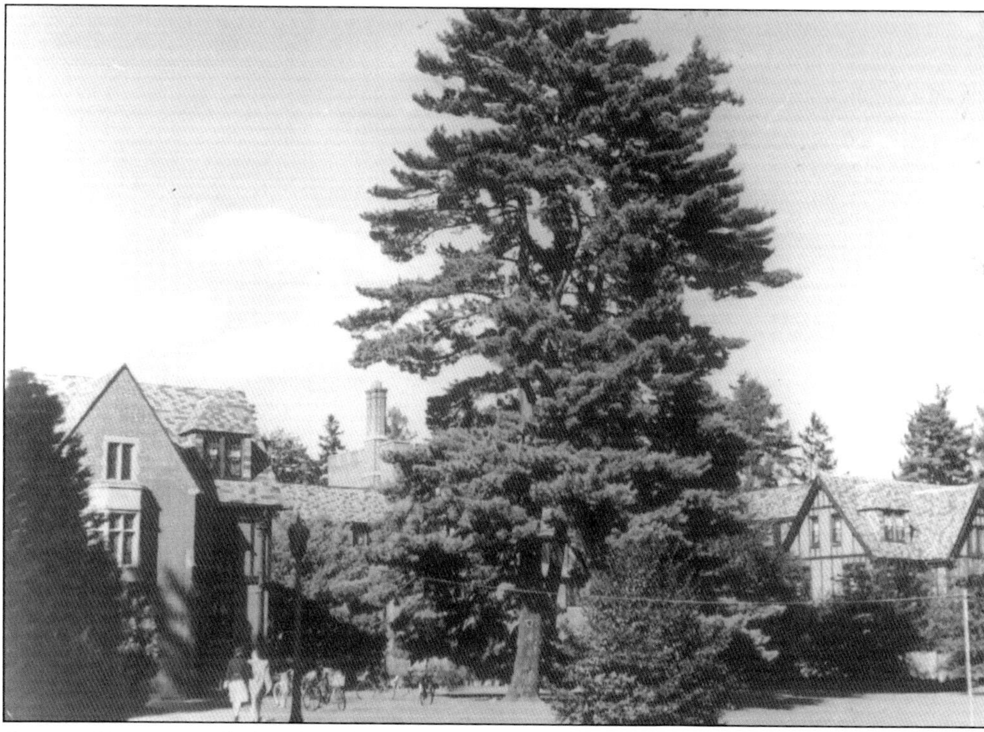

Cushing Hall. Intended at first for freshman, Cushing Hall was added to the growing list of dormitories in 1927. It was the gift of Florence Cushing (Class of 1874). In 1887, Cushing was one of three women to be nominated to the all-male board of trustees. The others were Elizabeth Poppleton (Class of 1876) and Helen Hiscock Backus (Class of 1873). (Courtesy Margaret DeM. Brown.)

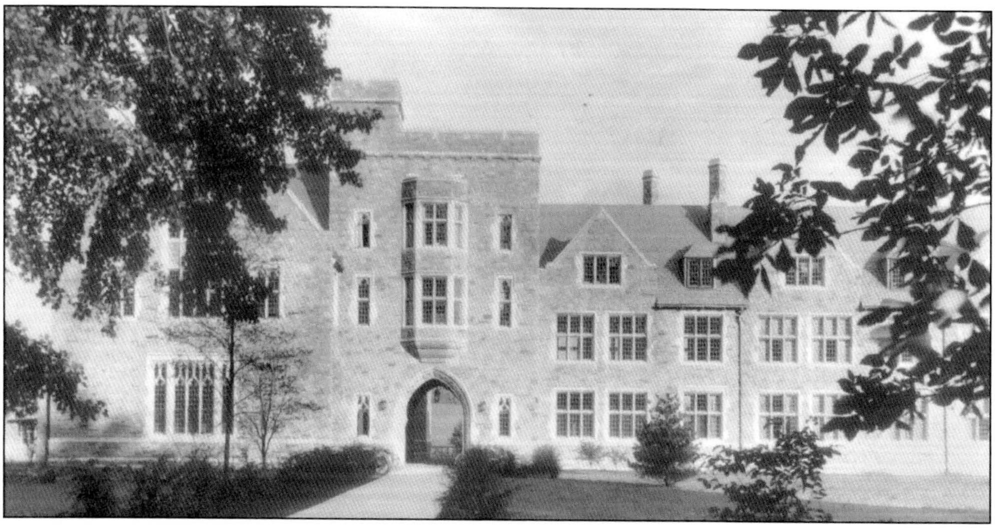

A Closeup of Blodgett Hall. Blodgett Hall, given by Mr. and Mrs. John Blodgett, was built in 1928. It was originally designed to house a multidisciplinary program in the social sciences, sciences, and arts. The title of this program, Euthenics, was coined by Vassar graduate Ellen Swallow Richards (Class of 1870) to denote the improvement of the quality of life. However, the program was not readily accepted by the faculty, and the building was modified for other uses.

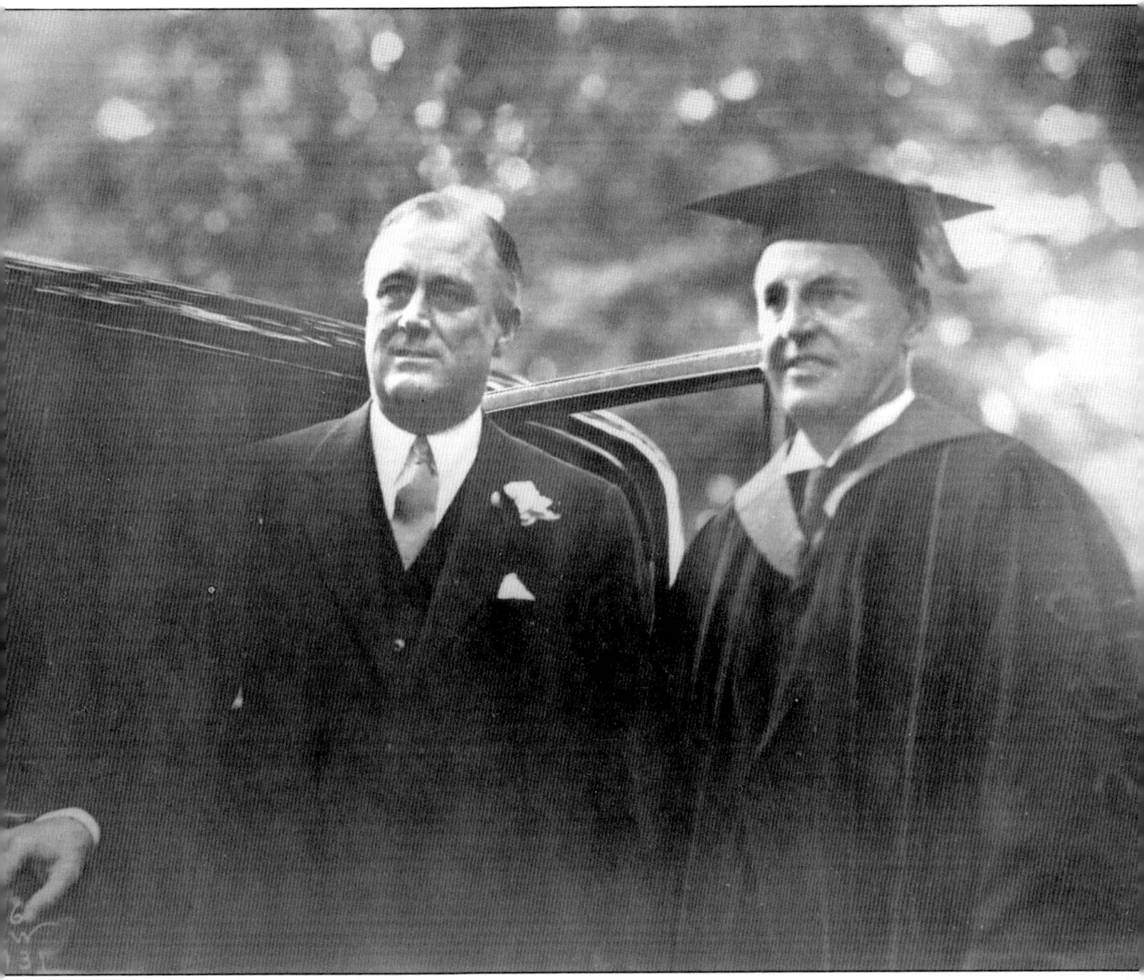

FDR, Vassar Trustee. Franklin Delano Roosevelt, governor of New York from 1929 to 1933, was a trustee of the college from 1923 until his death in 1945. He spoke at the 1931 commencement exercises. Roosevelt served on several trustee committees, including the 1926 committee that decided to end the requirement of attending chapel. Roosevelt and his wife, Eleanor, made appearances on the Vassar campus and often entertained Vassar students at the Summer White House (the Roosevelt estate) in Hyde Park, New York. In the late 1930s, the Vassar choir, under the direction of E. Harold Geer (professor of music), was asked to sing for the Prince and Princess of Norway, who were visiting the Roosevelts.

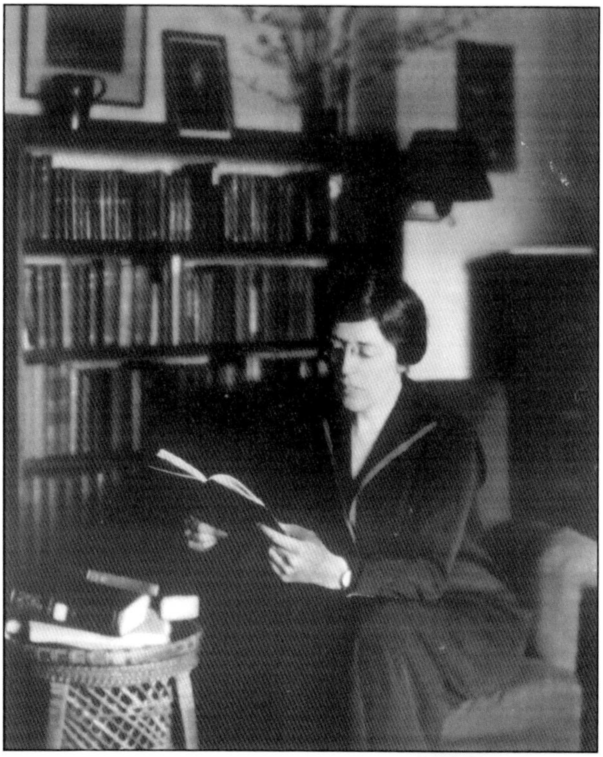

C. Mildred Thompson (Class of 1903). The day after his inauguration, MacCracken invited the presidents of three other women's colleges—Mount Holyoke, Smith, and Wellesley—to a working session in his office to establish a Four College Conference (the predecessor of the Seven Sisters organization) and look into chaotic admission procedures. That year, MacCracken chose C. Mildred Thompson, a young history professor, as secretary of Vassar College's newly formed Committee on Admission.

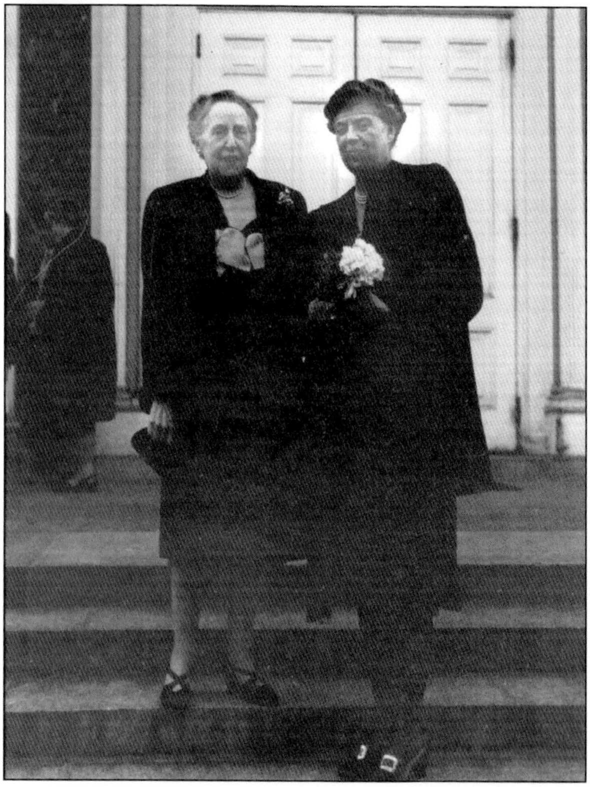

Eleanor Roosevelt (Right) and C. Mildred Thompson, Dean. Over the years, Dean Thompson and Mrs. Roosevelt became good friends. In 1944, Mrs. Roosevelt proposed Thompson as a delegate to the Conference of Allied Ministers of Education in London, a forerunner of UNESCO (United Nations Educational, Scientific, and Cultural Organization), where she joined the male delegates. Thompson was dean of Vassar College from 1923 to 1948.

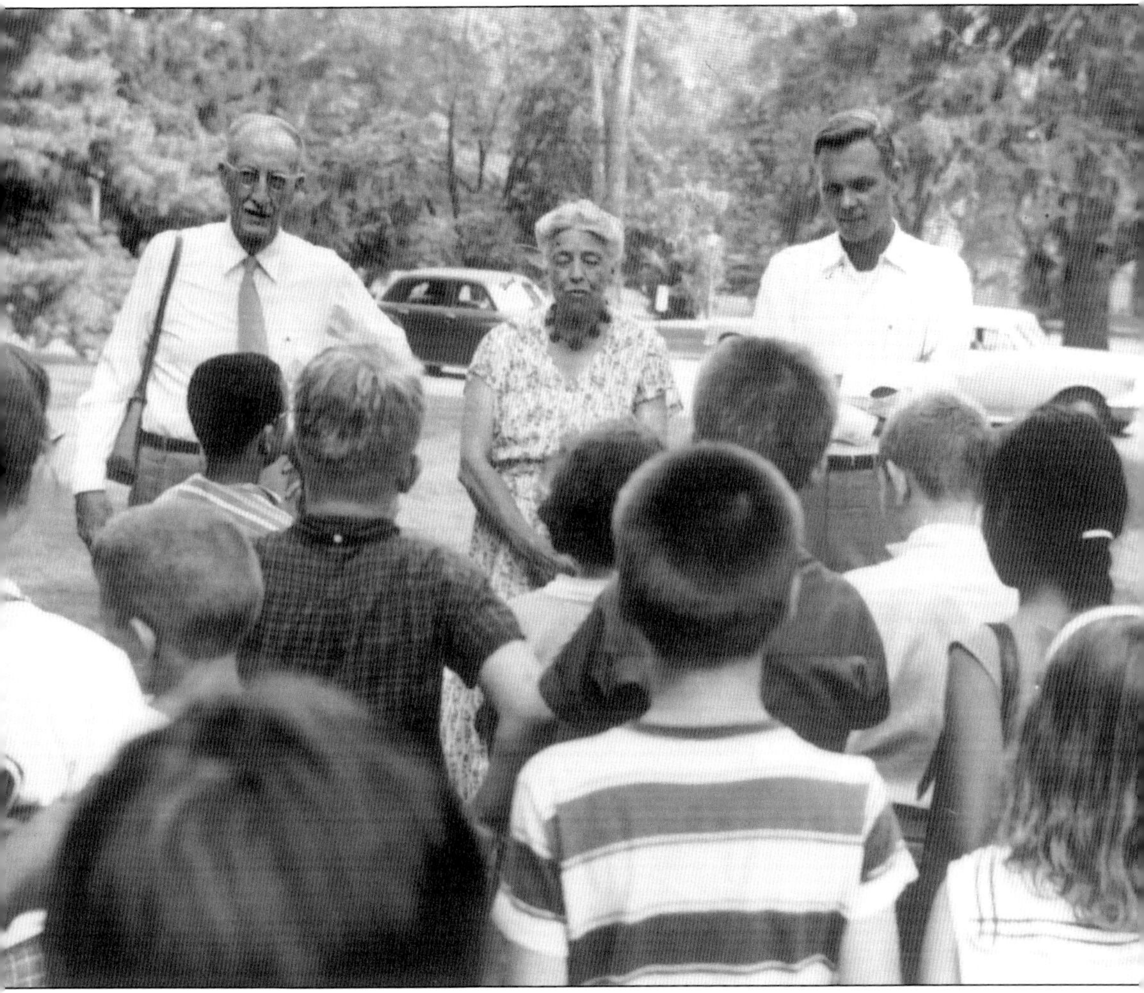

Eleanor Roosevelt Speaking Informally to Summer Institute Children. Professional adults, Vassar alumnae, their children and spouses, and a staff of educators gathered for six weeks every summer between 1926 and 1951 for the Summer Institute. Mrs. Roosevelt often dropped in from Val-Kill, her residence in Hyde Park, to talk with the children and adults. The Summer Institute was headed for many years by Prof. Mary Fisher Langmuir, the director of the Vassar College Nursery School.

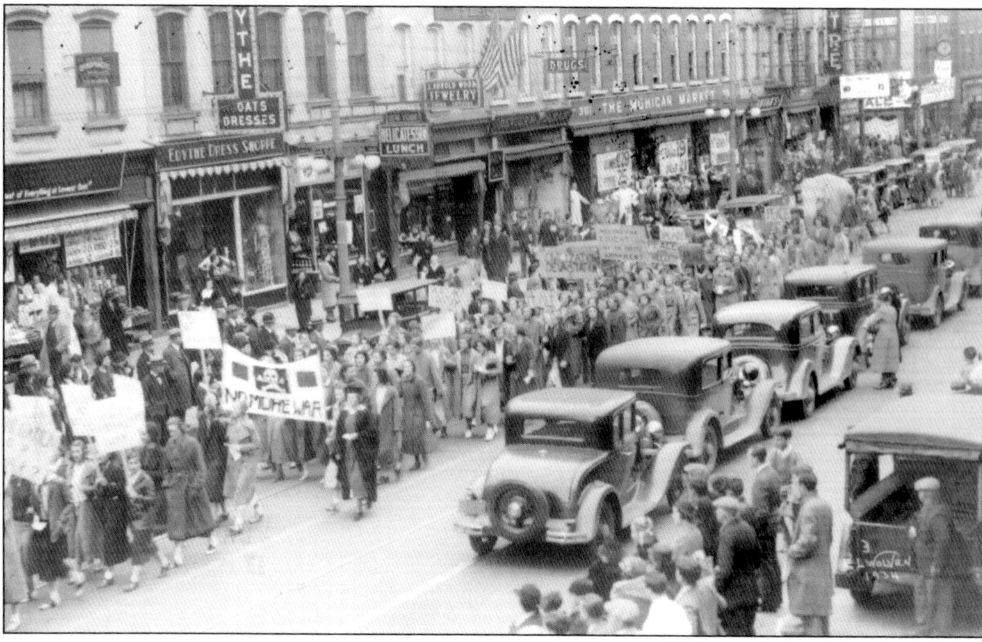

Peace Parade, Vassar Marching. Vassar students demonstrated for "no more war" in downtown Poughkeepsie in 1934. This photograph shows a lively crowd of onlookers watching an impressive line of marching students. Maintaining order in her cap and gown was Warden Eleanor Dodge, who upheld the students' right to demonstrate.

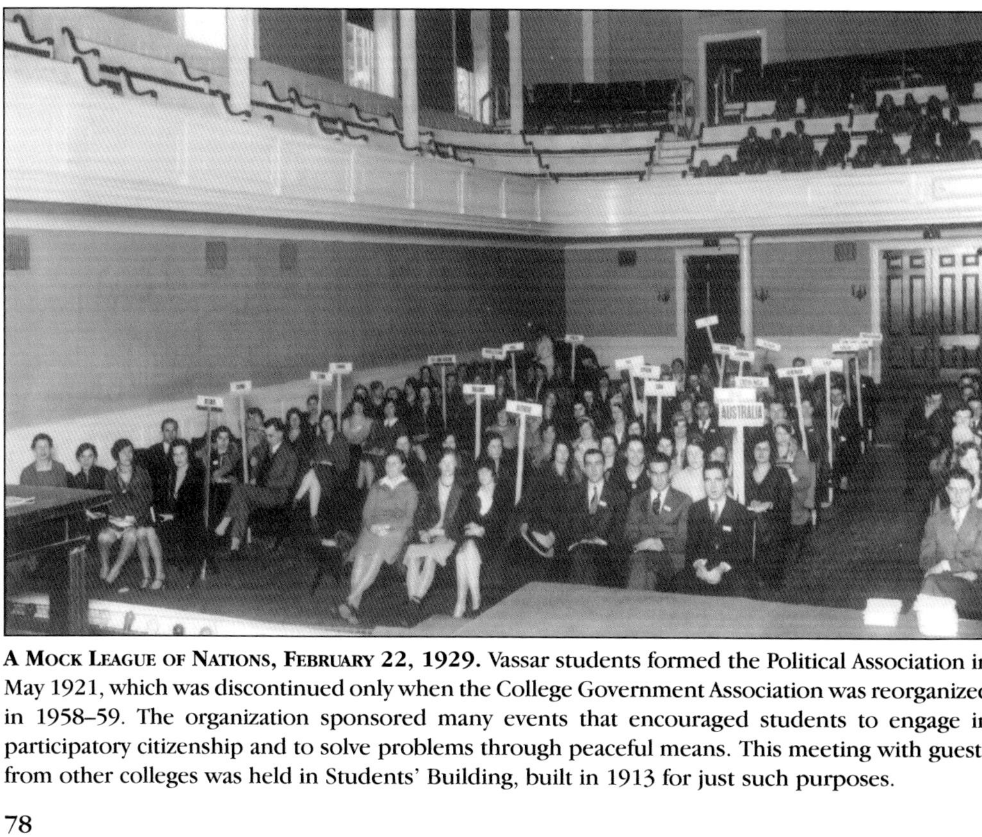

A Mock League of Nations, February 22, 1929. Vassar students formed the Political Association in May 1921, which was discontinued only when the College Government Association was reorganized in 1958–59. The organization sponsored many events that encouraged students to engage in participatory citizenship and to solve problems through peaceful means. This meeting with guests from other colleges was held in Students' Building, built in 1913 for just such purposes.

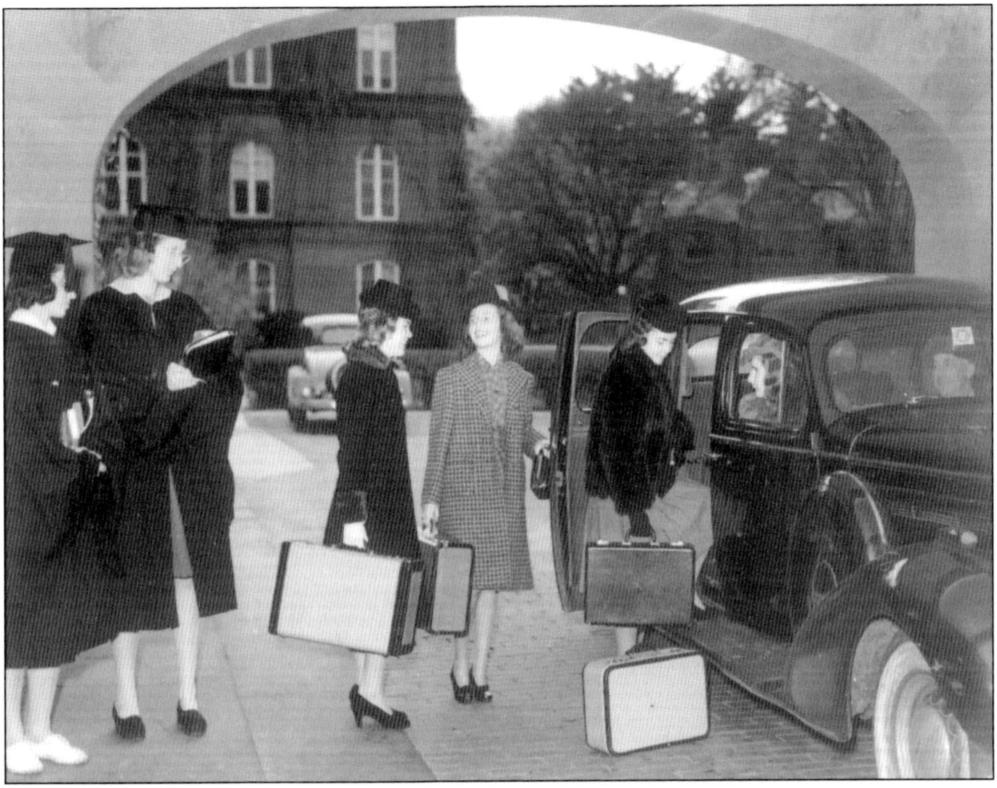

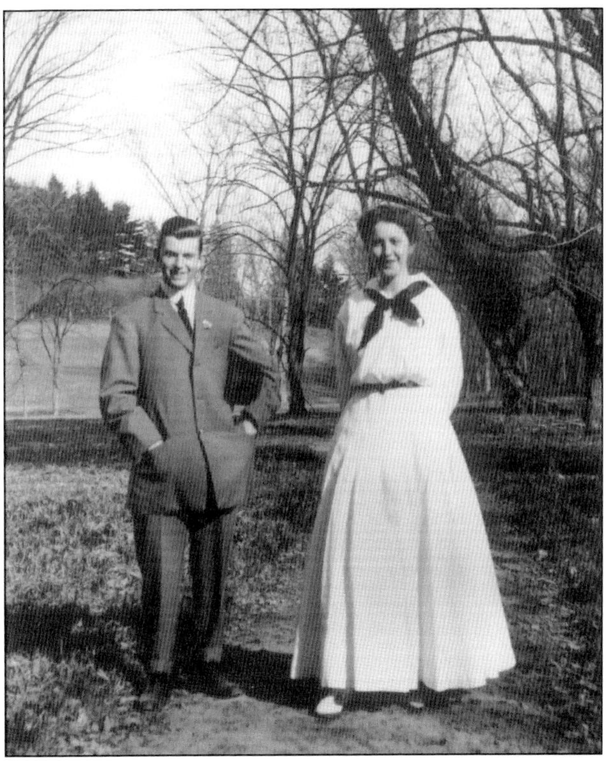

LEAVING FOR THE WEEKEND IN 1940 (ABOVE), AN EARLIER TWOSOME (RIGHT). The man and woman on the right are enjoying a walk on the path along the Casperkill before the stream was dammed in 1912. The middy blouse was in vogue at the time. Dating customs changed rapidly after World War I. By 1940, "weekends" at men's colleges were "in." The college more or less shut down at the end of the academic week as students joined an exodus to Yale, West Point, Williams, Princeton, or simply to meet their beaux "under the clock at the Biltmore" in Manhattan. Weekend time sometimes dragged for those students left back in the library.

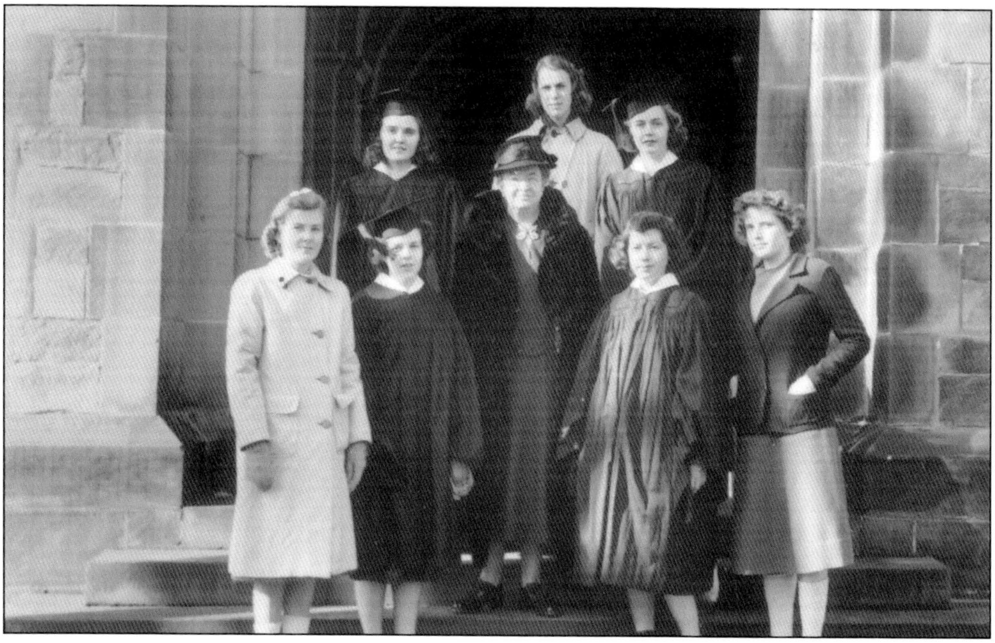

Carrie Chapman Catt with Students in 1941. Politically minded students meet on the steps of the chapel with Carrie Chapman Catt, probably before her lecture. In February 1941, the Political Association sponsored a conference entitled "Higher Education and the Defense of Democracy," with speakers and panel discussions from various points of view.

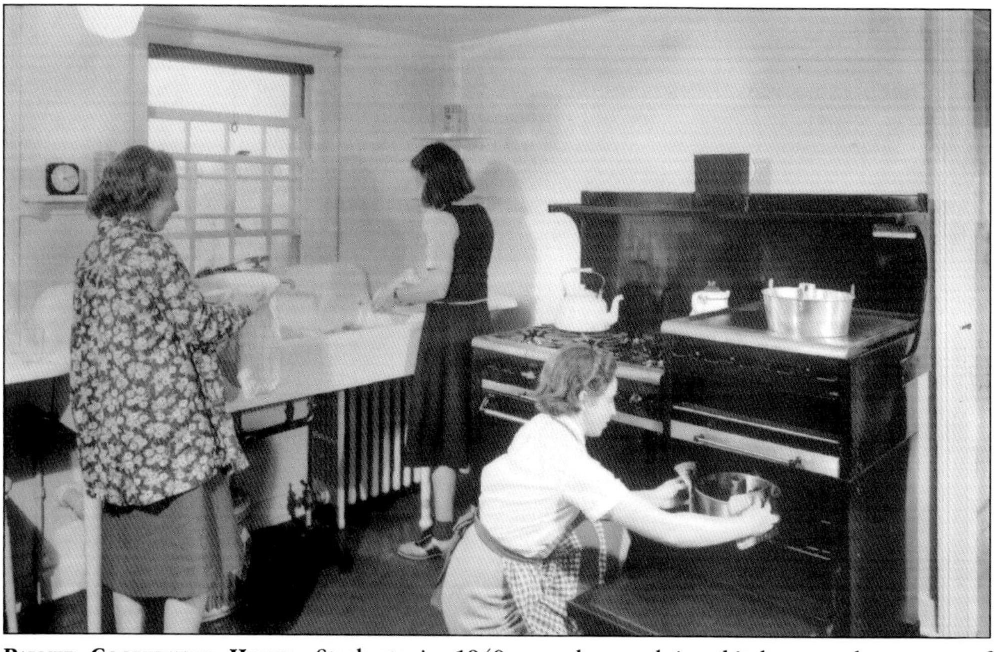

Palmer Cooperative House. Students in 1940 are shown doing kitchen work as part of cooperative living in Palmer House. About 30 students lived together in Palmer, the college's second cooperative house, purchasing their food and cooking their meals. Vassar has had three cooperative houses altogether: the first in a section of Blodgett Hall; the second, the remodeled Wing farmhouse, renamed Palmer House; the third, Ferry House, designed by Marcel Breuer.

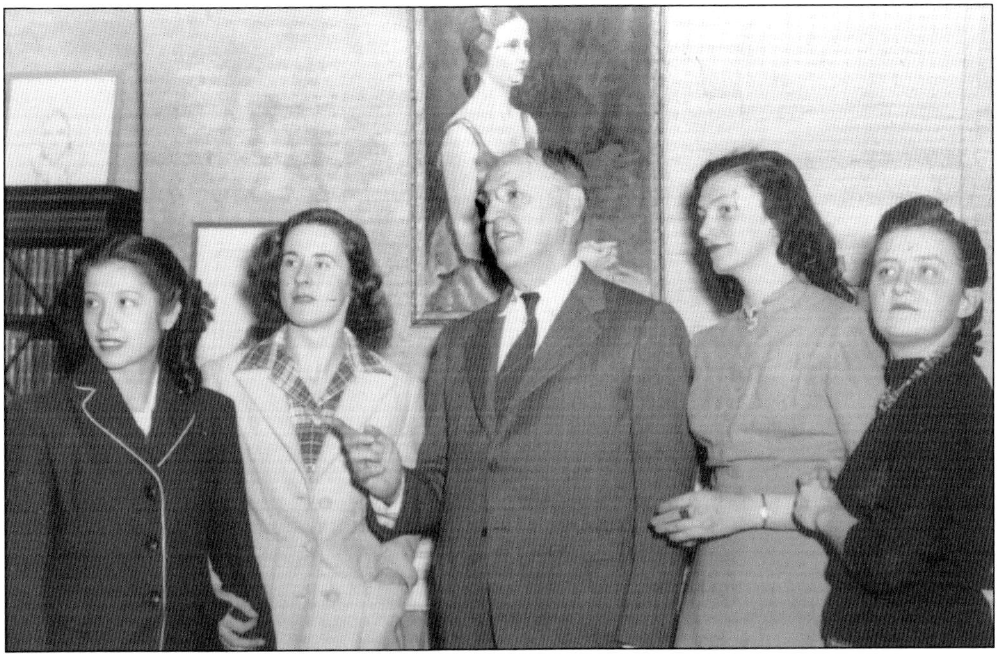

MacCracken with a Group of Foreign Students. This photograph shows MacCracken entertaining a group of foreign students. Beginning in the 1920s, when five Czechoslovakian students were enrolled at Vassar, the college sought out students from abroad. In the years after World War II, both displaced students and faculty members from Europe were welcomed into the Vassar community, along with students from other parts of the world.

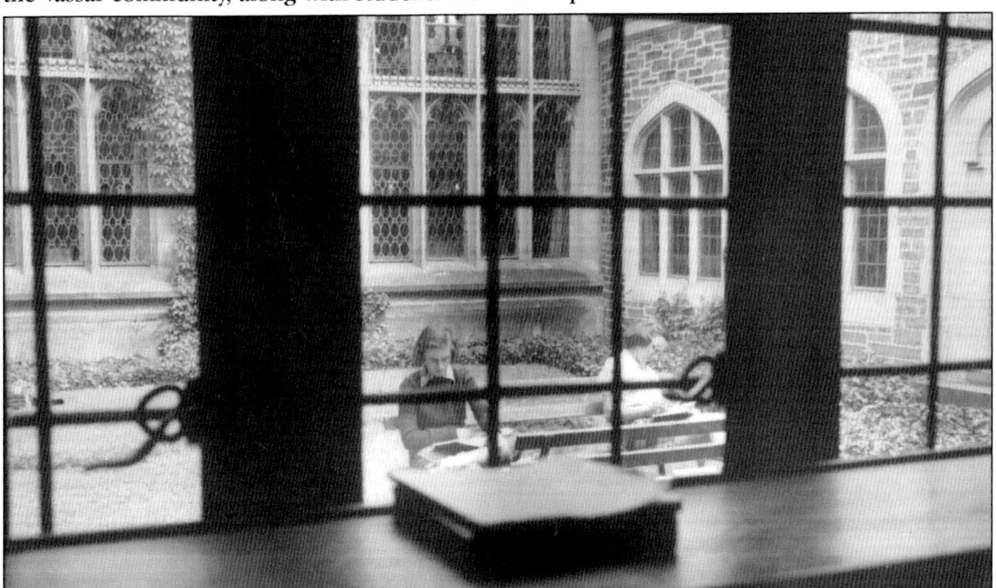

Absorbed Readers. The Thompson Library as it was in the 1940s, with grassy interior courtyards, afforded privacy for quiet reading. The library has been remodeled several times since it was built in 1905. Just completed is the Martha Rivers and E. Bronson Ingram Library, which has added archival space and many technological innovations. The recent renovation of the library has created a new grassy courtyard.

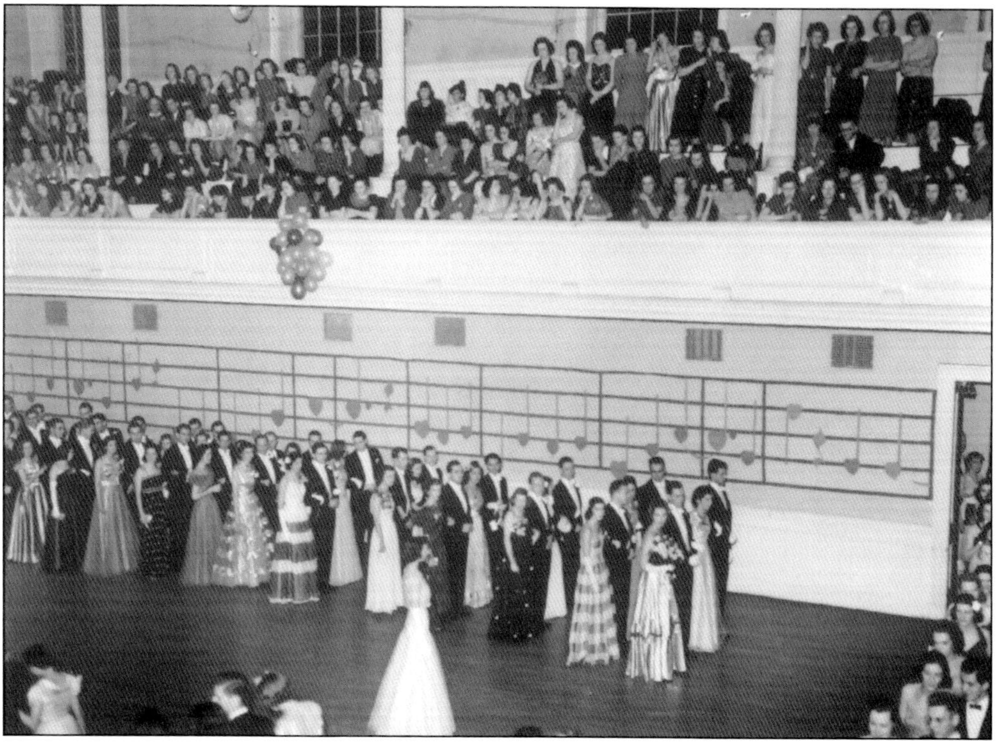

The Vassar Junior Prom, 1940. In February of any given mid-20th-century year, the rituals of the junior prom took place in Students' Building. The juniors and their dates opened the prom with a grand march while the rest of the college watched from the balcony. It was a weekend when hearts were won and broken.

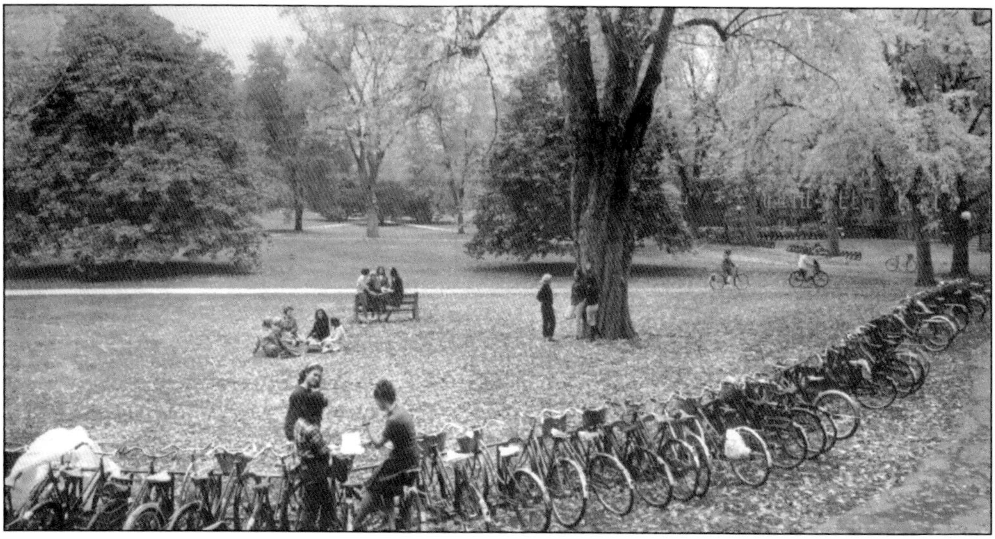

Bicycles. Before students were allowed cars on the campus, they rode bicycles or walked. There was a bicycle exchange in the basement of Students' Building, and there was Sam's Fixit Shop on Collegeview Avenue, where tires could be checked and bicycles repaired. The faculty members who lived nearby sometimes rode to class, and licenses were issued to bicycles instead of stickers to cars.

Four

REGROUPING FOR CHANGE: 1946–1967

In 1946, Sarah Gibson Blanding, who had been dean of the New York State College of Home Economics at Cornell, became Vassar's first woman president. During Blanding's administration, Vassar tripled its investment portfolio, introduced an extensively revised curriculum that emphasized independent work, added the number of men on the faculty, and more than doubled faculty salaries.

In her 18 years as the sixth president of the college, enrollment grew to 1,500 students, new buildings were constructed, and Main Building underwent substantial renovation. With the aid of the Mary Conover Mellon Fund for the Advancement of Education, student counseling services were extended and improved, and Vassar pioneered in basic research into psychological changes during the college years—research that proved valuable to Vassar as well as other institutions.

In a historic all-campus meeting on April 4, 1962, President Blanding told the Vassar students that disciplinary action would be taken against those who did not follow the moral standard of the college, for she believed that sexual promiscuity was "indecent and immoral." She advised those students who could not follow the rules to withdraw voluntarily from Vassar.

In 1961, as the college celebrated the centennial of its founding, Matthew Vassar's aims had been well realized. More than one-quarter of the graduates held advanced degrees, and hundreds had distinguished themselves. Not only had the name of Vassar become a byword for the educated woman, but the college was considered one of the foremost liberal arts colleges in the country.

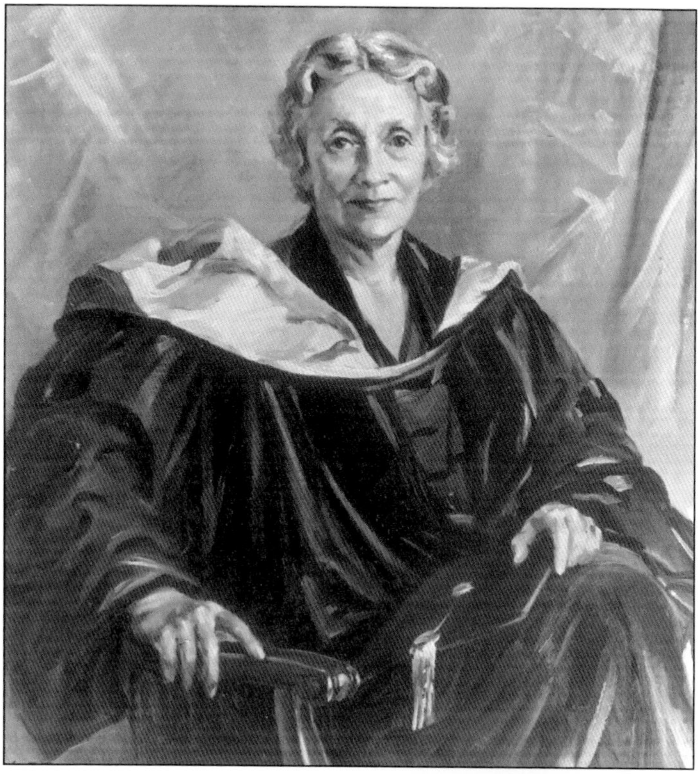

SARAH GIBSON BLANDING, THE DRAPER PORTRAIT. This portrait of Blanding, the first woman president of Vassar (1946–1964), was the gift of the trustees to the college. Painted by William F. Draper (1956), the painting hangs in the Gold Parlor of Main Building.

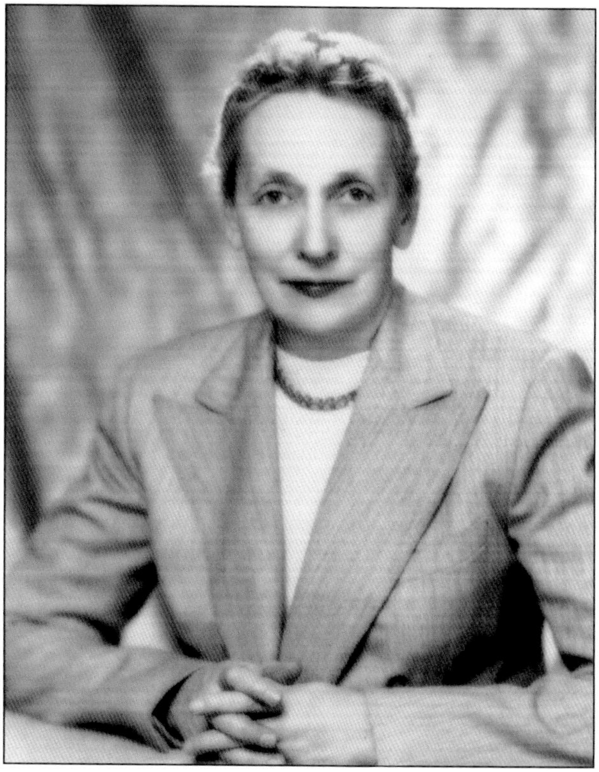

SARAH GIBSON BLANDING. President Blanding is seen in this photograph in an earlier, less formal pose than in the Draper portrait.

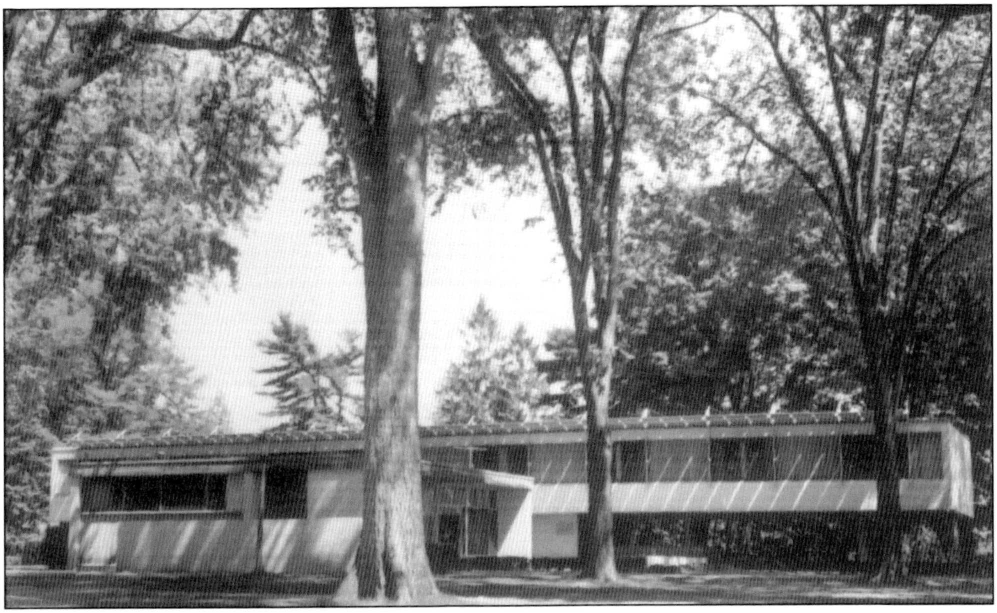

Ferry House. The Dexter M. Ferry Cooperative House, designed by architect Marcel Breuer, was dedicated on October 5, 1951. Twenty-seven students took up residence and housekeeping in Ferry House that fall. The ground floor provides common rooms for cooking, eating, and socializing. The elevated area offers bedroom and study accommodations. "In appreciation of all Vassar has meant to the Ferry family," the house was given by Dexter M. Ferry of Detroit, brother of Blanche Ferry Hooker (Class of 1899) and Queene Ferry Cooper (Class of 1896), who together gave the Vassar Alumnae House in 1924.

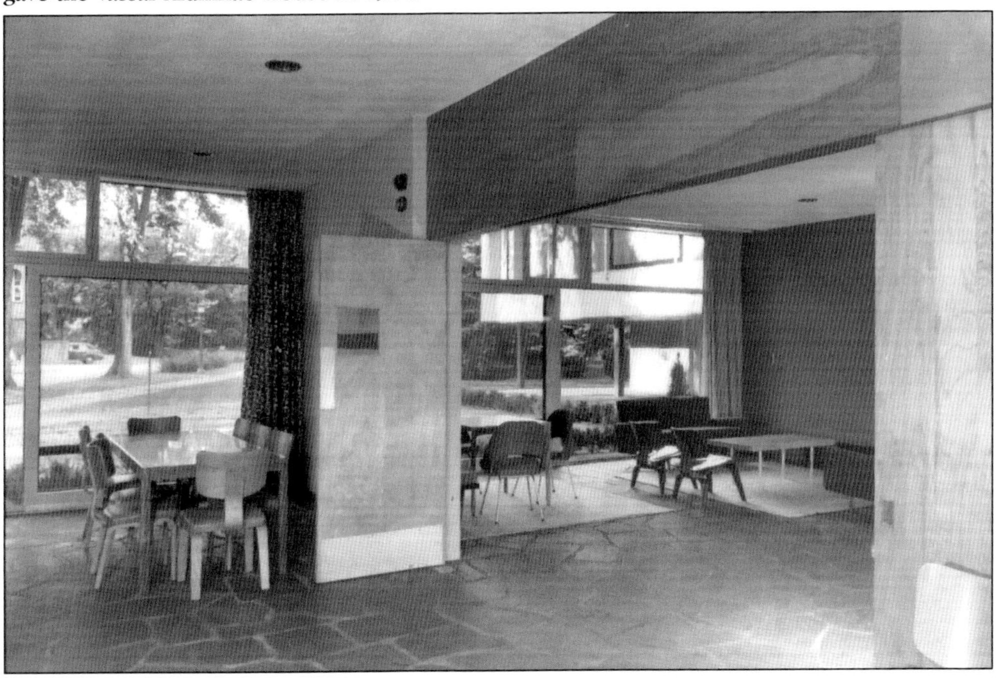

Ferry House, Interior. The building has a wall of glass to bring the outdoors into the interior of the building and doors to separate the common rooms.

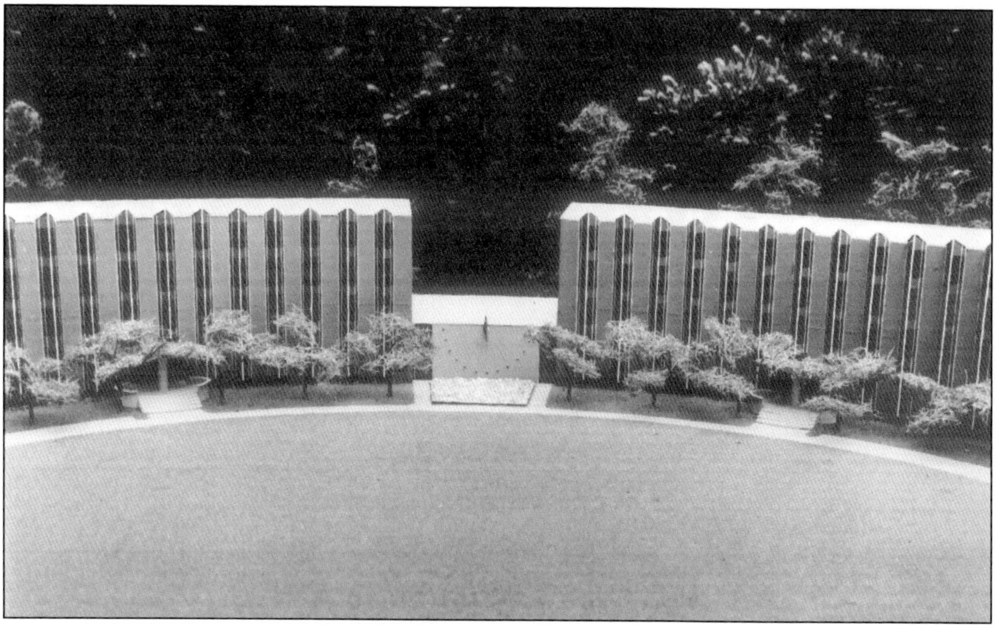

A Model of Noyes House. The Emma Hartman Noyes House, the last residence hall to be built, opened in the fall of 1958. It was given by the descendants of Emma Hartman Noyes (Class of 1880) and designed by Eero Saarinen, husband of Aline Saarinen (Class of 1935). The handsome building was intended to be the first of two identical units that would have formed a semicircle, as pictured here, thus reinforcing the form of the circle. After determining on coeducation, the college decided not to build the second building but to build the Town Houses and Terrace Apartments as alternative, apartment-style living space.

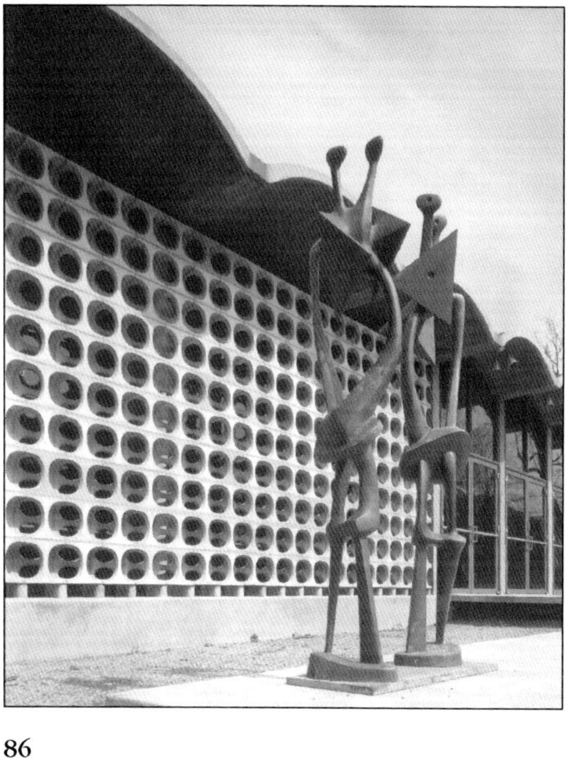

Chicago Hall. Designated for language study, Chicago Hall was dedicated on April 24, 1959. Winston Elting and Paul Schweikher were the architects for the building, the third on the campus at that time to be built in a contemporary style. Building funds were raised by alumnae of the Chicago area, under the leadership of Marion Musser Lloyd (Class of 1932). Pictured is Henry Moore's sculpture *Double Standing Figure* on loan to Chicago Hall in the 1960s. The sculpture is now part of the permanent collection of the Frances Lehman Loeb Art Center.

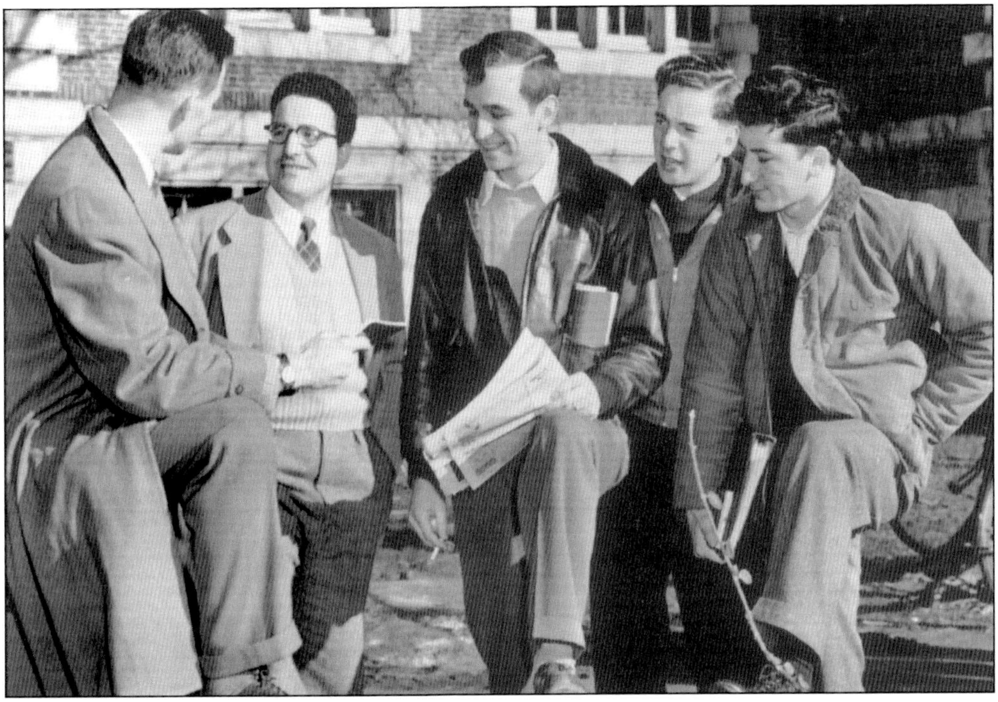

The First Vassar Men. From 1946 to 1950, there was a program at Vassar for veterans of World War II that enabled them to attend classes on campus under the GI Bill. The State University of New York granted their degrees, as Vassar's charter prevented the college from granting degrees to men.

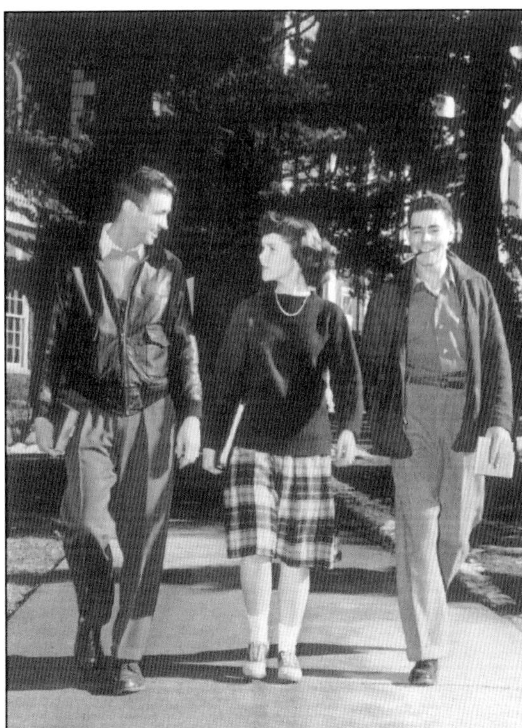

A Rare Sight in the 1940s. Of the 40 GIs who arrived on campus in 1946, 16 completed the college course and received their degrees.

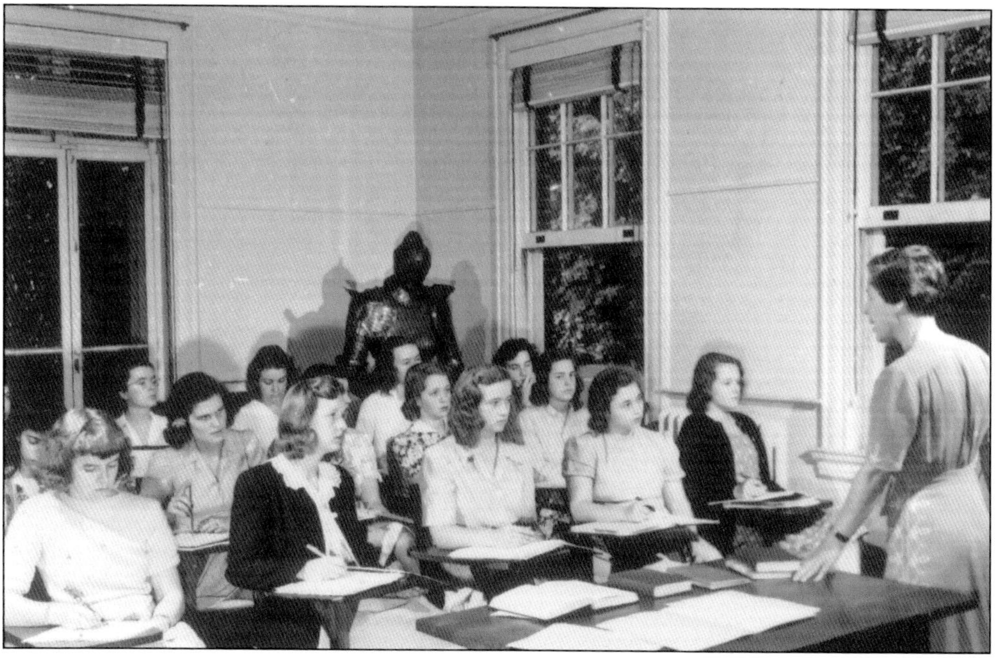

A History Class. In this traditional class setting, Prof. J.B. Ross (Class of 1925) lectures to her students. Ross was professor of history from 1935 to 1937 and from 1940 to 1966. She served as assistant dean from 1944 to 1949. Note the knight in armor at the back of the room.

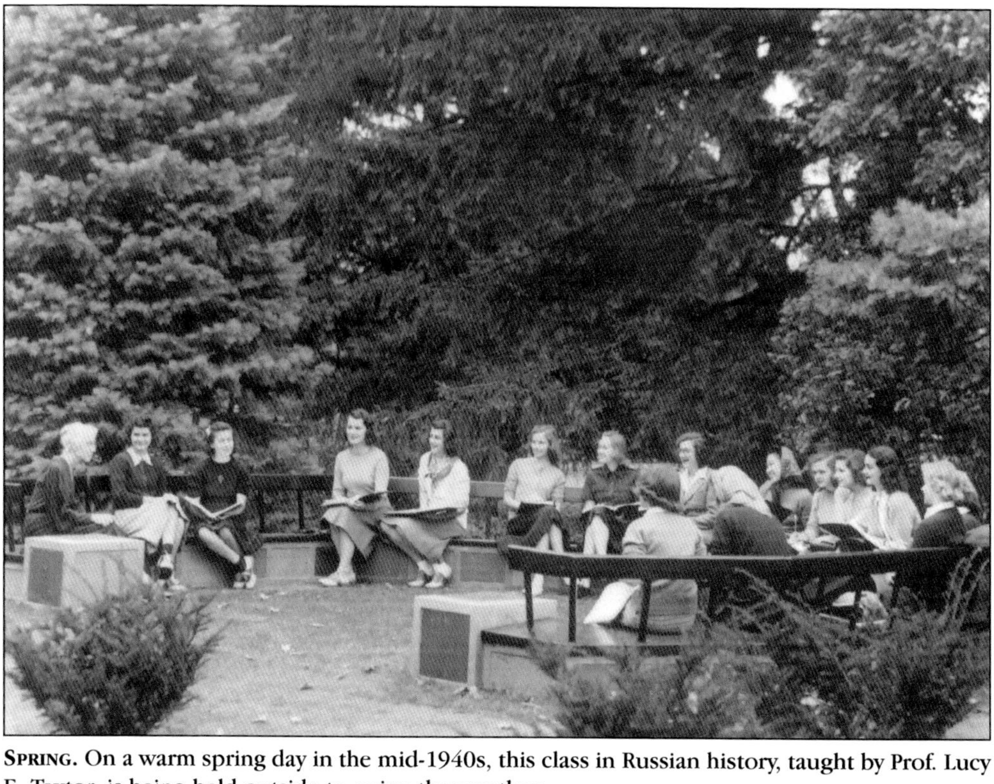

Spring. On a warm spring day in the mid-1940s, this class in Russian history, taught by Prof. Lucy E. Textor, is being held outside to enjoy the weather.

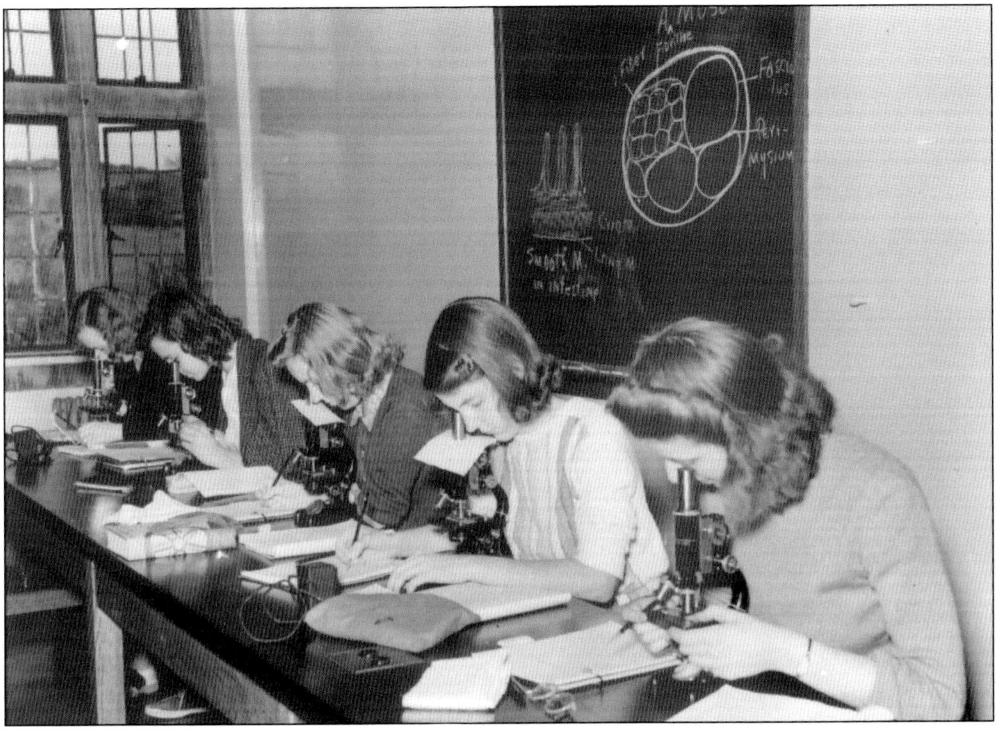

ZOOLOGY CLASS. Students examine specimens in a zoology class.

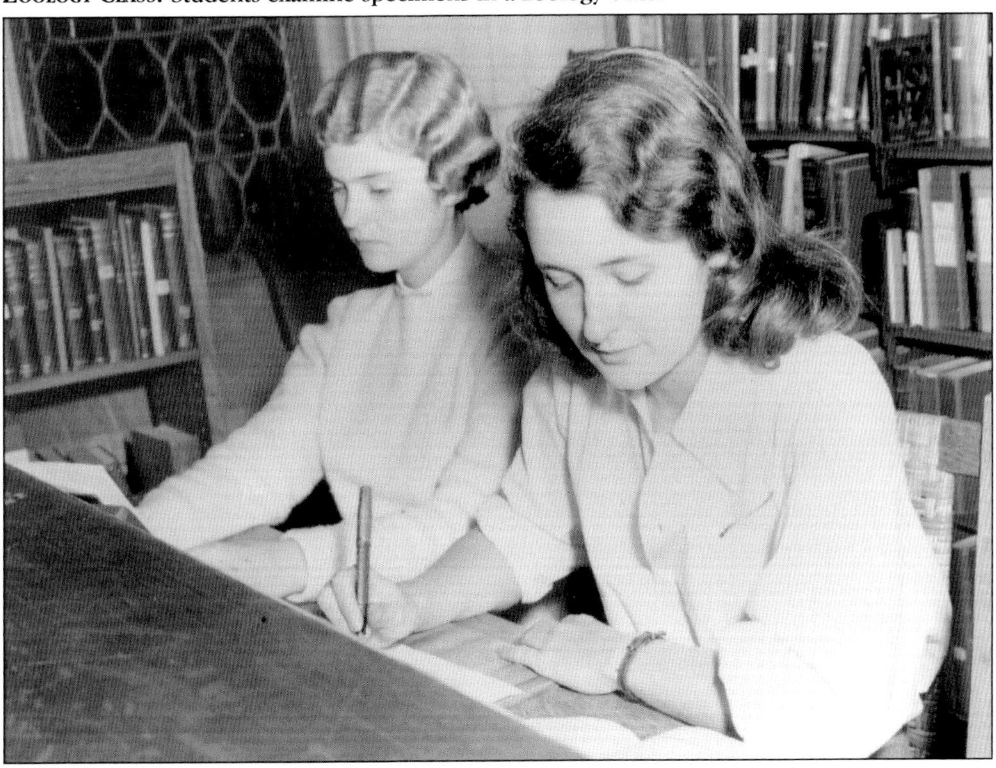

A FAVORITE SPOT TO STUDY, 1952. Students often enjoyed quiet time in the library to study.

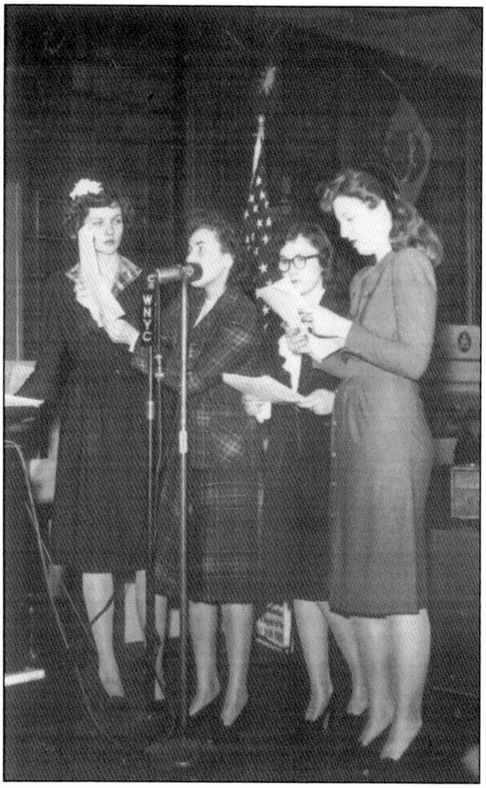

THE VASSAR RADIO WORKSHOP, 1944. Students of the Vassar Radio Workshop broadcast at a radio station office in Pershing Square, New York City. The broadcast was entitled "College Girl! What Are You Doing?"

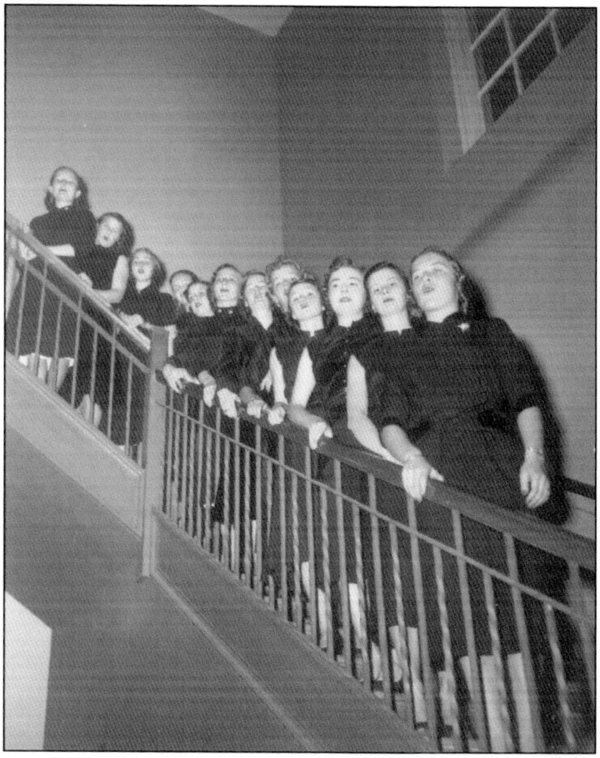

THE NIGHT OWLS. One of the nation's oldest continuous a capella singing groups, the Night Owls were formed at Vassar in 1942. The story is that the group was founded when several young women broke a polio quarantine at the college. Dressed in black, they sneaked out of their rooms at night to sing in the basement of the library. Notable Night Owls include actress Meryl Streep (Class of 1971). In 1993, the group was chosen to sing in the parade celebrating President-Elect Bill Clinton's inauguration in Washington, D.C., on January 20. Their repertoire includes songs from the 1930s and 1940s.

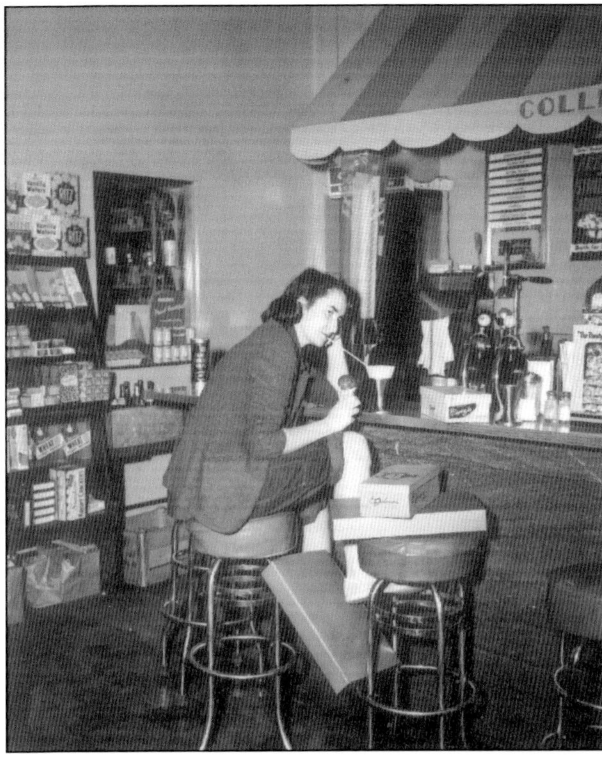

AN OLD-FASHIONED SODA COUNTER. Students in the 1950s would relax with a soda in the College Drug Store on Raymond Avenue.

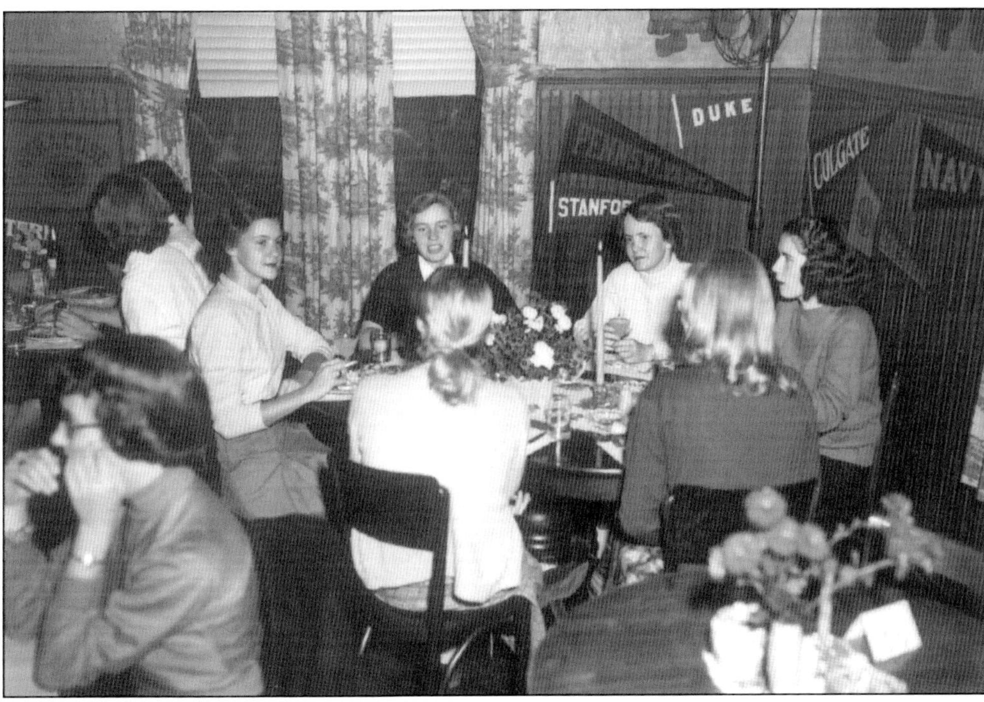

THE DUTCH CABIN. Always a favorite gathering place for students, the Dutch Cabin restaurant on Fairmont Avenue, across the street from the north end of campus, offered food, drinks, and good times with friends.

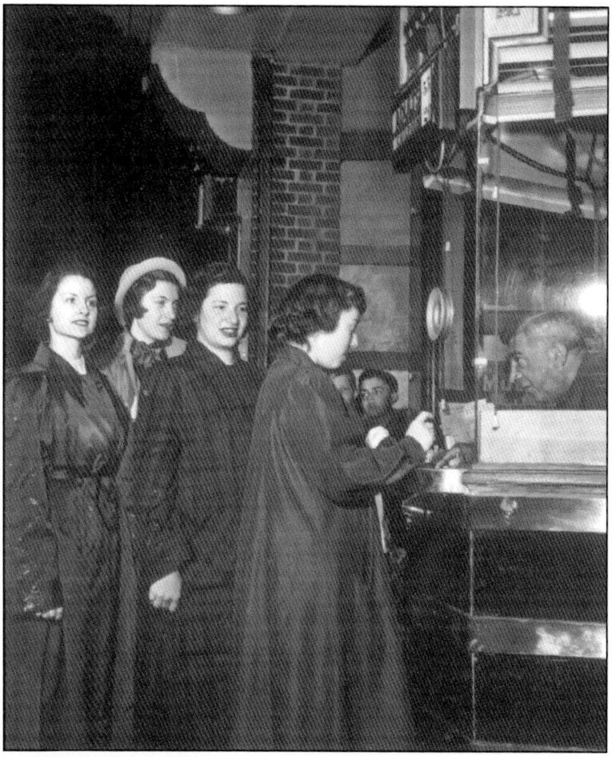

The Juliet Theater. Students line up in the 1950s to purchase tickets at the Juliet Theater on the corner of Raymond and Collegeview Avenues.

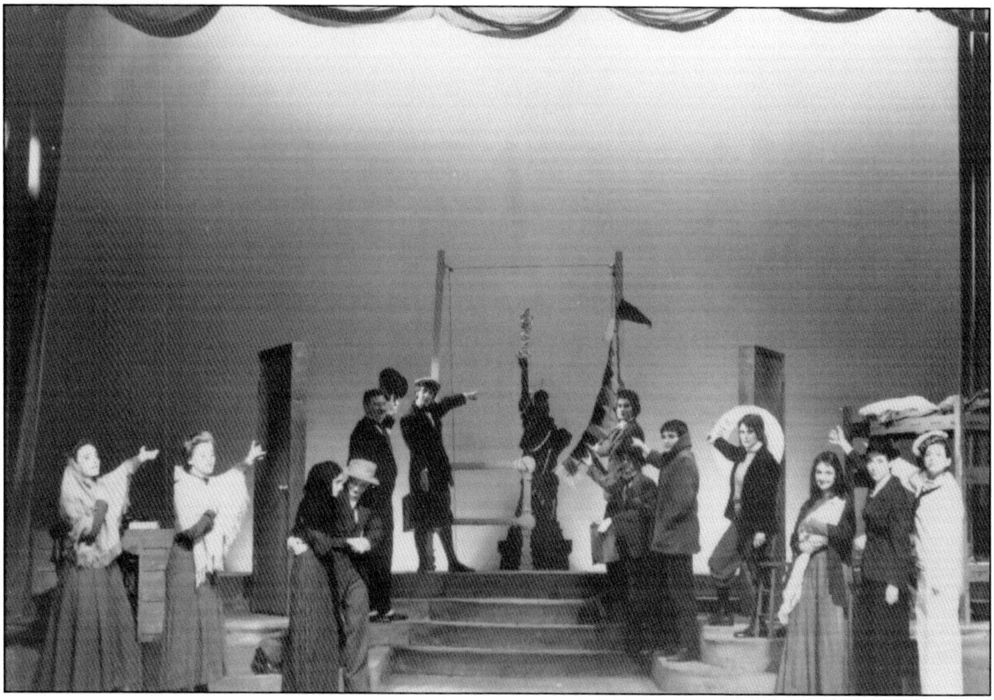

A Dramatic Production. On May 8, 1958, the Vassar Experimental Theatre presented the first American performance of Franz Kafka's *Amerika,* dramatized by Leon Katz and directed by George B. Dowell, both of the drama department.

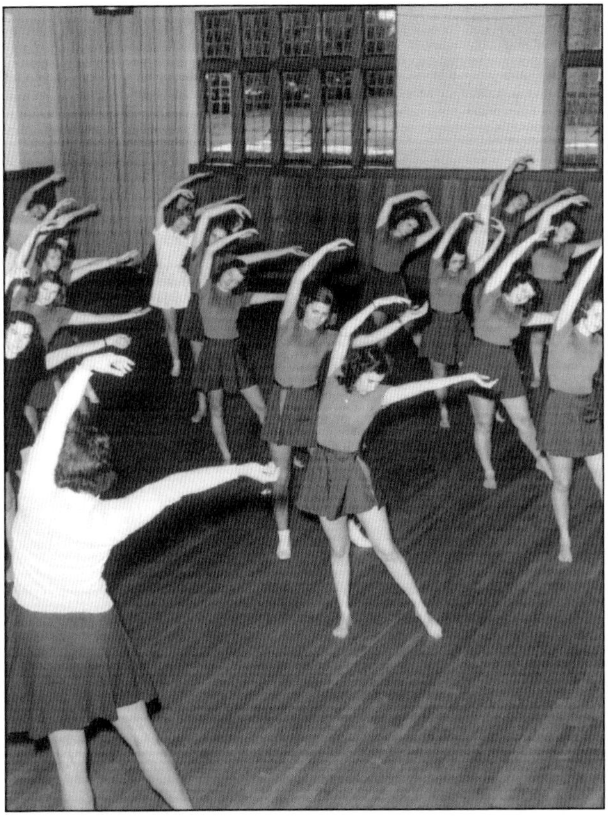

Body Mechanics Class. Pictured is a body mechanics class, which was required of all freshmen since the college began. Matthew Vassar was very interested in physical education for women. In 1893, seniors had asked that compulsory gymnastics be abolished for the senior class, but the faculty thought there was "not sufficient reason" to grant their request. During the early 1970s, physical education as a requirement for all students was dropped.

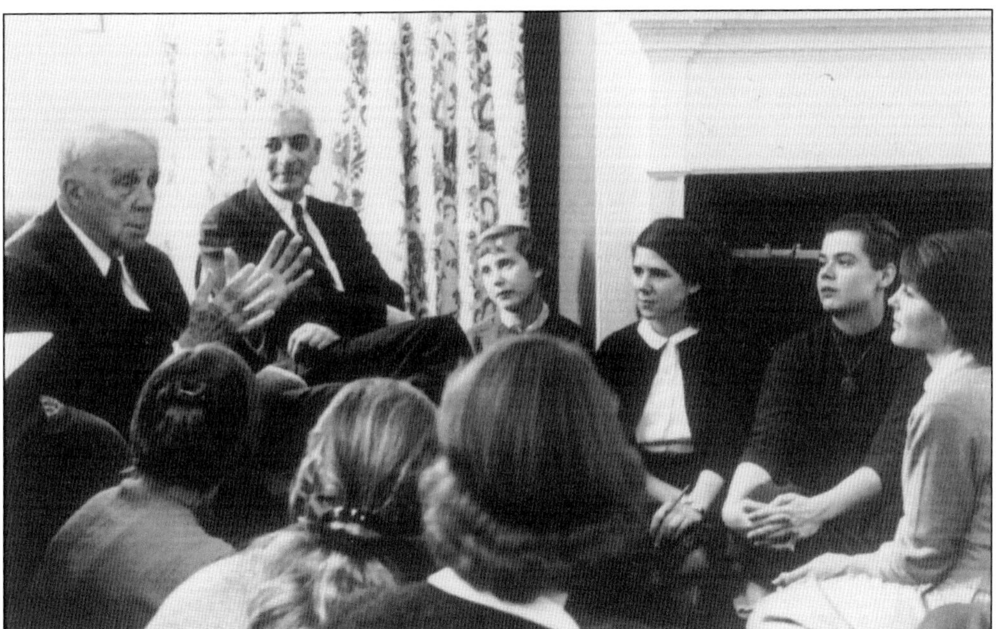

Poet's Visit, 1959. American poet Robert Frost (left) visited the campus two days in December 1959. He gave a lecture entitled "The Peril of Newness" and talked informally with English department majors. To Frost's right is Richard A.E. Brooks, professor of English at Vassar.

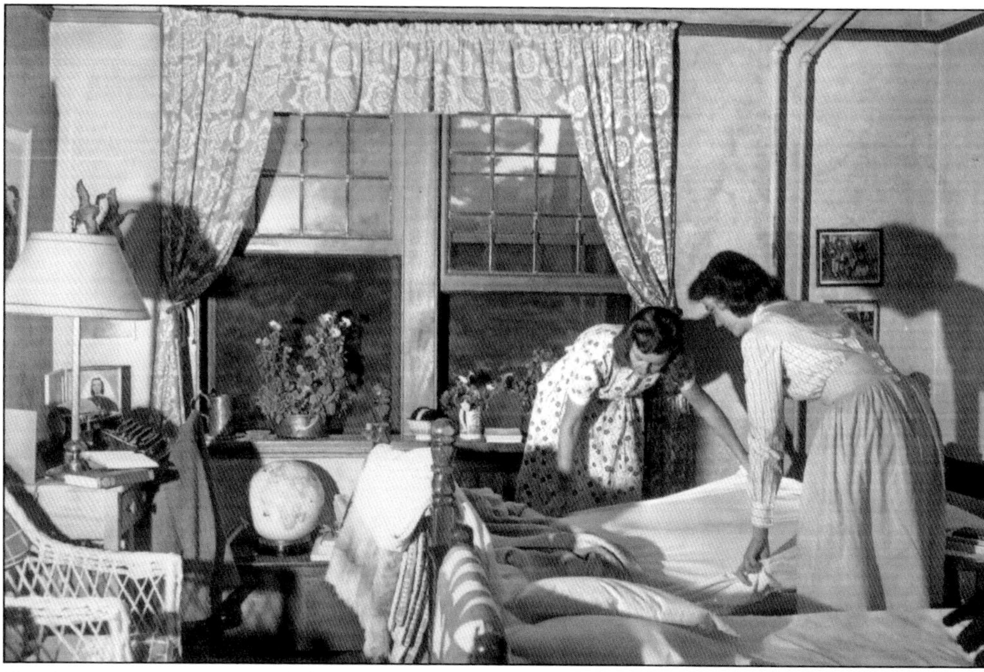

The Student Room. A typical dormitory room in the 1950s had chintz curtains, wicker furniture, and plants. In spite of rumors that students brought their own maids to campus, they have always been responsible for their rooms.

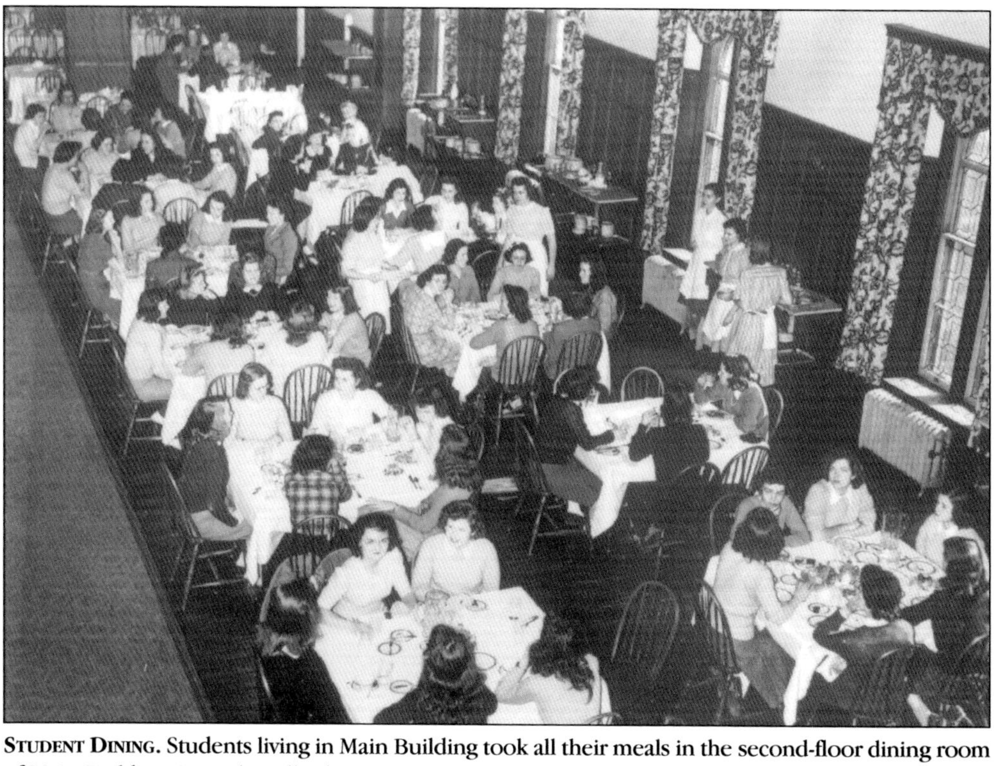

Student Dining. Students living in Main Building took all their meals in the second-floor dining room of Main Building (now the Villard Room). Shown here is a bird's-eye view of the dining room.

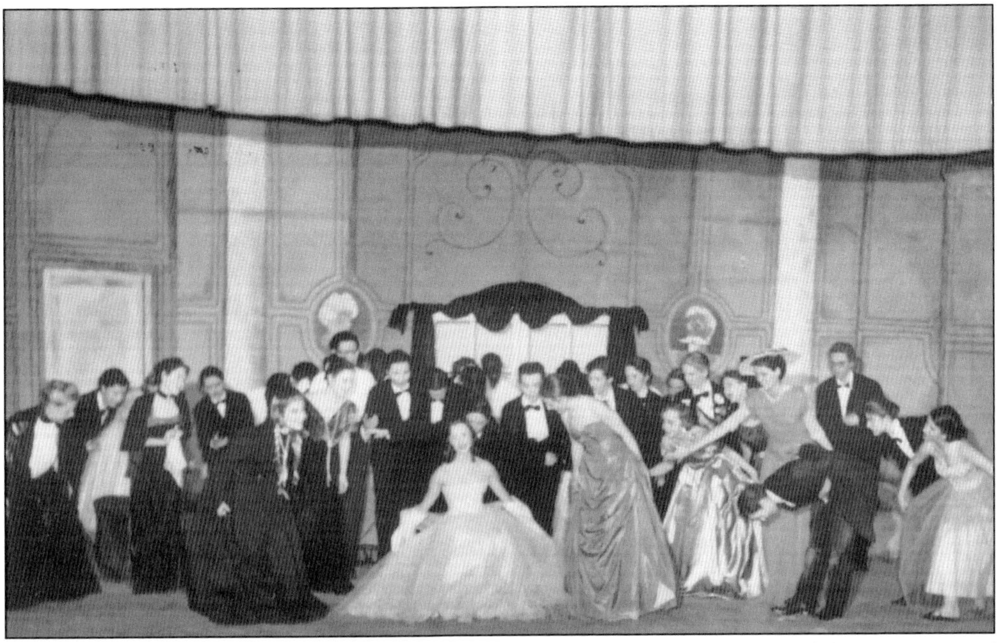

A Sophomore Party, 1953. It wasn't all work and no play. The sophomores had their own special party, apart from juniors and seniors.

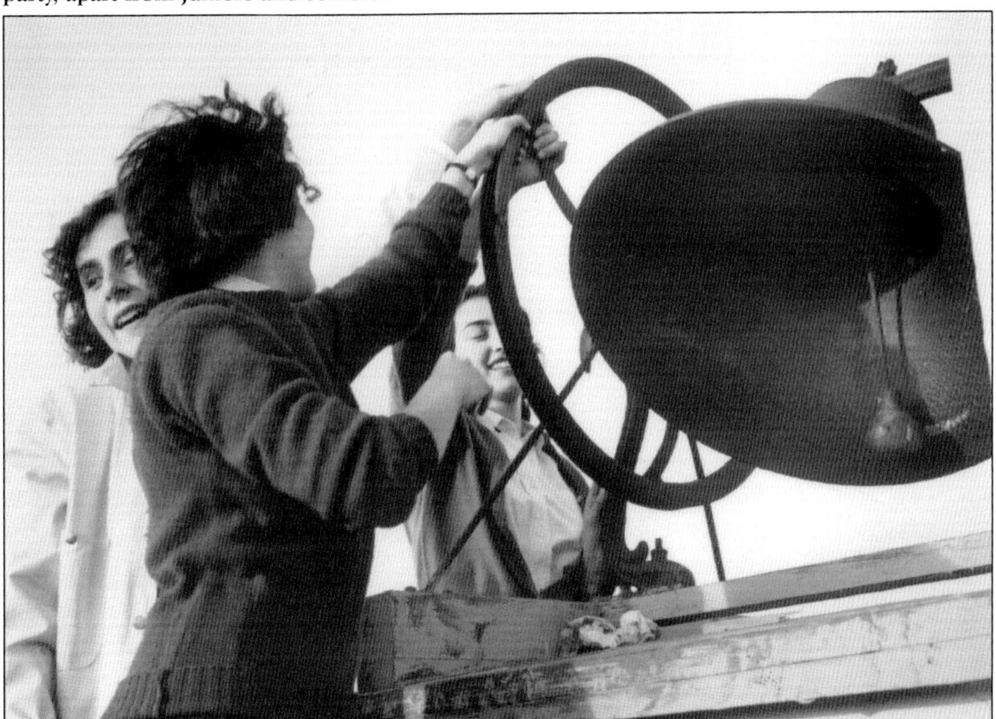

Salve Night, 1957. Salve Night (*salve* means "hail" in Latin) is traditionally the Wednesday of the last week of classes. Juniors officially become seniors, and the new officers of the student government take office. Tradition decrees that all juniors must ring the bell on the roof of Main Building in order to become seniors.

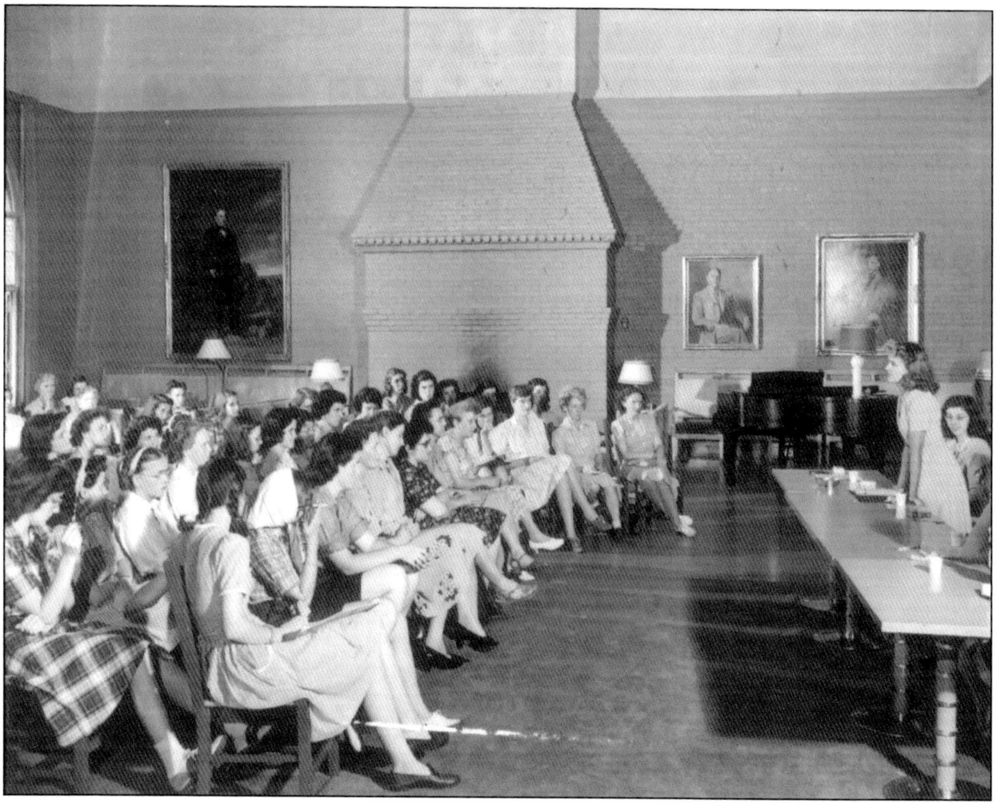

Student Government. Pictured is a student government meeting in the 1950s, held in the Aula in Ely Hall. Part of the old gymnasium, the Aula had been created by President McCracken as a room for faculty meetings. The space is now a cafe for the campus community.

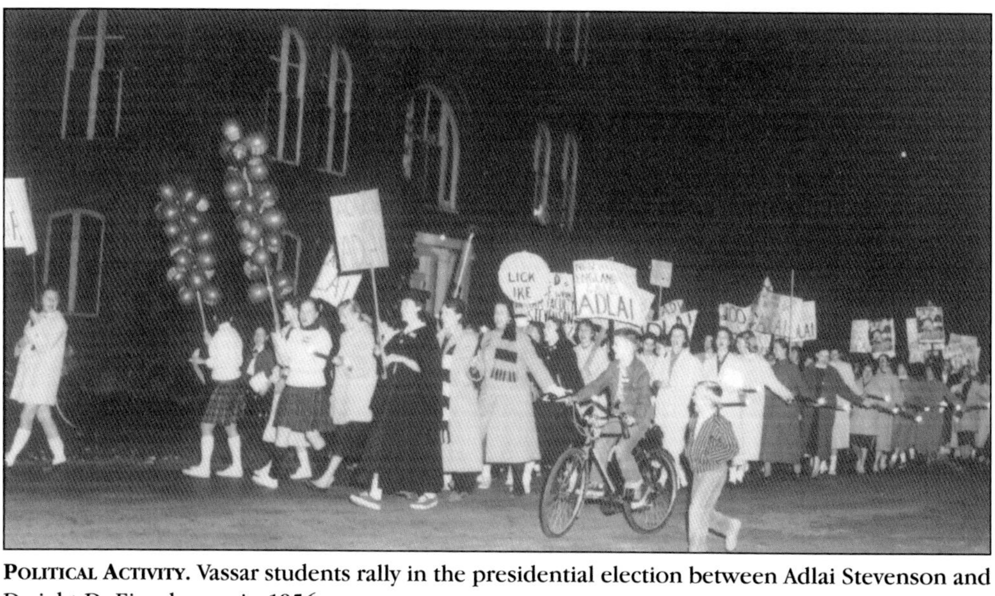

Political Activity. Vassar students rally in the presidential election between Adlai Stevenson and Dwight D. Eisenhower in 1956.

MARION TAIT. Dean of the college (1948–1961) and dean of the faculty (1961–1965), Marion Tait was also professor of classics from 1948 to 1977.

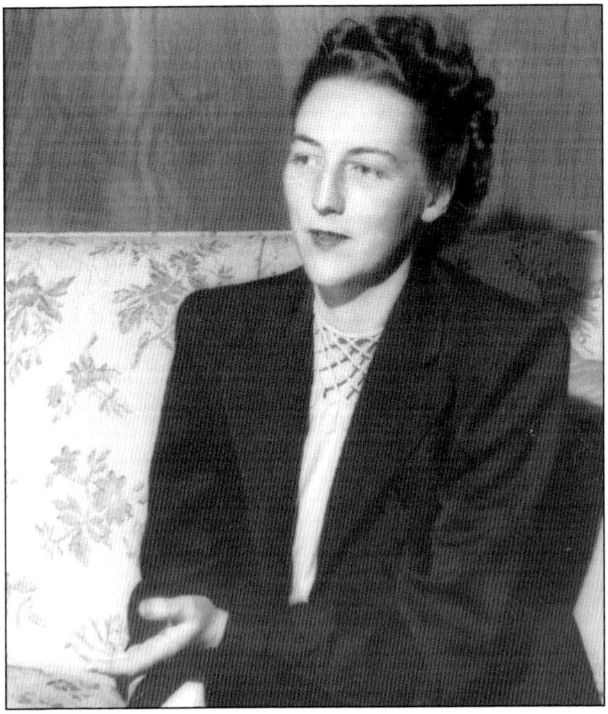

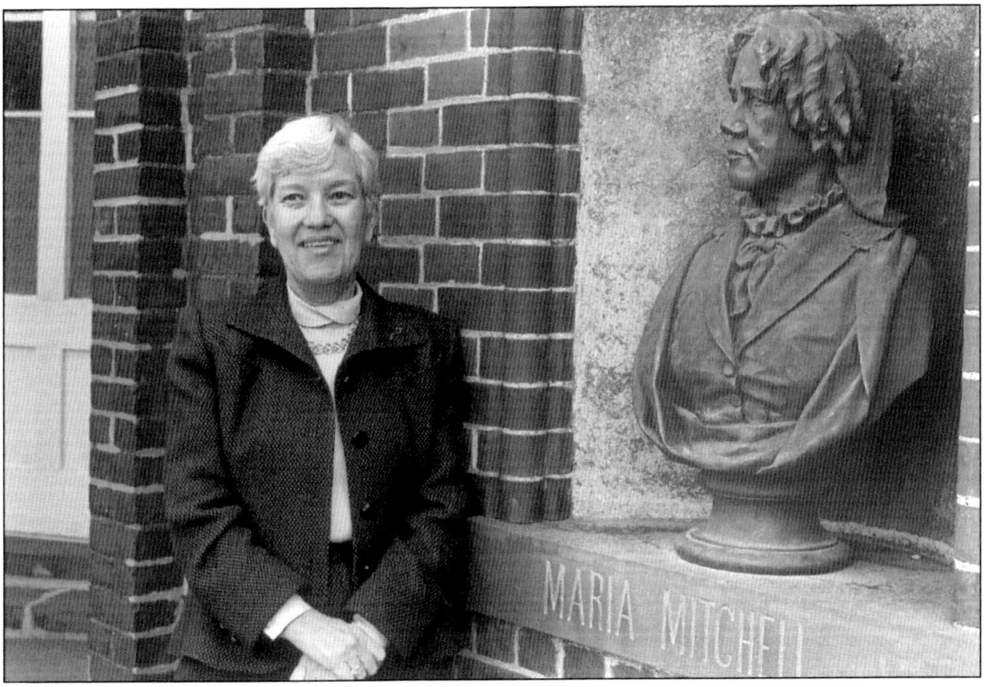

VERA COOPER RUBIN (CLASS OF 1948). At the time of her induction, Rubin was one of three women astronomers in the National Academy of Sciences and one of 57 women elected to the 2,610-member academy since it was chartered in 1863. Rubin is credited with proving the existence of "dark matter," or nonluminous mass. Here, she is standing before the bust of astronomer Maria Mitchell in the original observatory, now a National Historic Landmark.

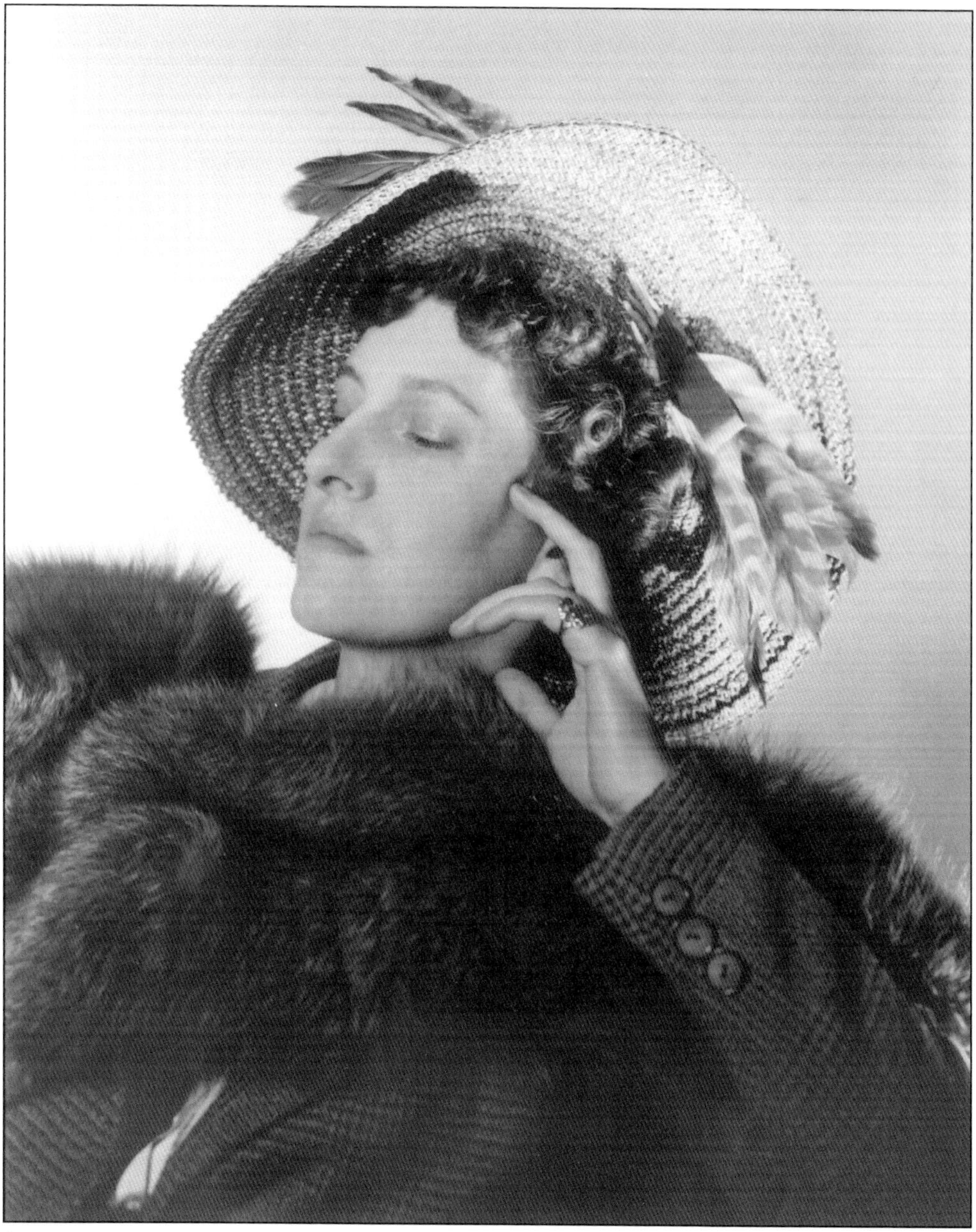

Agnes Rindge Claflin. A well-known figure in the international art world and a prominent art historian, Claflin was a professor of art from 1923 to 1965. She served as chair of the art department and director of the art gallery from 1944 until 1963. She is shown here in a dramatic photograph by George Platt Lynes. (Courtesy Frances Lehman Loeb Art Center; gift of Leila Cook Barber, professor of art.)

Five

Coeducational Vassar: 1968 to the Present

In 1966, Alan Simpson (president of Vassar College) and Kingman Brewster (president of Yale University) asked their boards to undertake a yearlong study to determine the feasibility and desirability of uniting the two institutions in a coeducational venture. After the study revealed extreme opposition to the merger from many Vassar alumnae, John Wilkie (chair of Vassar College's board of trustees) announced in November 1967 that the Vassar board had declined Yale's invitation. At the same time, however, the board had determined that the college would move as soon as possible to educate men as well as women. A few months later, in the spring of 1968, the college amended its charter and gradually moved into the recruitment of Vassar men.

Virginia B. Smith became the second woman president of Vassar in 1977, eight years after the transition to coeducation was initiated. Since 1969, Vassar has become fully coeducational, but the Vassar traditions live on, some of them translated into new forms or adaptations to accommodate the inclusion of men.

Under the leadership of Pres. Fances Daly Fergusson, an art and architectural historian who assumed office in 1986, the college has become more heterogeneous, has reexamined its goals as a liberal arts college, and has continued to excel at the forefront of American undergraduate education. The college now has some 2,400 students. Quite a few single-sex colleges became coeducational in the 1960s and 1970s, but Vassar College's bold step toward coeducation, which followed a century and a half of educating women, was without precedent in encouraging a new equality between the sexes.

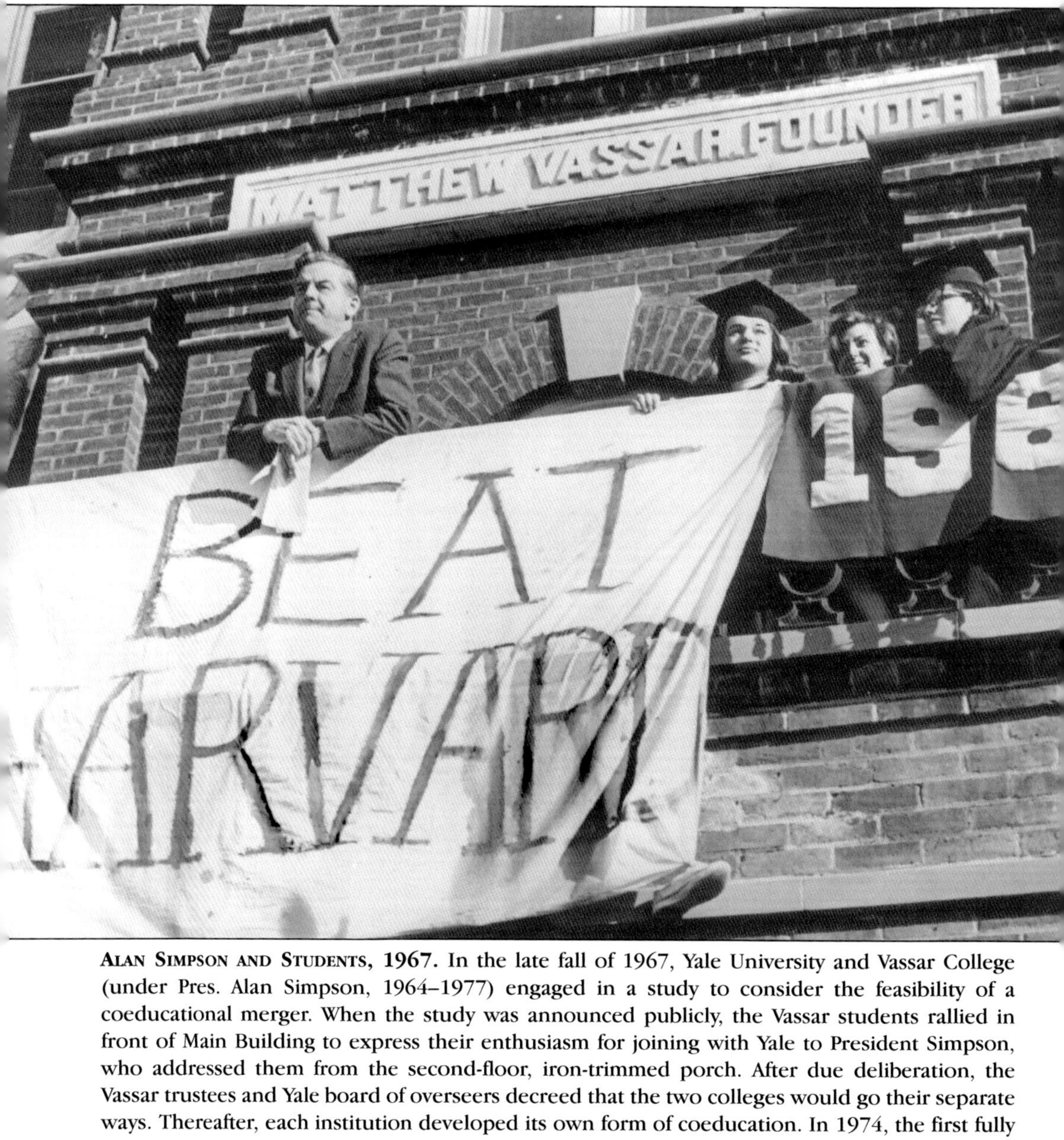

Alan Simpson and Students, 1967. In the late fall of 1967, Yale University and Vassar College (under Pres. Alan Simpson, 1964–1977) engaged in a study to consider the feasibility of a coeducational merger. When the study was announced publicly, the Vassar students rallied in front of Main Building to express their enthusiasm for joining with Yale to President Simpson, who addressed them from the second-floor, iron-trimmed porch. After due deliberation, the Vassar trustees and Yale board of overseers decreed that the two colleges would go their separate ways. Thereafter, each institution developed its own form of coeducation. In 1974, the first fully coeducational Vassar class graduated. In the 1999–2000 academic year, the college celebrated 30 years of successful coeducation. (Photograph by Charles Porter.)

MERYL STREEP (CLASS OF 1971) IN A VASSAR COLLEGE DRAMA DEPARTMENT PRODUCTION OF *MISS JULIE*. Meryl Streep, who was then an undergraduate drama major, performed the leading role in Strindberg's *Miss Julie* in December 1969. The play was translated by Evert M. Sprinchorn, professor of drama, and directed by Clinton Atkinson, whose idea it was to have Streep play the role of Miss Julie. The male lead was Prof. Lee Devin. (Courtesy Vassar College Drama Department.)

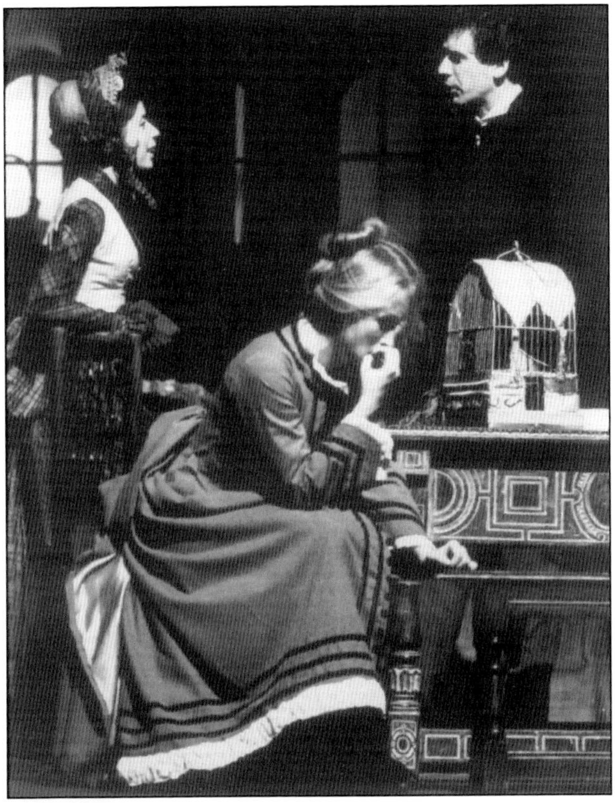

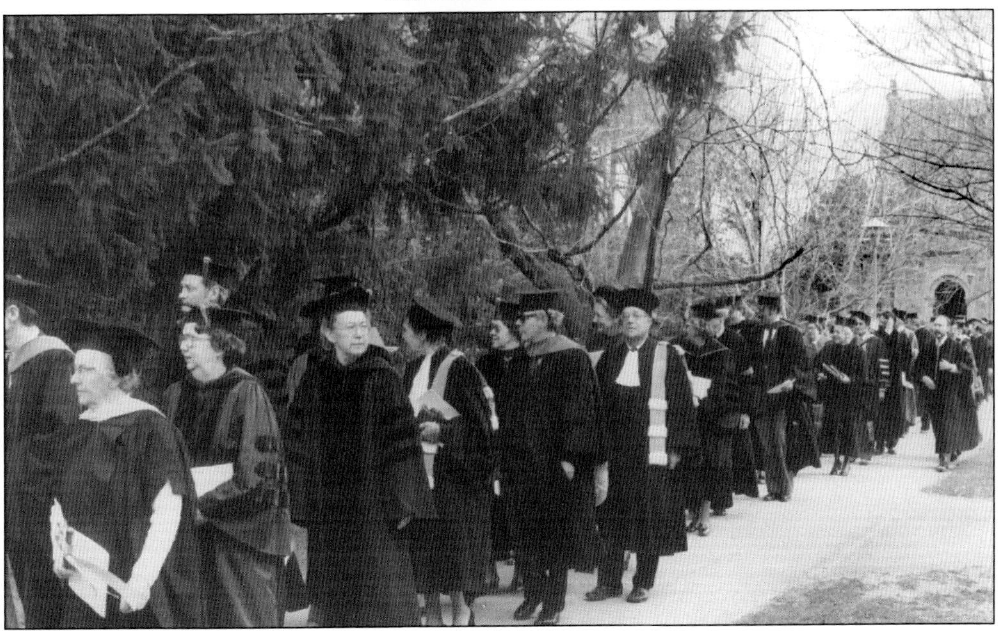

AN ACADEMIC PROCESSION IN THE EARLY 1970S. The custom of wearing academic regalia for convocations began just before World War I as President MacCracken was inaugurated. The marching order of the faculty is determined by length of academic service to the college. In this case, the faculty is marching away from the chapel, where ceremonies were held.

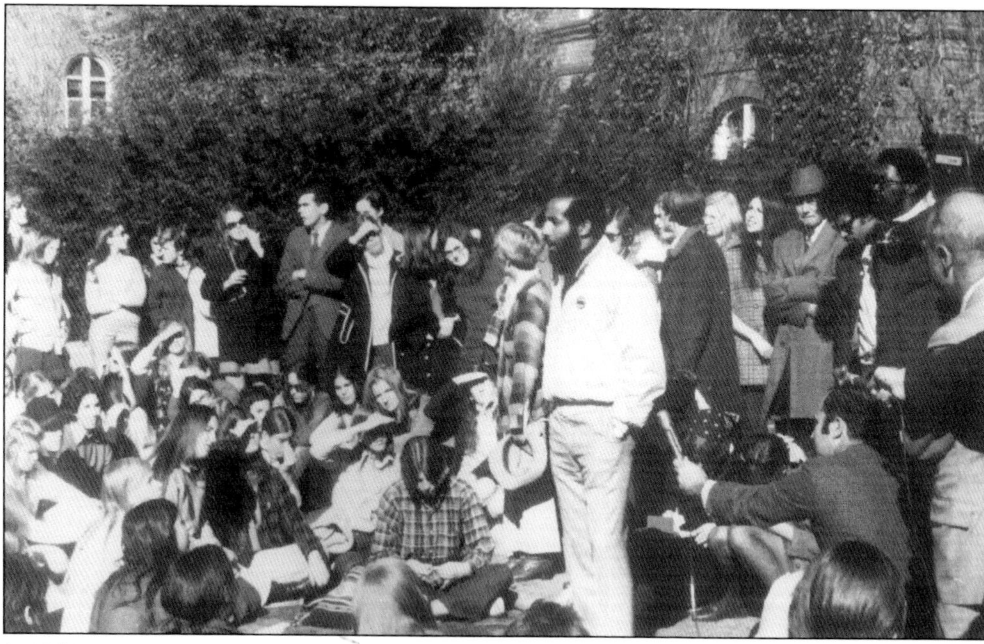

A 1960s Demonstration. The issues of the 1960s fostered discussions and demonstrations on most college campuses, and Vassar was no exception. Pictured here is a sizeable gathering of faculty, students, and administrators discussing issues related to the development of the Africana Studies program. Prof. Milfred Fierce, head of the program, is speaking into the microphone.

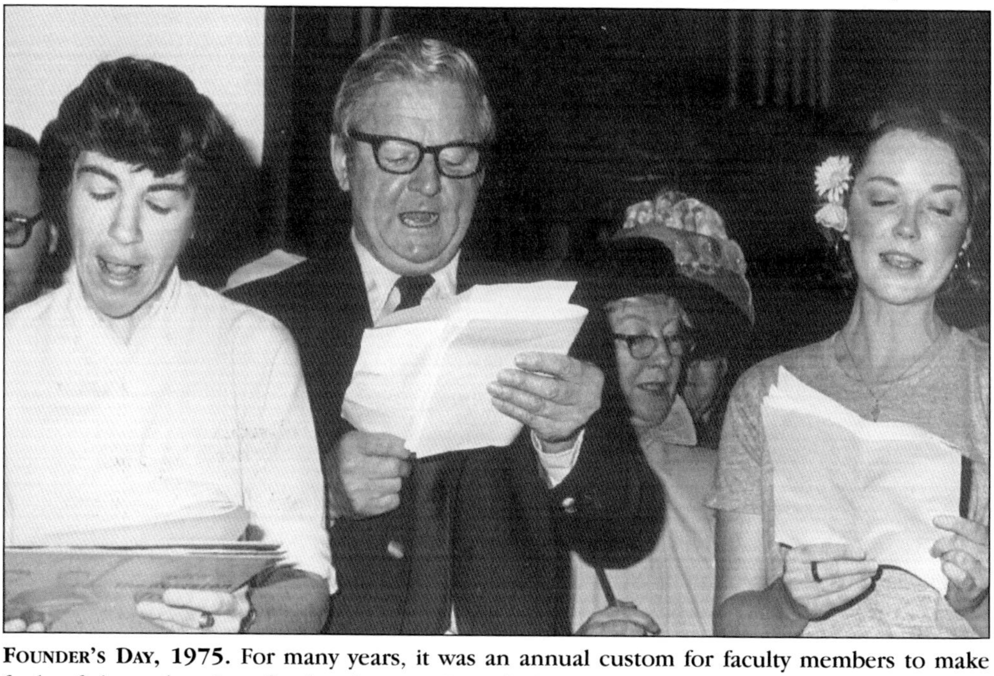

Founder's Day, 1975. For many years, it was an annual custom for faculty members to make fools of themselves in a faculty show on Founder's Day, a campus celebration to honor the founder's birthday on April 29, 1792. Here, those participating in the show include, from left to right, Prof. Anne Constantinople, President Simpson, instructor Joanne Dempsey, and Dean Barbara Wells (in background with hat). (Photograph by Kenneth Chandler.)

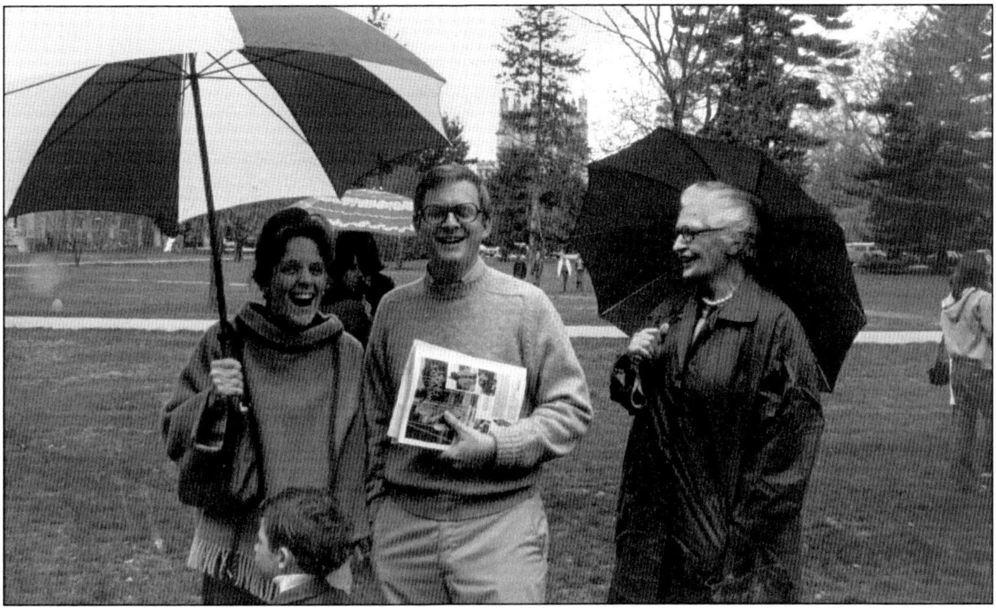

Founder's Day, 1976. Enjoying a laugh on a rainy Founder's Day are, from left to right, Christine Fahlund (assistant professor of biology), Gregory Fahlund (assistant to the president), and Dean Elizabeth Drouilhet. Nicknamed "the Dru" by the students, Drouilhet was a formidable leader in the administration from the early 1940s until her retirement in the 1970s. Her foresight and keen sense of the students' point of view facilitated Vassar's move into coeducation.

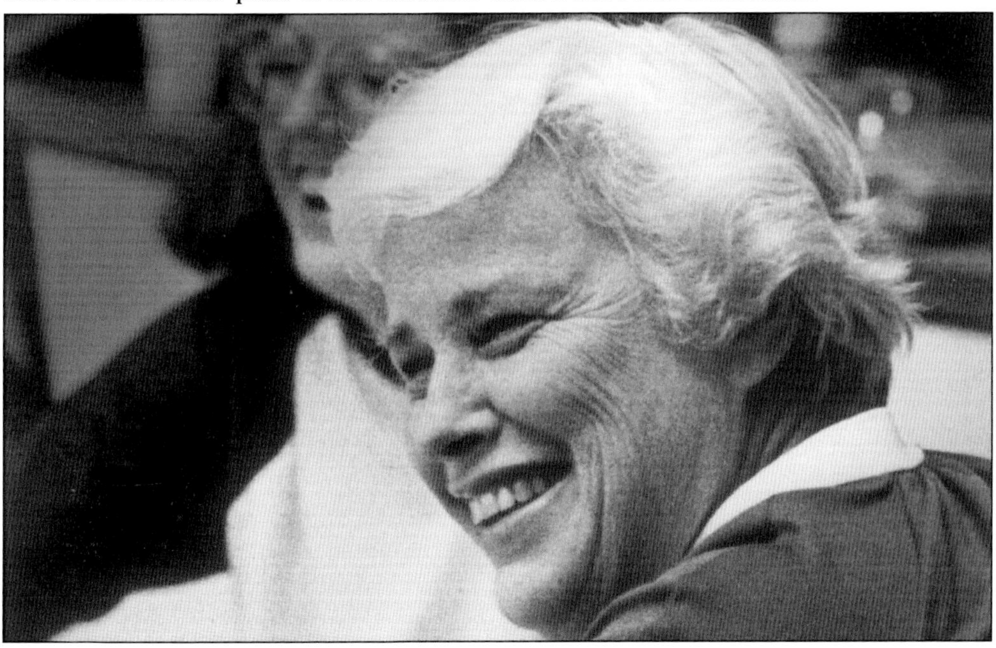

Virginia B. Smith, Vassar President from 1977 to 1986. The second woman president of Vassar, Virginia B. Smith took office eight years after the transition to coeducation. During her tenure in the 1980s, she led a $100 million fundraising drive, $74 million of which was raised by 1986, when she retired. She established the President's Distinguished Visitor program and invited Mary McCarthy to be her first visitor in 1982.

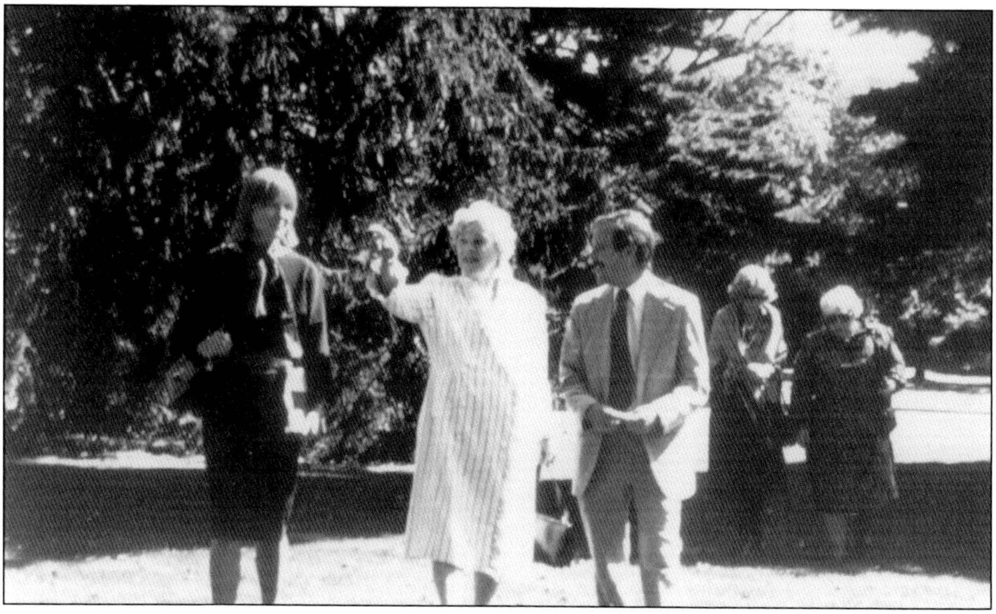

Mary McCarthy. Walking across the lawn toward the Thompson Library are, from left to right, writer Frances FitzGerald, Mary McCarthy, and presidential assistant Robert Parks. Behind them are author Elizabeth Hardwick (left) and Virginia B. Smith (right). The occasion was the acquisition of the McCarthy papers. Smith also enriched the Vassar manuscript collection by acquiring the Burroughs and Elizabeth Bishop (Class of 1934) papers. At the time of Smith's retirement, the board of trustees honored her commitment to the collection by naming it after her. (Photograph by Dixie Sheridan.)

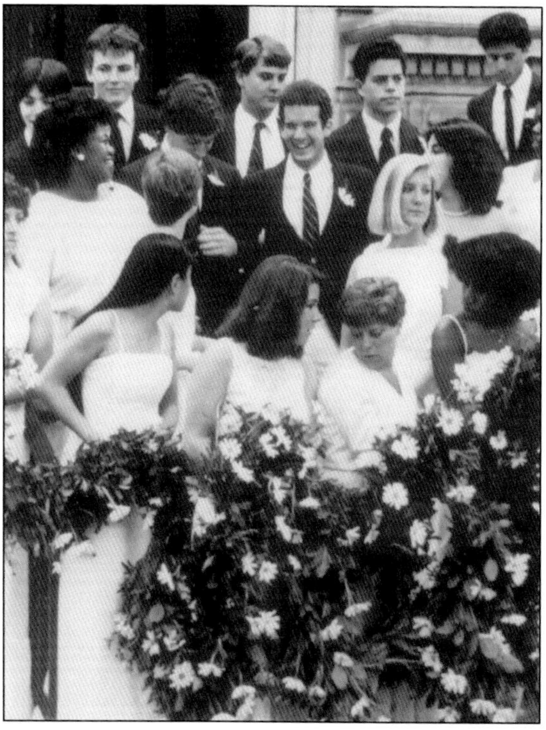

A-Coeducational Daisy Chain, May 1984. Daisies were first used to decorate the chapel in 1884. Exactly 100 years later, the custom of celebrating graduation with students carrying a daisy chain still prevailed. By 1984, however, males had joined the females as their escorts. (Photograph by Ben Rayfield.)

A Repertory Dance Theater Presentation, October 21, 1983. The Dance Theater, a group of dance students first directed by Prof. Ray Cook, perform in front of the Thompson Library. Since 1984, the group has given performances annually in the Bardavon Theater in Poughkeepsie. In 1998, its program was "Appalachian Spring," staged by Assistant Prof. Stephen Rooks, a former Martha Graham dancer. (Photograph by Ben Rayfield.)

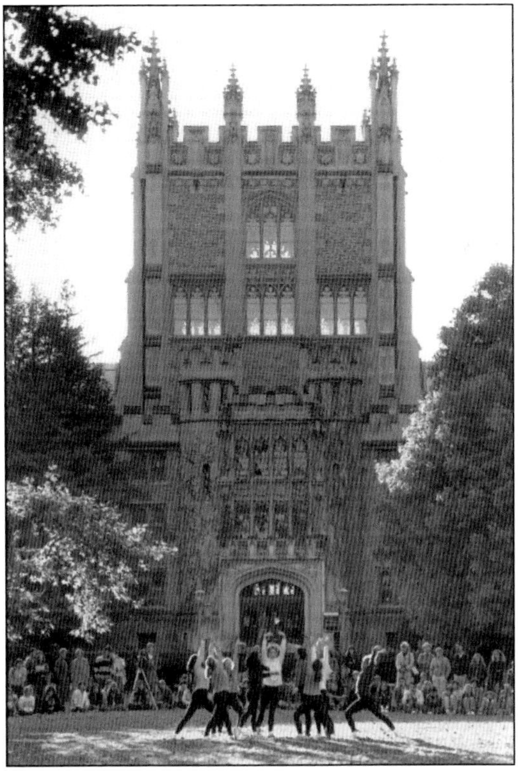

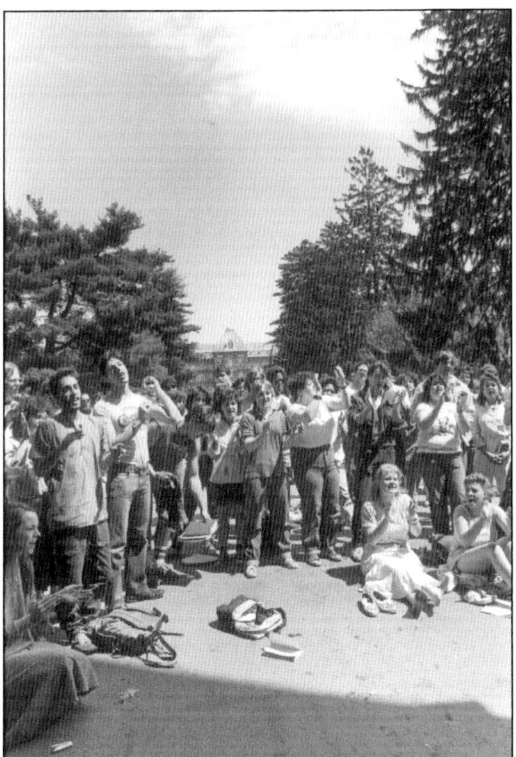

An Apartheid Demonstration. On April 16, 1985, students gathered at the front gate of the college to signify their support of measures against apartheid in South Africa. Dropping their book bags, they peacefully sang and chanted.

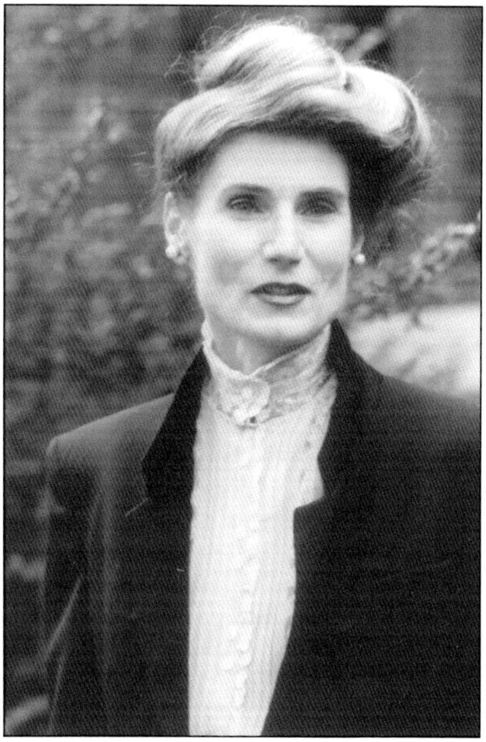

Nancy Graves (Class of 1961), Distinguished Visitor. Artist Nancy Graves was the President's Distinguished Visitor in April 1986. Graves was invited to the campus to meet with students and talk with classes for a few days. (Photograph by Dixie Sheridan.)

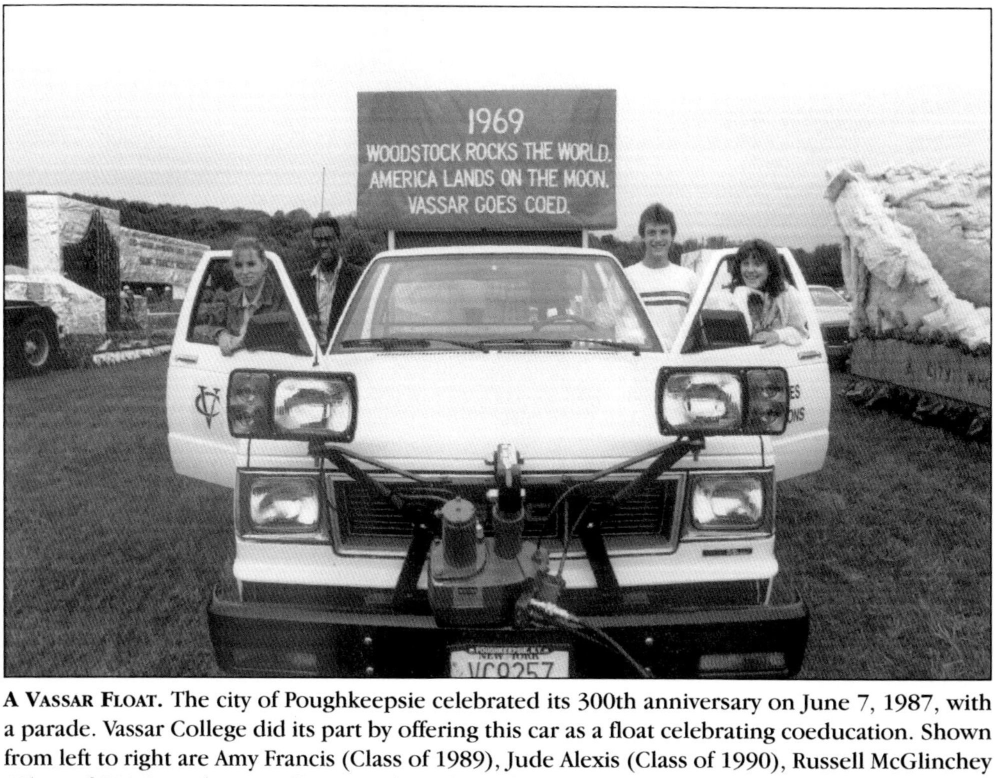

A Vassar Float. The city of Poughkeepsie celebrated its 300th anniversary on June 7, 1987, with a parade. Vassar College did its part by offering this car as a float celebrating coeducation. Shown from left to right are Amy Francis (Class of 1989), Jude Alexis (Class of 1990), Russell McGlinchey (Class of 1991), and Nancyellen Uniacke (Class of 1989). (Photograph by Ben Rayfield.)

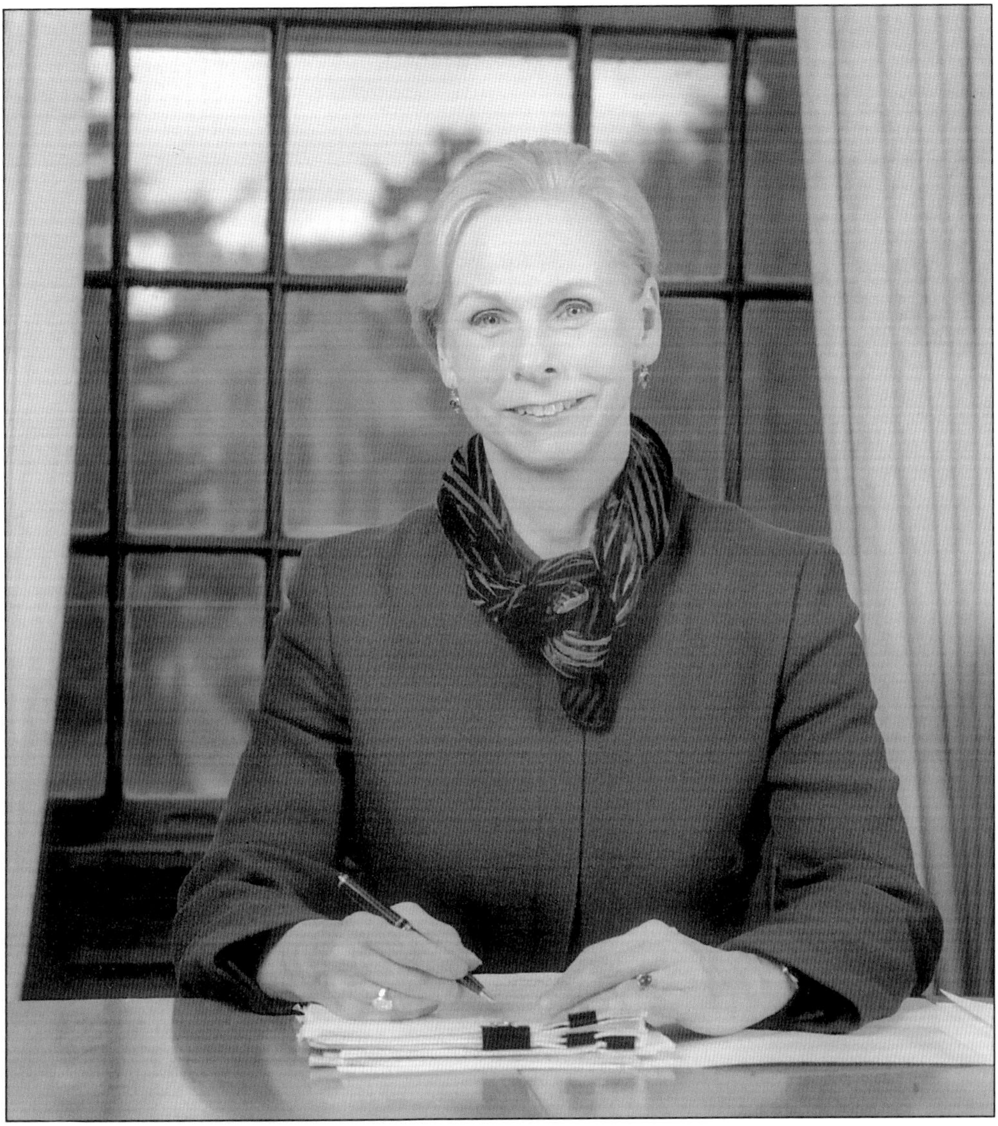

FRANCES D. FERGUSSON, VASSAR PRESIDENT. Frances Daly Fergusson became the ninth president of Vassar College in 1986. An art and architectural historian, President Fergusson is the third woman to head the college. During her tenure, a $200 million fundraising campaign was completed in excess of its goal. Under her leadership, the curriculum has been expanded and the beauty of the campus has been enhanced. Several important buildings have recently been added: the Frances Lehman Loeb Art Center, the Class of 1951 Observatory, three new laboratories in Blodgett Hall, the athletic center, and the Martha Rivers and E. Bronson Ingram Library. Construction will soon begin on a new center for drama and film. Active in community and national affairs, Fergusson was awarded the Eleanor Roosevelt Center at Val-Kill Medal in 1998. She is chair of the board of the Mayo Foundation–Mayo Clinic and a member of the board of trustees of the Ford Foundation. She has published widely in her academic specialty of architectural history and is the recipient of the Founders' Award of the Society of Architectural Historians. (Photograph by Will Faller.)

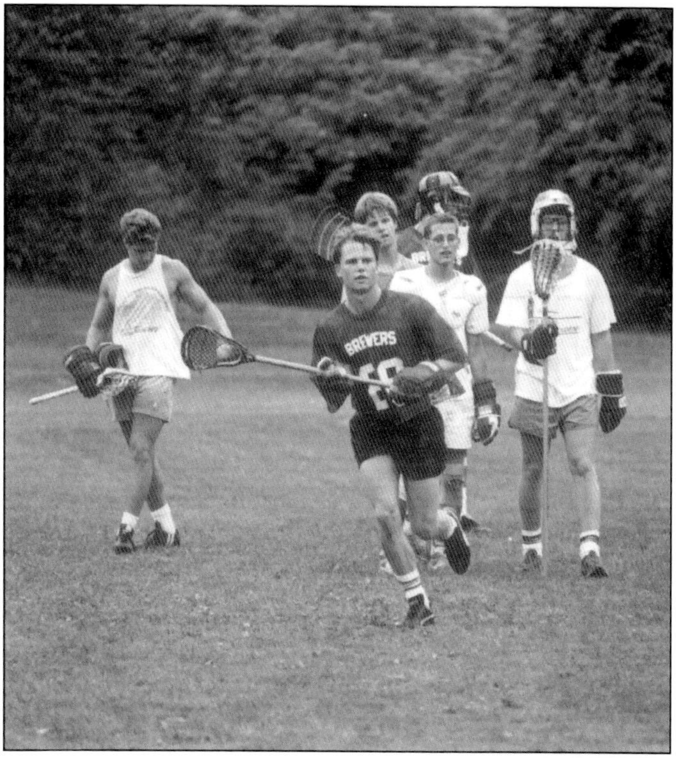

The Vassar Brewers Varsity Lacrosse Team. Although their first outing as a varsity team would not occur until the following spring, the lacrosse men met informally twice a week in the fall of 1987 for line drills. Here, the team's co-captain, Tim Ognisty (Class of 1988), is out front in the dark jersey. The other co-captain, Jason Pickering (Class of 1988), is not shown. Today, Vassar athletics can count 22 varsity teams. (Photograph by Ben Rayfield.)

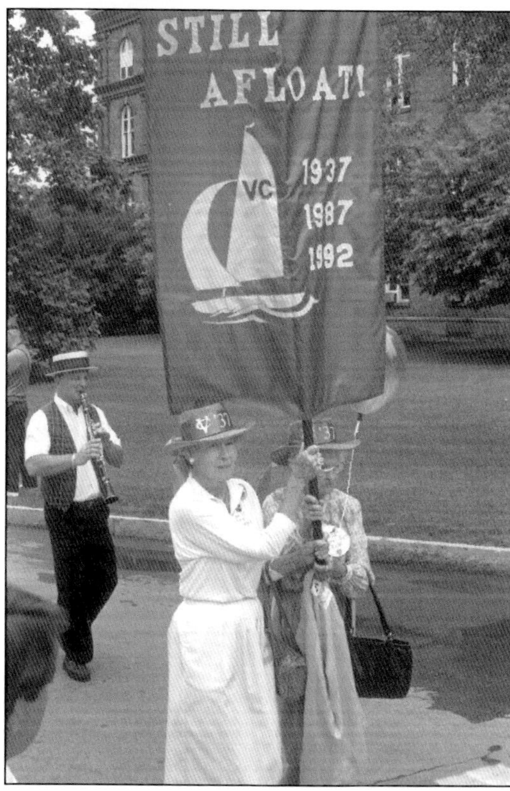

A Reunion, June 7, 1992. Every year, two weeks after the graduating seniors leave the campus, reunion classes take over for the weekend. Veronique Vaillancourt (Class of 1994), who assisted in making alumni and alumnae feel at home at the 1992 reunion, caught members of the Class of 1937 celebrating their 55th reunion to the beat of a Poughkeepsie marching band. (Photograph by Veronique Vaillancourt.)

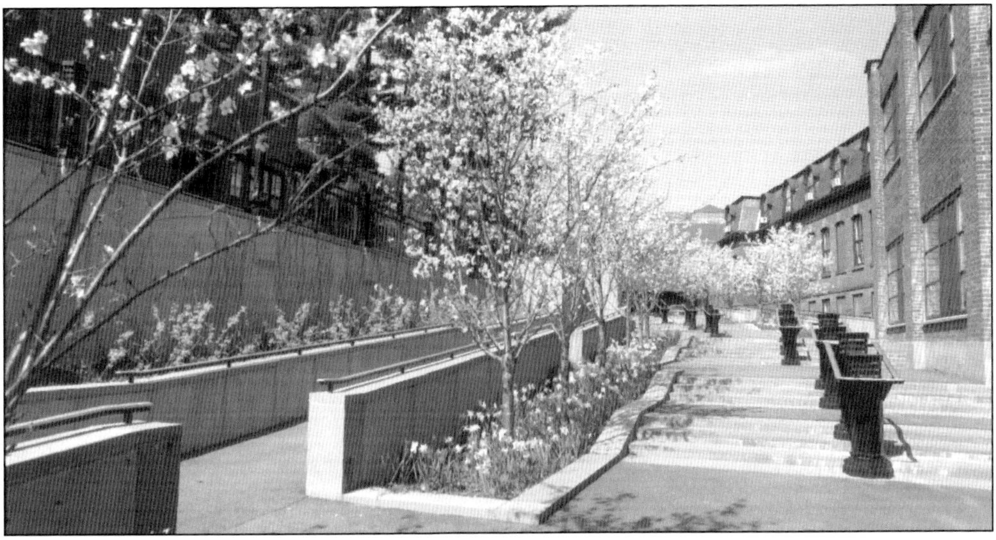

The Emily Hargroves Fisher and Richard Fisher Passage, 1994. Designed by architects Roth and Moore, with landscaping by Diana Balmori, the Fisher Passage helps create a new look for what Frances Fergusson once called Vassar's "backyard." This area of the campus behind Main Building is now a vital hub. The building in the right foreground was once a service building and now houses the computer center. The remodeled college laundry in the background now serves as offices for development and space for the computer science department. (Photograph by Dixie Sheridan.)

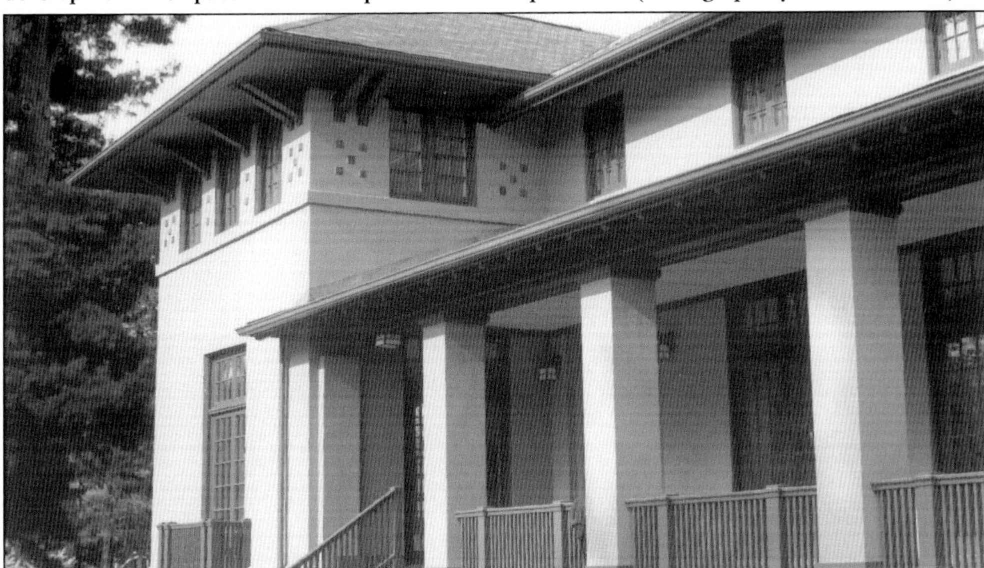

The Carol and James Kautz Admission House. In 1908, the Vassar Student Association gave funds to the college to build the Goodfellowship Clubhouse. The Goodfellowship Club was organized in 1902–1903 for maids and students. (The Steadfast Club, formed in 1890, was the first club of maids, students, and faculty.) The Goodfellowship Clubhouse provided employees with a place for gatherings and classes as well as for recreation and rest. In the early 1990s, the building was accurately restored to become the elegant and much needed Kautz Admission House. Carol Kautz was a member of the Class of 1955, and James Kautz was a member of Vassar's board of trustees from 1983 to 1995 and chair from 1989 to 1995. (Photograph by Dixie Sheridan.)

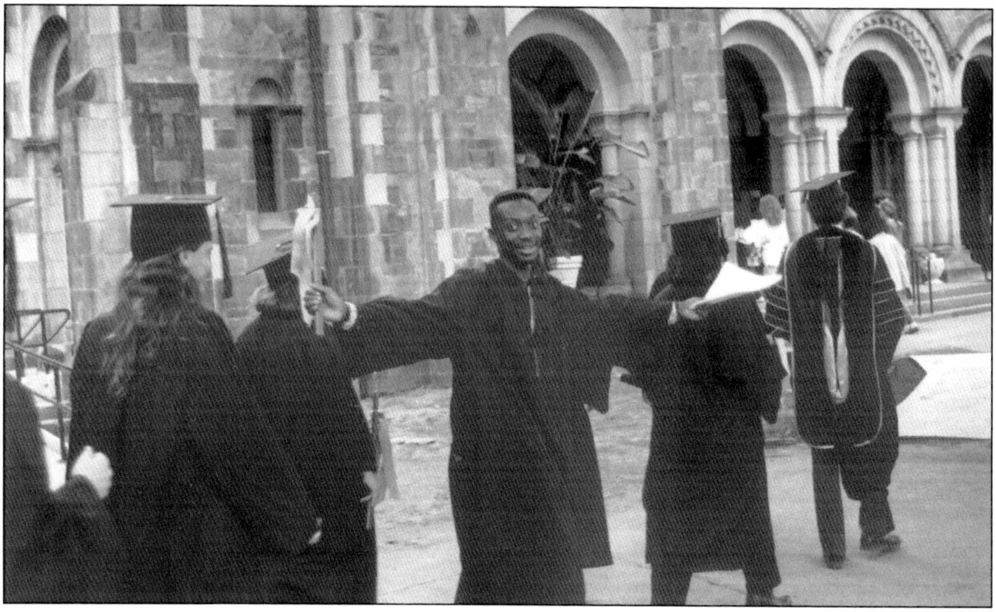

FALL CONVOCATION, 1991. Each fall, students, faculty, and officers of the college gather in the chapel for convocation. The formal ceremony began in 1915 under President MacCracken's administration. Shown here is the president of the Vassar Student Association for the academic year of 1991–92, Pascal St. Gerard, who addressed the audience at the convocation. (Photograph by Susan DeKrey.)

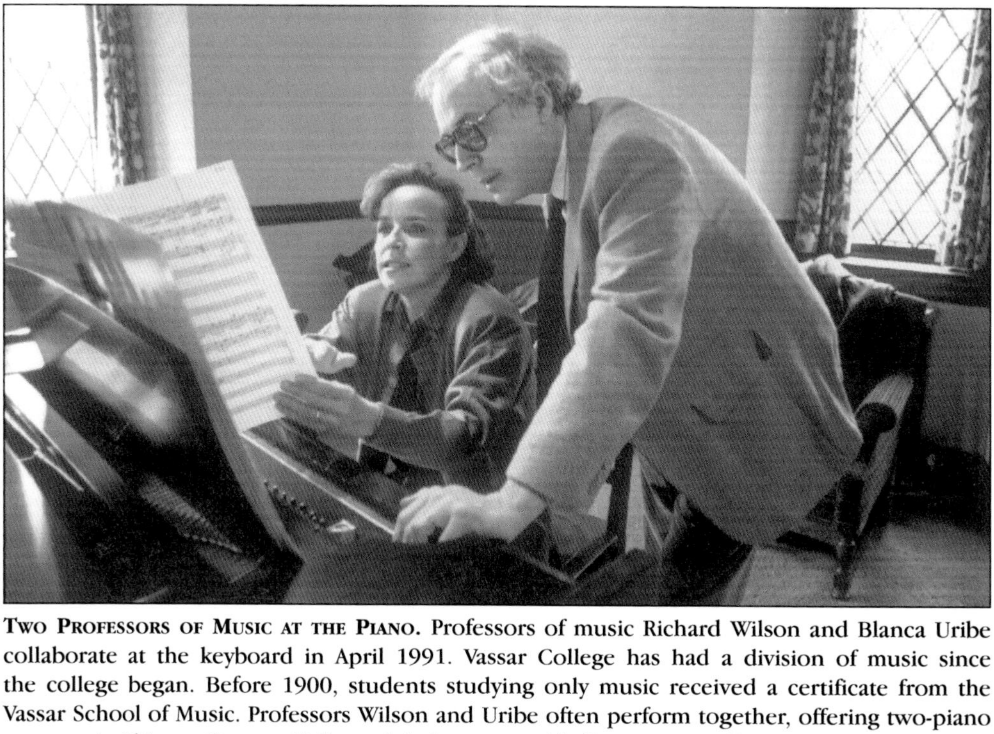

TWO PROFESSORS OF MUSIC AT THE PIANO. Professors of music Richard Wilson and Blanca Uribe collaborate at the keyboard in April 1991. Vassar College has had a division of music since the college began. Before 1900, students studying only music received a certificate from the Vassar School of Music. Professors Wilson and Uribe often perform together, offering two-piano concerts in Skinner Concert Hall, modeled on a grand hall in a Loire Valley chateau. (Photograph by Ben Rayfield.)

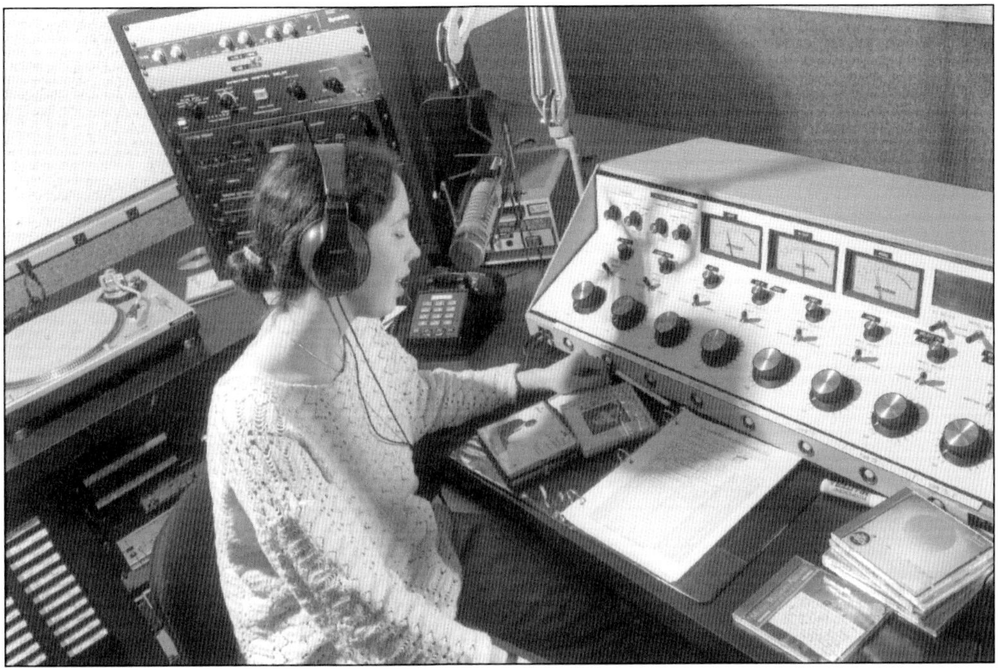

WVKR, THE VASSAR RADIO STATION, 1995. Vassar first broadcast in 1938 courtesy of a Poughkeepsie radio station. In October 1972, the college's own station, WVKR, began broadcasting from Main Building. Operated by the Student Government Association, it is a voice of the Vassar community to the outside world. (Photograph by Martin Dixon; courtesy the College Board.)

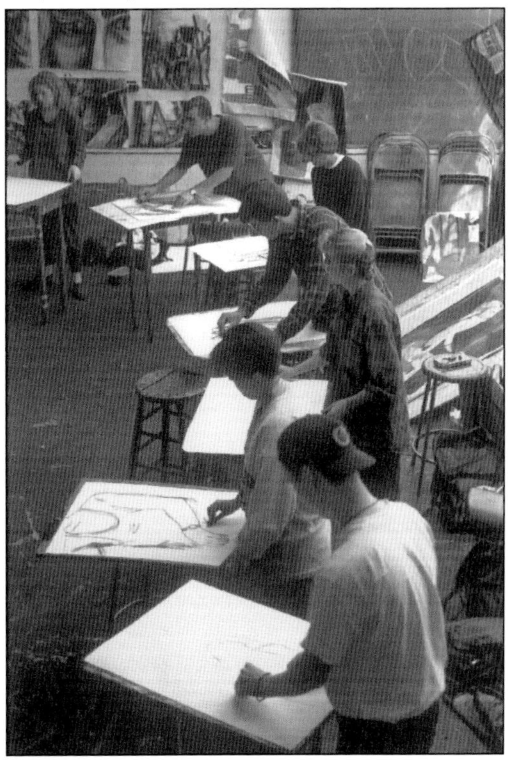

"BIRTHDAY SHOOTOUT," APRIL 29, 1992. The 200th birthday of Matthew Vassar was celebrated in various ways on Founder's Day in 1992. "Birthday Shootout" was a battery of campus photographers who ranged the campus taking impromptu photographs. Ann Daley's drawing class is shown in this picture taken by sculptor-photographer Harry Roseman. (Courtesy Harry Roseman, associate professor of sculpture.)

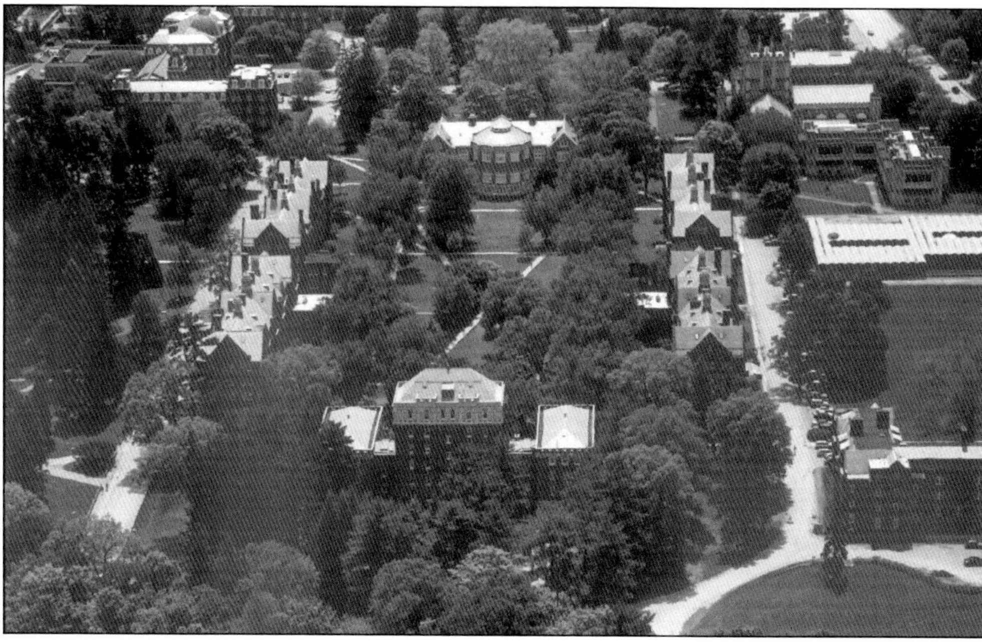

An Aerial View of Campus, 1990. The Vassar College campus in 1990 could be described as an arboretum. Owing to the generosity of Vassar classes and private donors over the years as well as the generations of caretakers, the campus offers up its beauty. This aerial photograph shows the quadrangle from the north, with Jewett Hall in the immediate foreground. (Photograph by Dixie Sheridan.)

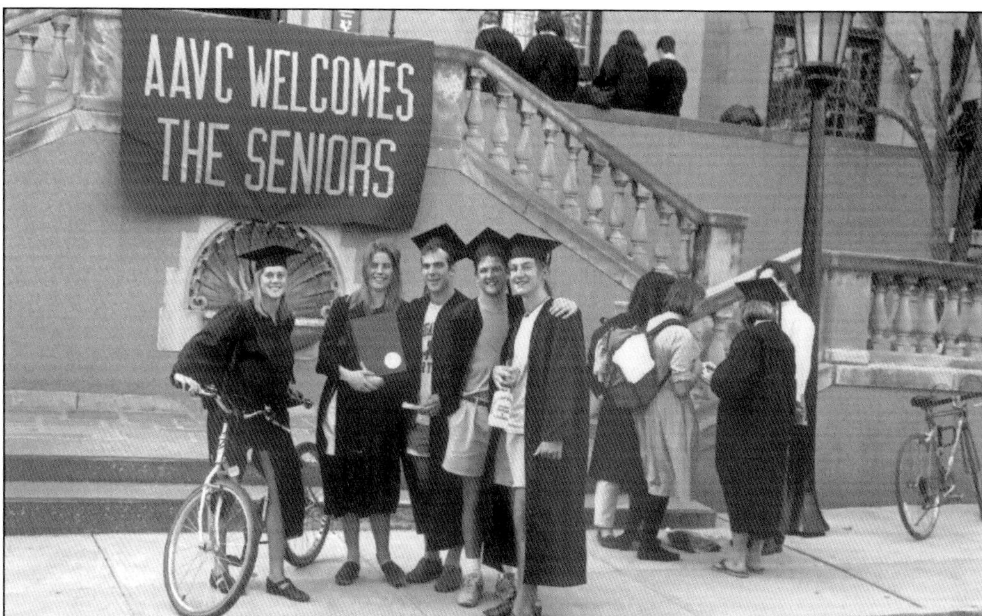

AAVC (Alumnae/Alumni of Vassar College) Welcomes Seniors. Every year after spring convocation, a ceremony in the chapel marks the changing of the guard in the student body. As part of the tradition, the junior class rings the bell atop Main Building to celebrate its coming seniority and the seniors are welcomed as alumnae at the Alumnae House. (Photograph by Charles Porter.)

"Birthday Shootout," Ringing the Bell. In a "Birthday Shootout" on April 29, 1992, Leila Nichols (Class of 1993) rings the old bell of Main Building in celebration of juniors moving up to the status of seniors. (Photograph by Kelly Wissman, Class of 1995.)

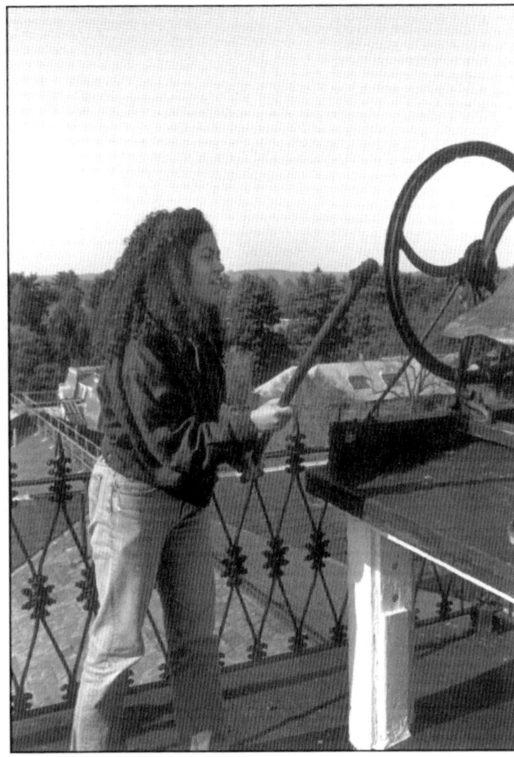

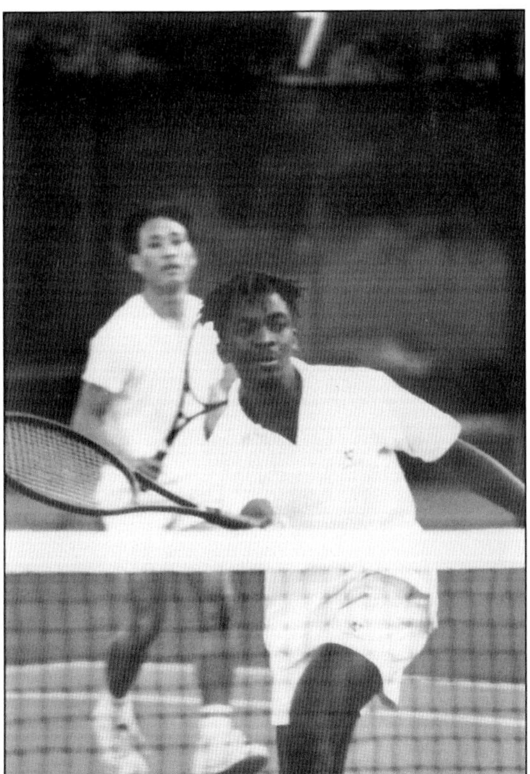

Men's Tennis, Spring 1994. These men's doubles partners are (front) Dalindyebo Shabalala (Class of 1998) and T.C. Changkachith (Class of 1995). (Courtesy Susan Colodny.)

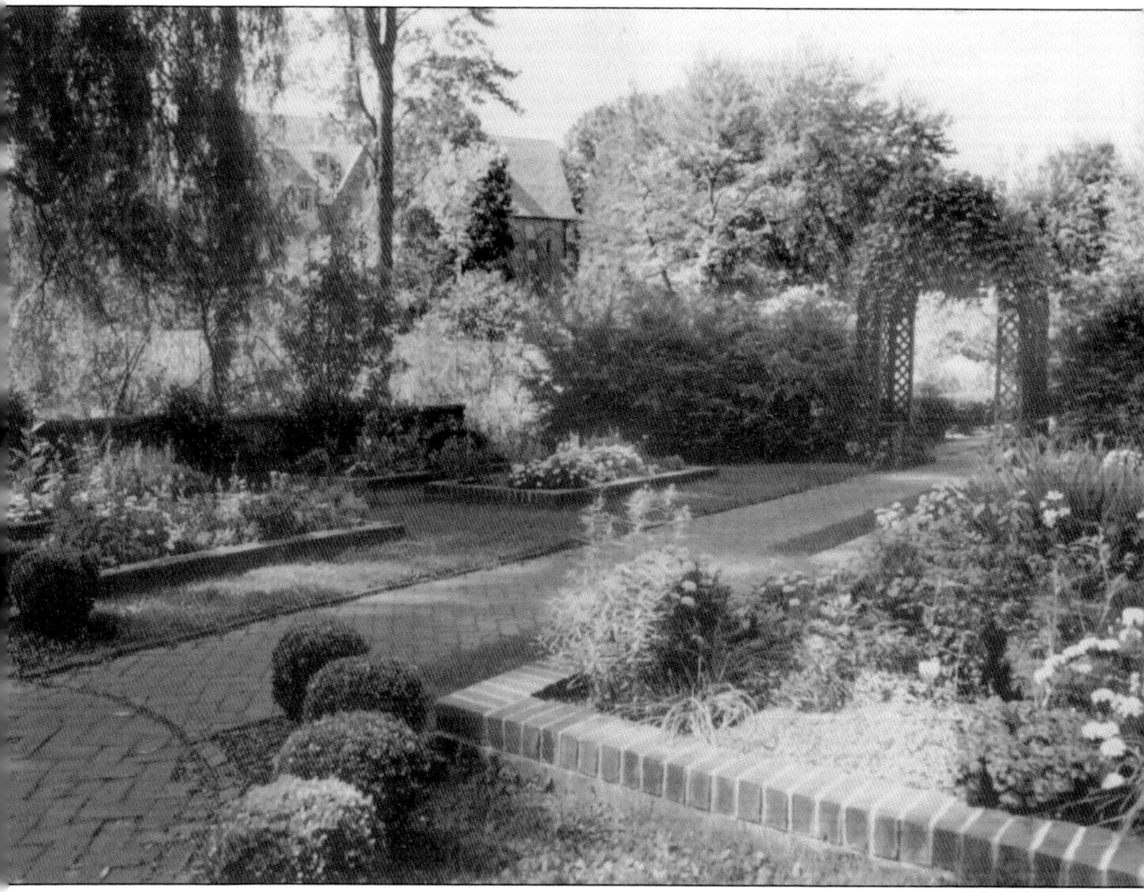

THE SHAKESPEARE GARDEN. The garden is in full bloom as the photographer catches the sunlight. The Skinner Hall of Music, modeled on a Loire Valley chateau, rises in the background. Belle Skinner (Class of 1887), whom Skinner Hall honors, financed the rehabilitation of the village of Hautenchatel in the Loire Valley after it was damaged during World War I. Brick framed beds now give form to the Shakespeare Garden plantings. (Photograph by Bill Denison.)

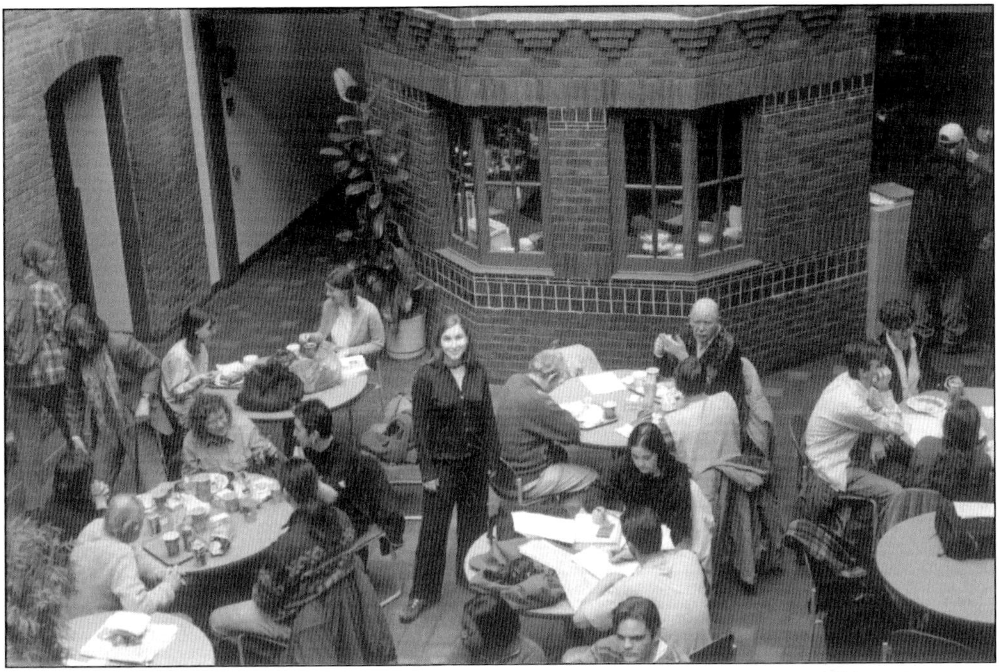

The Retreat, 1997. The Retreat has been an informal eating spot in Main Building for years. Even before the prizewinning College Center was created in 1977, there was the Retreat, where cooperative house students would sell brownies, sandwiches, and other delicacies for pocket money. Today, it is a favorite informal meeting and eating place for the entire college community. (Photograph by George Laws.)

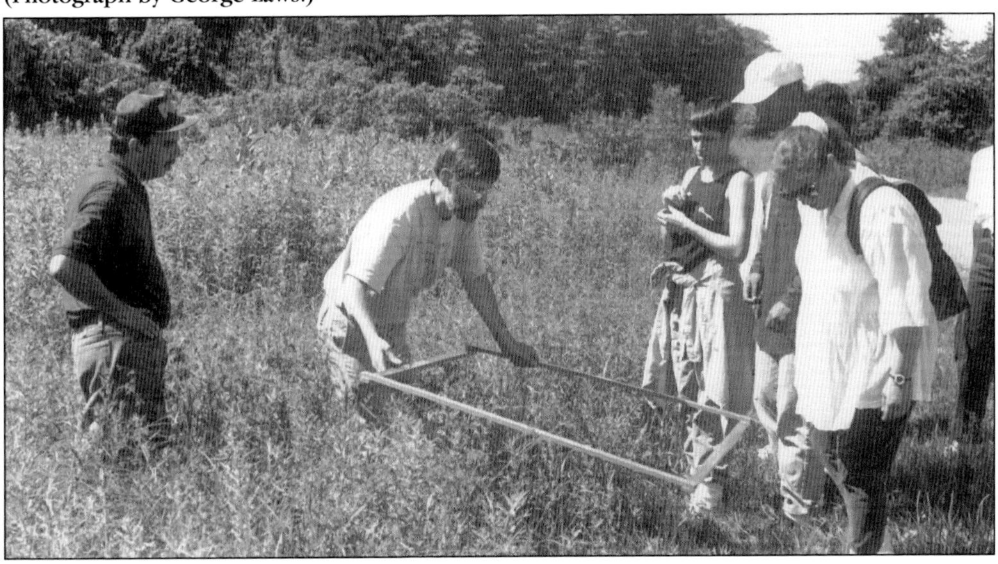

The Exploring Transfer Program, Prof. Bob Suter in the Field with Students, July 1994. The innovative summer program called Exploring Transfer was started in 1985 to give students at community colleges a five-week experience studying the liberal arts on the Vassar campus. Seventy percent of the students in the program have transferred to four-year institutions (including Vassar itself), and three of the five students who enrolled at Vassar graduated as members of Phi Beta Kappa. (Photograph by Sylvia Whitman.)

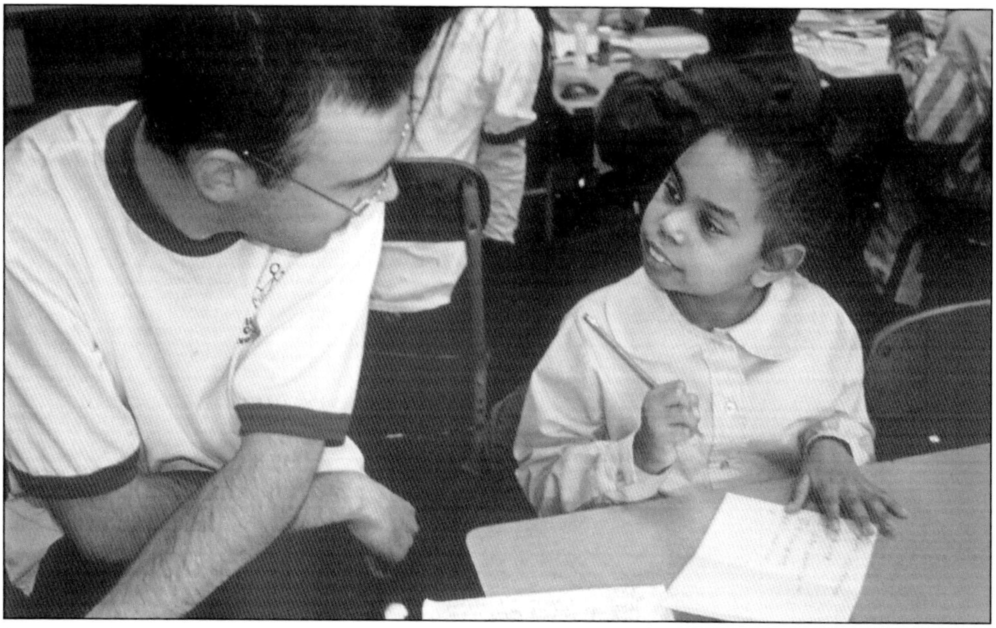

A Vassar Student Working with a Poughkeepsie Waring Academy Pupil. Michael Peluso (Class of 1999) worked with children in the public school system in February 1997 as part of his academic program. Students concentrating on education work with teachers in the classroom. (Photograph by Diane Zucker.)

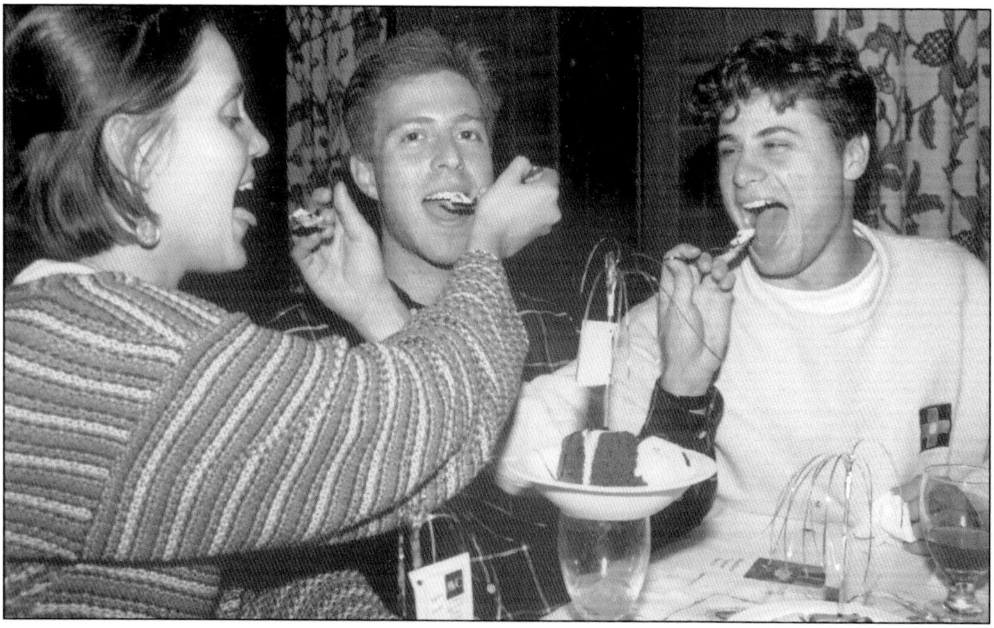

Vassar Devils at the Alumnae House Pub, 1995. The Flag Shop on Raymond Avenue catered to the sweet tooth of Vassar students in the early 20th century. There, students could indulge in "Vassar angels" (angel cake, ice cream, and chocolate sauce) and "Vassar devils" (devil's food cake, ice cream, and marshmallow sauce) on demand. When the "pub" was added to the Alumnae House restaurant services in the late 1930s, these confections naturally turned up on the menu. (Photograph by Jonah Sutherland.)

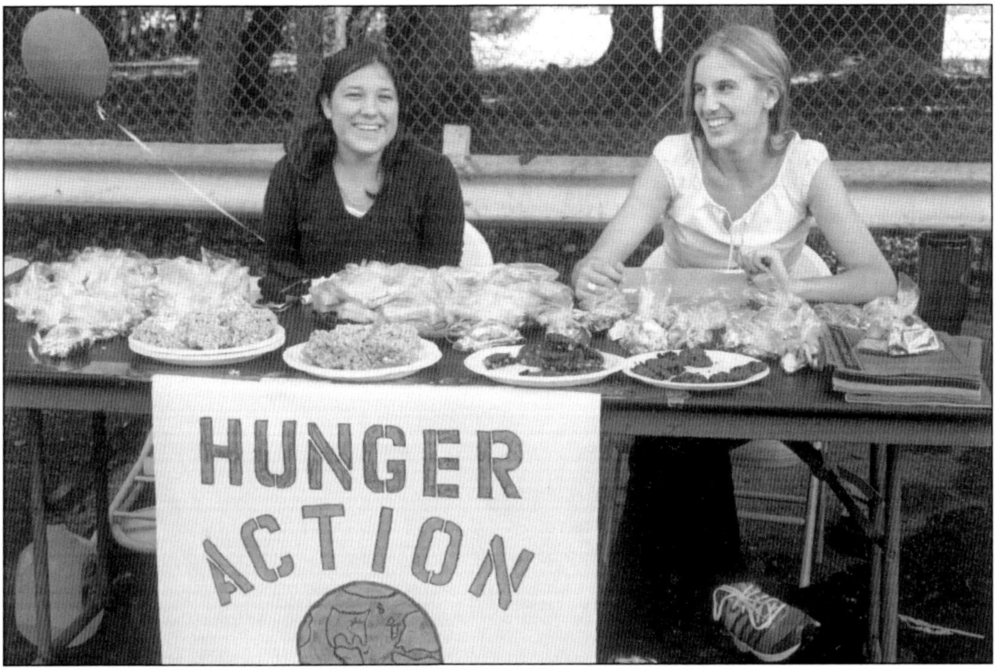

The Arlington Street Fair, Hunger Action, September 1999. Vassar and Arlington (the section of Poughkeepsie bordering the college to the north) have teamed up to form an association and work for the improvement of the area. The Arlington Business Association and Vassar College concentrate on beautifying storefronts and arranging events to draw people to the area. Pictured here is one of the booths manned by Vassar students for the street fair in 1999. (Photograph by Diane Zucker.)

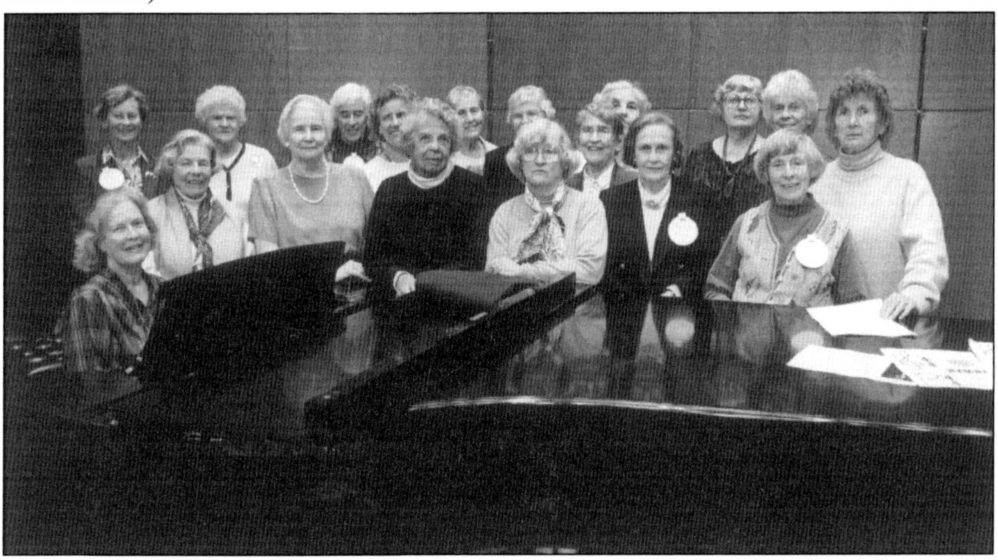

Singers from the Class of 1944 Tape Songs. Interested in preserving songs from their college days, a group of singers from the Class of 1944 gathered in Skinner Hall one fall day in 1997 to record songs for the music archives. Carol Saunders Robinette is at the piano. The songs included "The Pride of the Campus," "Clothes Make the Woman," "Conservation Song," "The Only Life to Live," "I'm in a Permanent Wave," and "All in Good Time." (Photograph by Diane Zucker.)

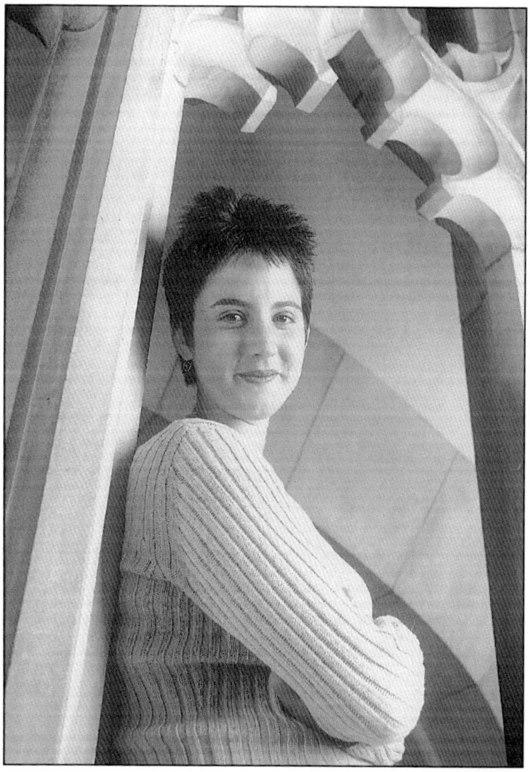

The Rhodes Scholarship. A double major in political science and women's studies, Rachel Simmons (Class of 1996) was one of the 32 graduates from across the country to join the Rhodes ranks in 1997. Simmons won the prestigious Rhodes Scholarship for graduate studies at Oxford University in England. (Photograph by Russell Monk.)

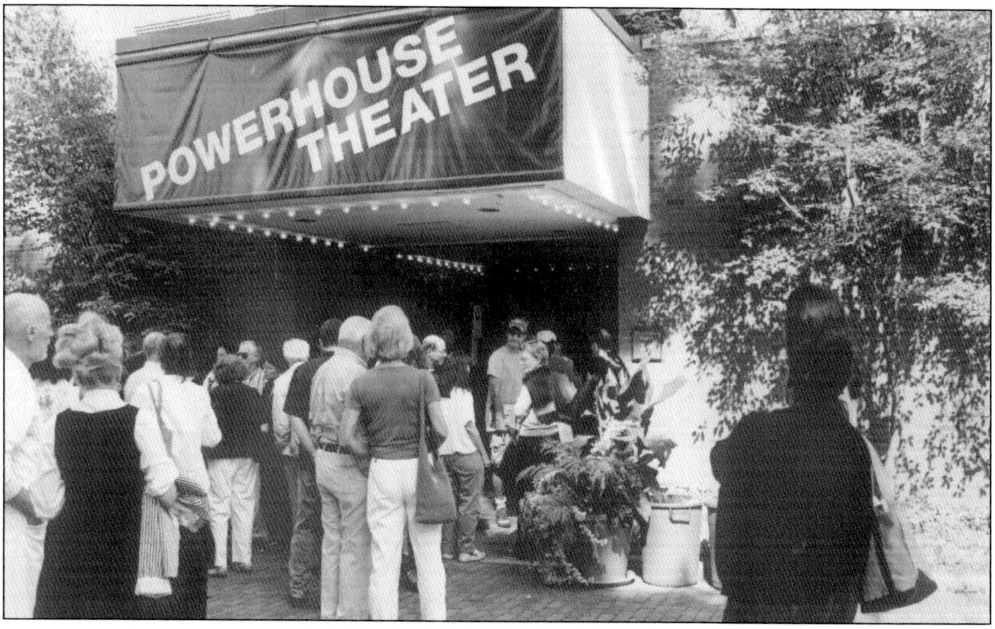

Before Showtime, 1999. The college began its summer theater program in the 1980s. In 1912, bidding goodbye to gas lighting, the college had built a powerhouse behind Main Building to provide electricity. After 1954, the plant stood idle for nearly three decades until it was converted into the Powerhouse Theater. Recently, the old coal bins were also remodeled into a black box theater for student productions, the Susan Stein Shiva Theater. (Photograph by Dixie Sheridan.)

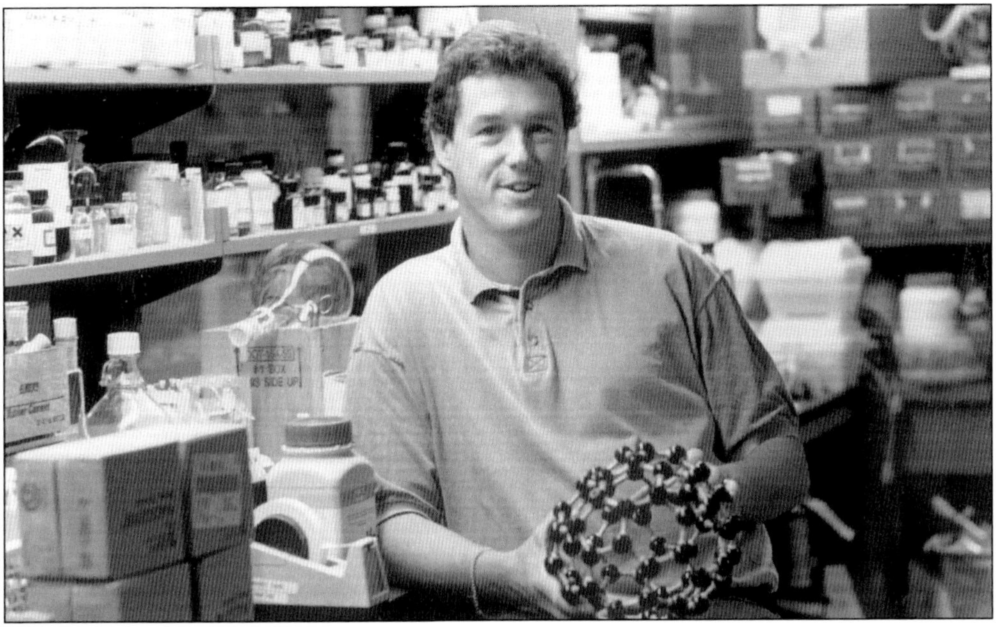

Chemist Christopher Smart (Class of 1984). Associate Prof. Christopher Smart specializes in organic chemistry. Chemistry has been taught at Vassar since the college began. The department moved from Main Building to Vassar Brothers Laboratory in 1880. In 1909, Sanders Chemistry (now Sanders Recitation Hall) opened, the first Vassar building to prepare for electricity. In 1984, the Seeley G. Mudd Chemistry Building was built, Smart's headquarters on campus. (Photograph by Dixie Sheridan.)

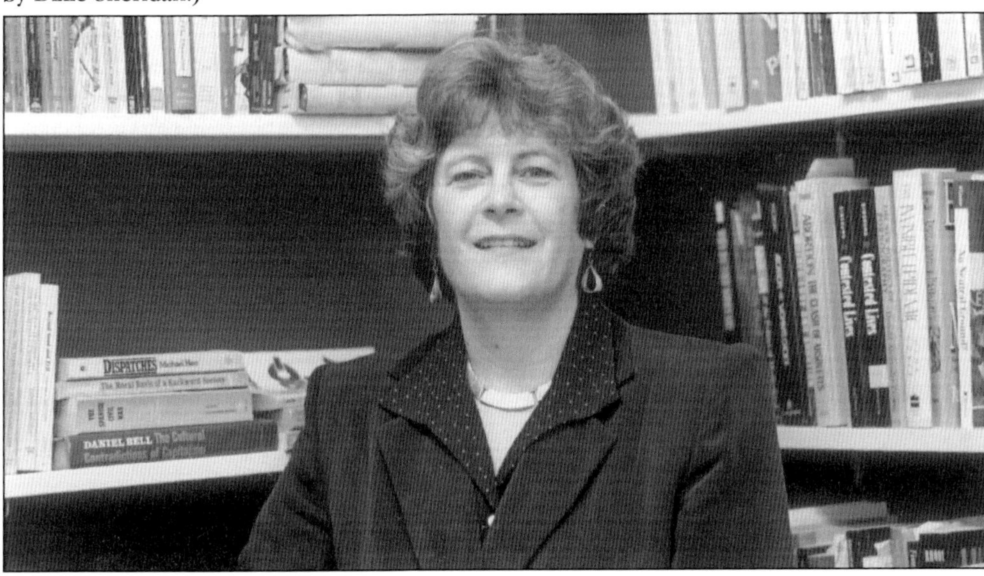

Mary Shanley, Professor of Political Science. Mary L. Shanley, professor of political science since 1973, is one of 13 members of the political science department, which is housed in Rockefeller Hall, Vassar's oldest classroom building. Her special interests lie in feminist theory and family law. She is the author of *Feminism, Marriage, and the Laws in Victorian England*. Her most recent book, *Making Babies, Making Families,* is on contemporary family law. (Photograph by Dixie Sheridan.)

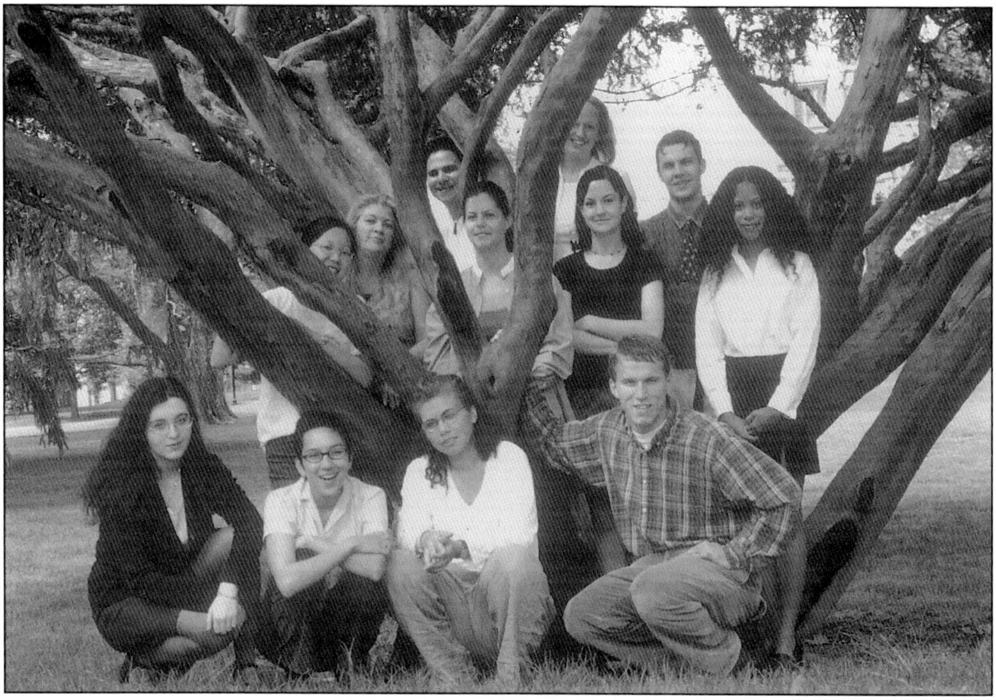

Fellowship and Award Winners. Every year, graduates from colleges and universities across the country vie for prizes, scholarships, fellowships, and travel grants from foundations and graduate schools. Vassar students win an incredible number of these prizes. Posing are 12 Vassar students who won some of these prizes. (Photograph by George Laws.)

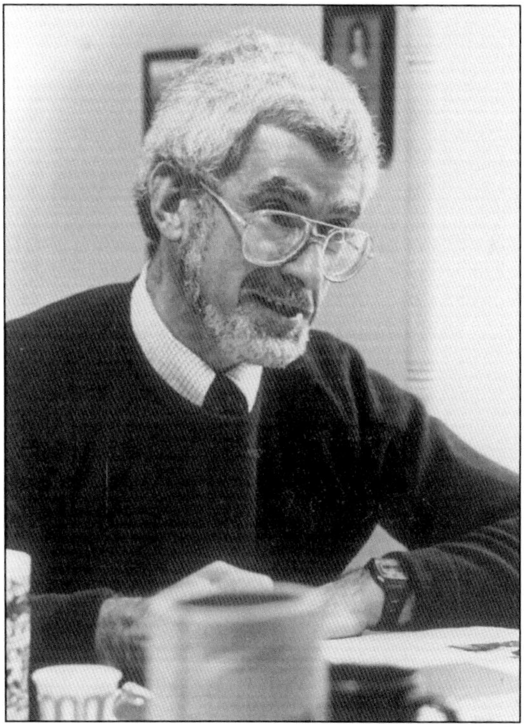

Anthony Wohl, Professor Emeritus. Professor Wohl sits in an accustomed position at a seminar table in Swift Hall. His field, in which he has many publications, is Victorian history and Victorian studies.

THE LONDON PLANETREE ON THE LIBRARY LAWN. A symbol of Vassar, the London planetree has been on the front lawn of the college for many generations of students. This picture was taken in October 1993. The tree was once identified as an American sycamore, but Vassar horticulturist Jeff Horst has revealed this identification to be incorrect. (Photograph by George Laws.)

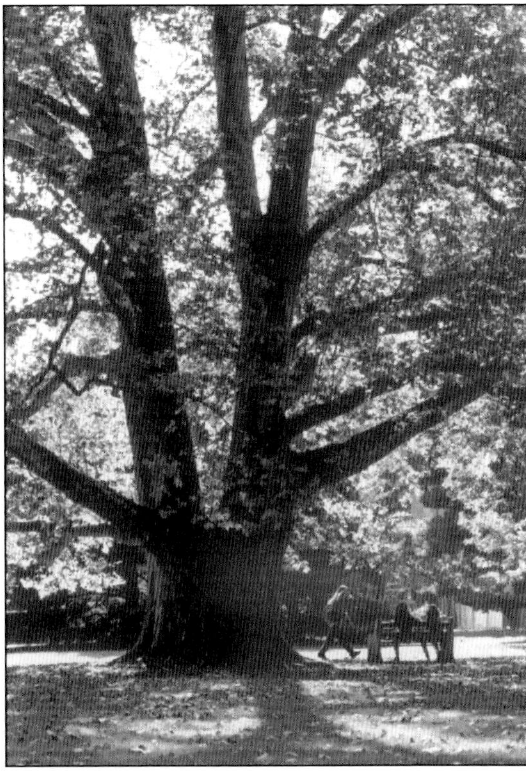

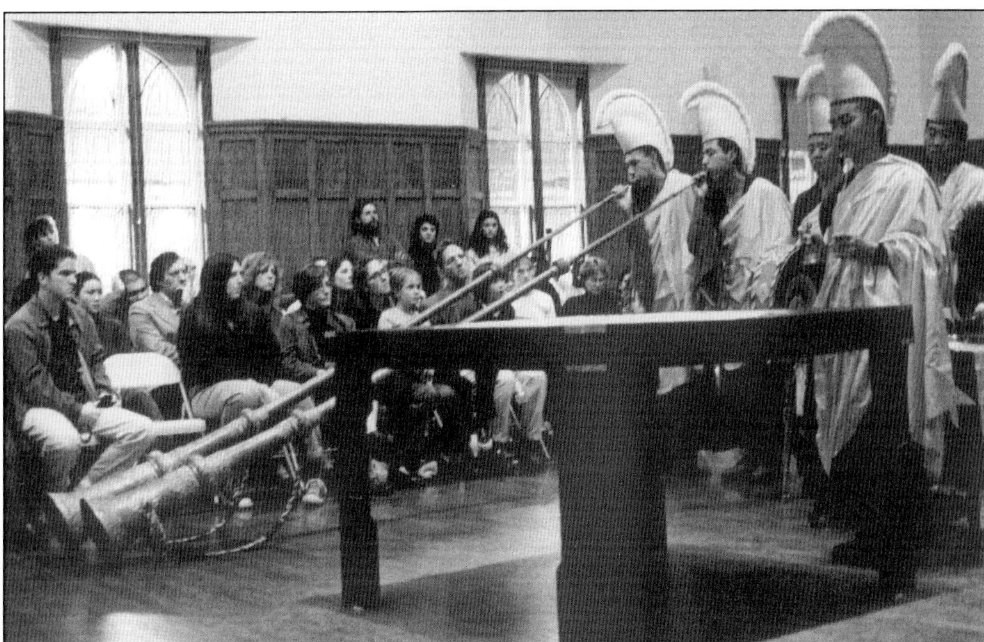

A VISIT FROM MONKS AT THE CLOSING CEREMONY, NOVEMBER 1999. A group of Tibetan monks from Deprung Loseling Monastery visited the college in November 1999 and created a ceremonial mandala in the Villard Room. They taught members of the college community about their beliefs and traditions. (Photograph by Diane Zucker.)

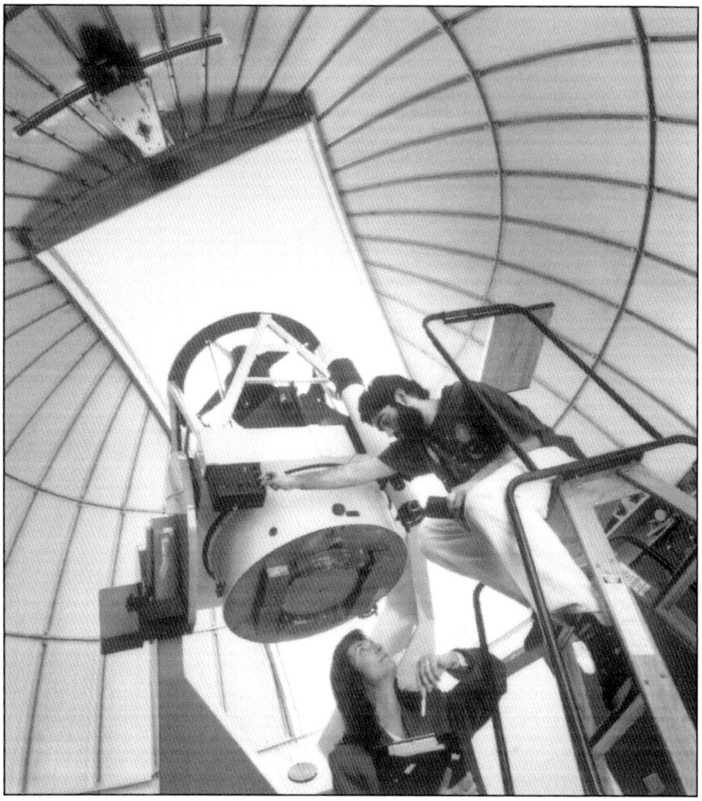

The Class of 1951 Observatory. Dedicated in 1997, the Class of 1951 Observatory houses 32- and 20-inch reflecting telescopes. The 32-inch telescope is used for researching supernovae, variable stars, and the structure of galaxies, while the smaller one is used for instruction. Shown at the left is Prof. Debra Elmegreen, who holds an appointment to the Maria Mitchell chair. (Photograph by Will Faller.)

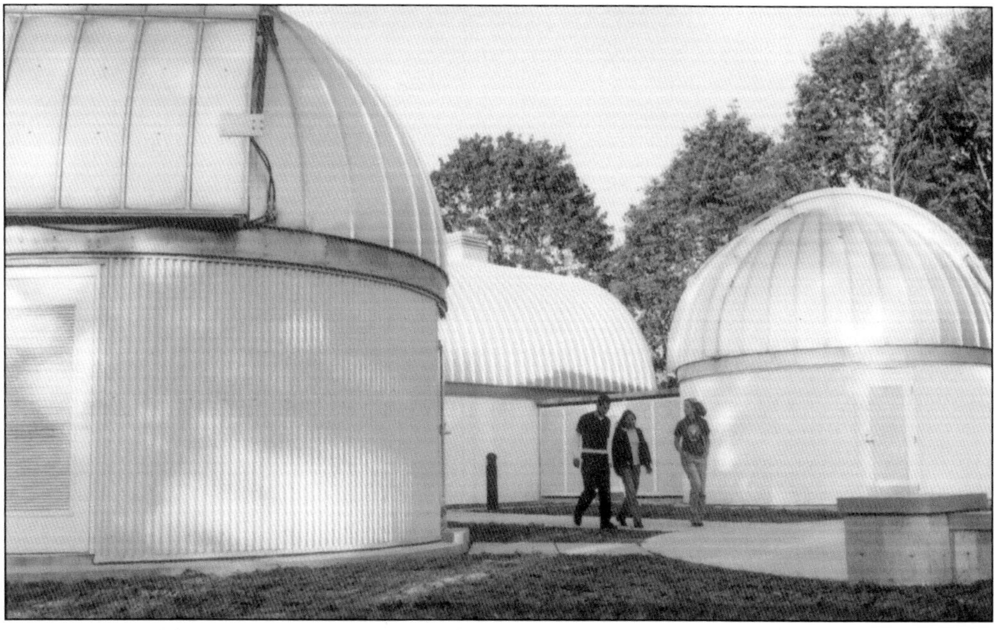

The Class of 1951 Observatory Domes. Students walk the path toward campus. The observatory is located at a far end of campus, away from lights and interference. Maria Mitchell's original observatory is now on the National Register of Historic Landmarks and is used for other academic purposes. (Photograph by Will Faller.)

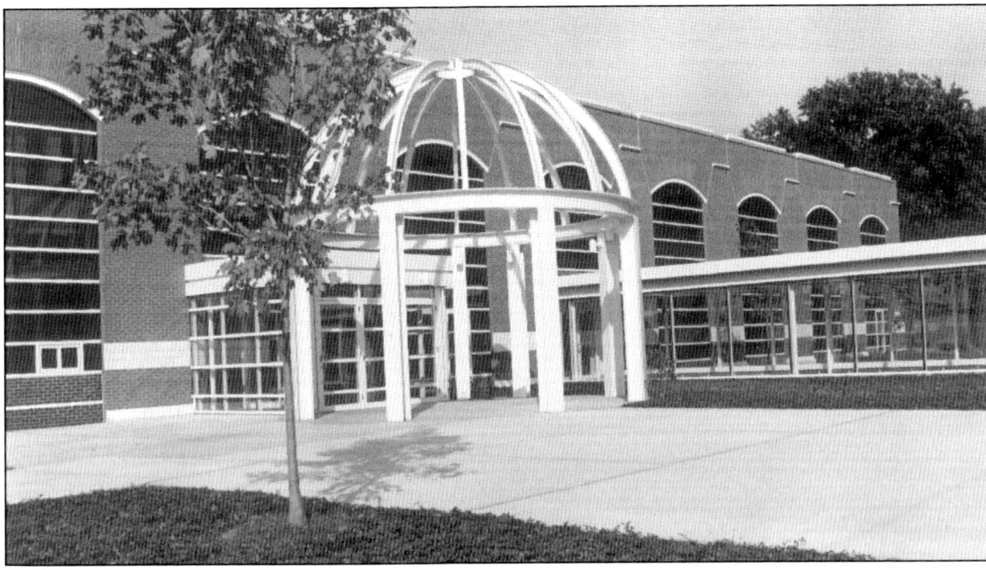

The Field House Addition. As part of a comprehensive plan to expand the college's athletic facilities, a new athletic center was dedicated in October 2000. The 52,000-square-foot building includes a gymnasium large enough for practice courts for basketball and a competition court with seating for 2,000 spectators. The new gymnasium also includes an elevated running track, a 5000-square-foot exercise and fitness area, an aerobics room, offices for faculty and coaches, and an atrium for refreshments. (Photograph by Diane Zucker.)

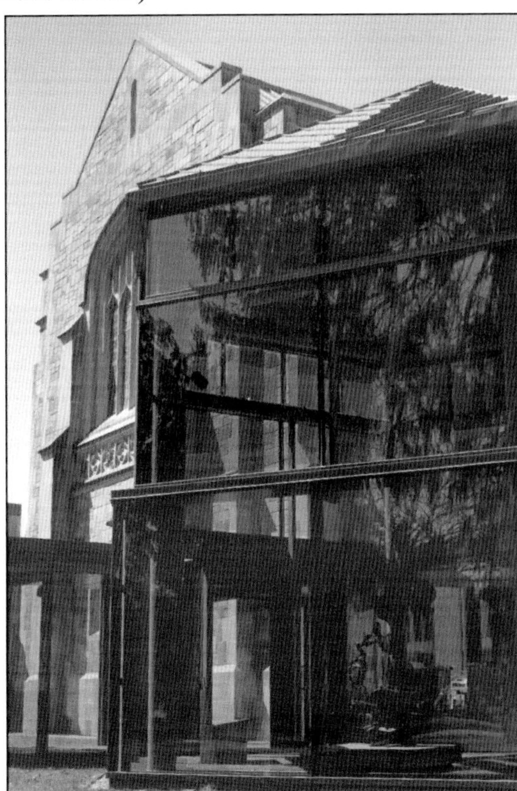

The Frances Lehman Loeb Art Center. Designed by Cesar Pelli, the art center at Vassar opened in the fall of 1993. Frances Lehman Loeb gave $7.5 million toward the construction of a new art center and the renovation of existing art facilities. Since the founding of Vassar in 1861, the art gallery has been a prized part of the college and its curriculum. Today, the gallery's collection contains more than 14,600 paintings, prints, drawings, and photographs. It is noted for its Hudson River School paintings, old-master prints (especially Rembrandt and Durer), 19th-century English drawings, and 20th-century art. (Photograph by Dixie Sheridan.)

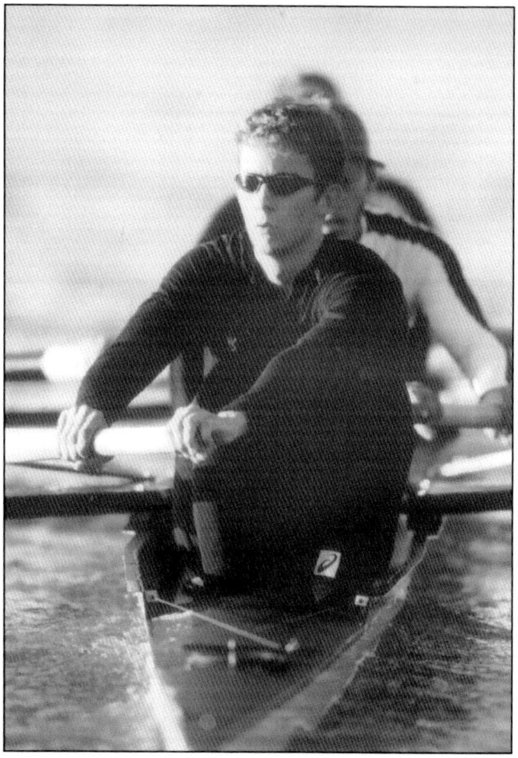

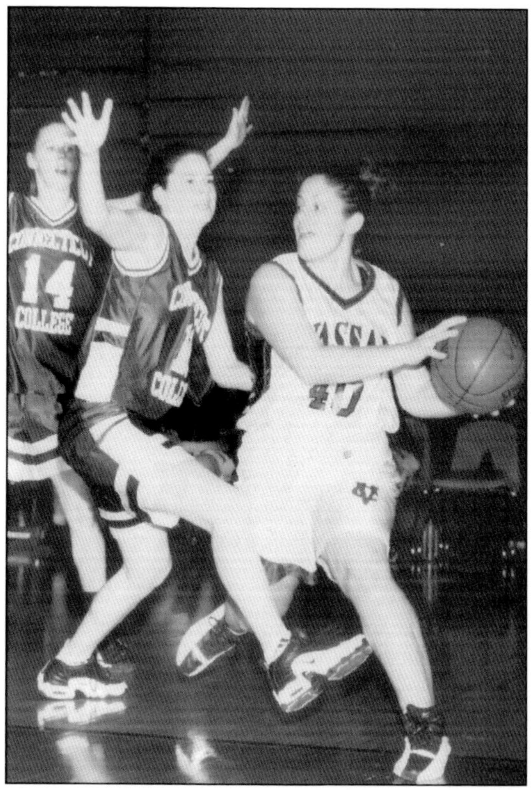

Playing Hard. The athletics program, an integral component of the Vassar educational experience, embraces a wide range of intercollegiate varsity teams, club sports, and intramurals. The college fields 22 varsity teams that compete in Division III of the National Collegiate Athletic Association (NCAA) as well as men's and women's club rugby. In 1996, the college acquired property on the Hudson River (not far from where Matthew Vassar had his large brewery in the 19th century) and now has a boathouse there. Among the many shells is one named the Frances Fergusson, after the current president. In 1998, women's soccer won the Eastern Collegiate Athletic Association Mid-Atlantic Championship. Also that year,-women's tennis won the Seven Sisters Championship and distance runner James McCowan was named All-American and NCAA regional champion. (Courtesy Carlisle Stockton.)

THE MARTHA RIVERS AND E. BRONSON INGRAM LIBRARY. The Martha Rivers and E. Bronson Ingram Library adds new resources, including archives, to the Vassar libraries. The library system encompasses the Frederick Ferris Thompson Memorial Library, the Van Ingen Library, the art library, the Helen D. Lockwood Library, and the George Sherman Dickinson Music Library. (Photograph by Diane Zucker.)

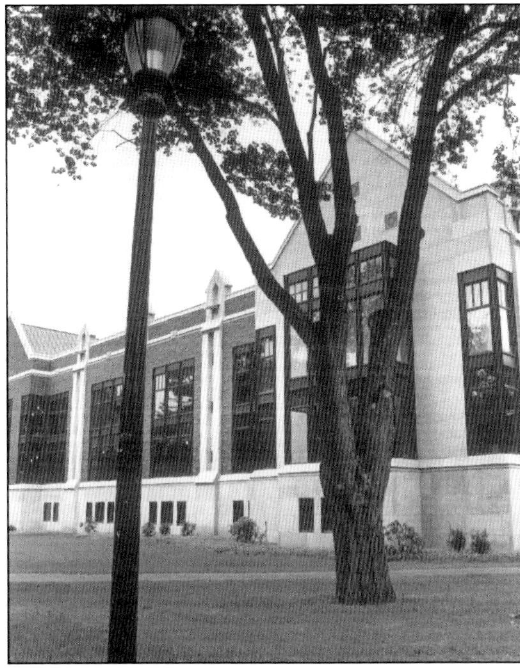

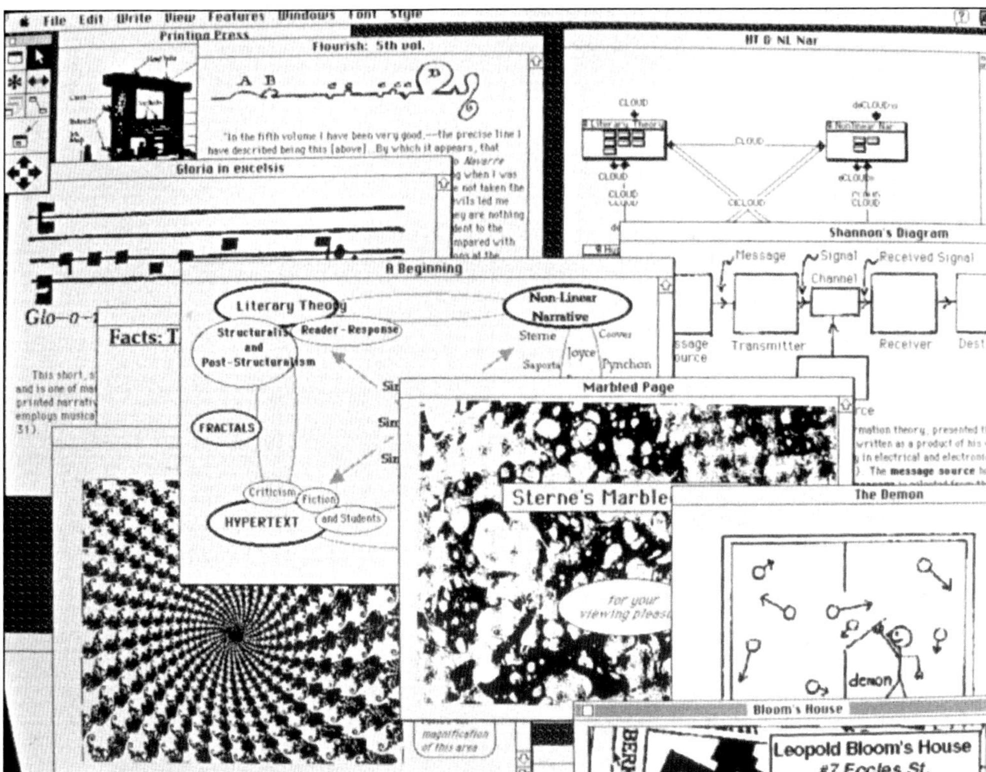

A HYPERTEXT SCREEN. By the 1990s, computers had become omnipresent on the campus. They were used both privately and in the classroom as a medium between students and teachers. This hypertext screen from December 1992 illustrates some classroom texts. (Photograph by George Laws.)

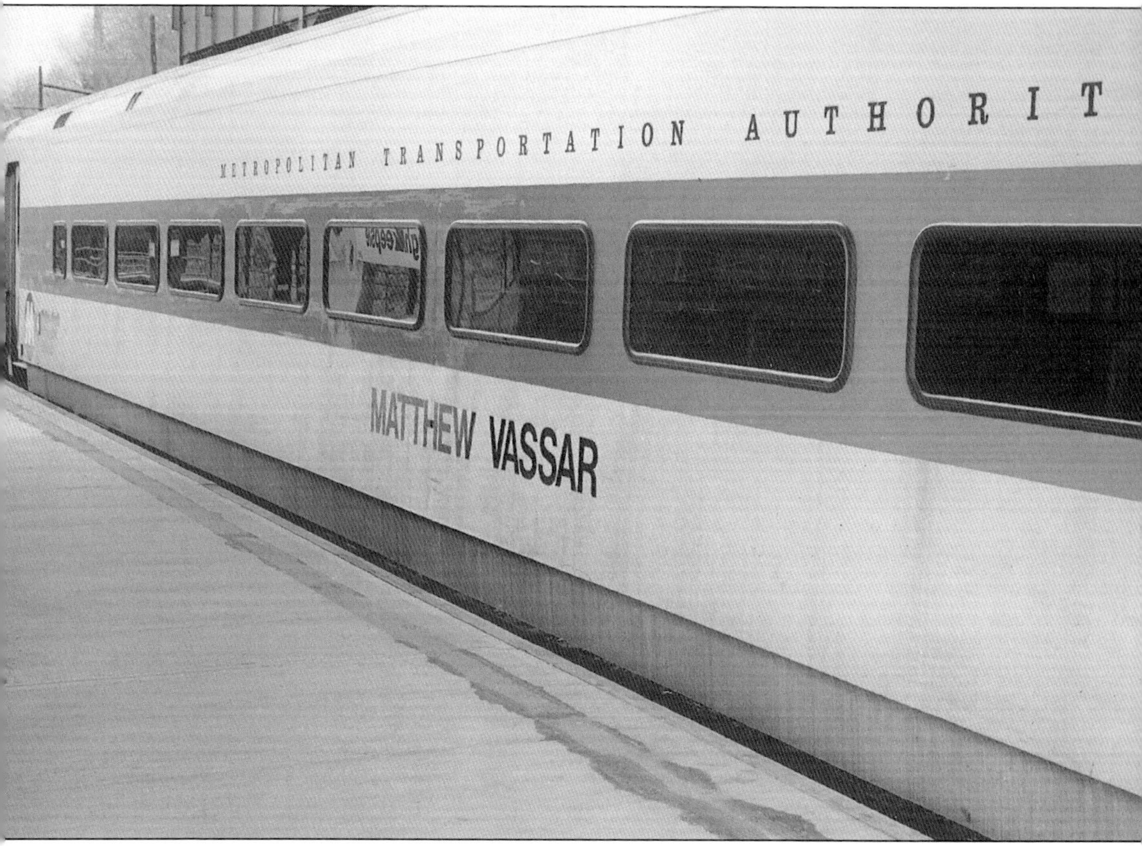

The Founder Would Have Been Impressed. One of Matthew Vassar's most important commitments was to the development of the Hudson River Railroad, of which he was president beginning in 1842. By 1849, regularly scheduled trains were traveling between New York City and Poughkeepsie, making the run in an hour and 45 minutes. In April 1994, an observant

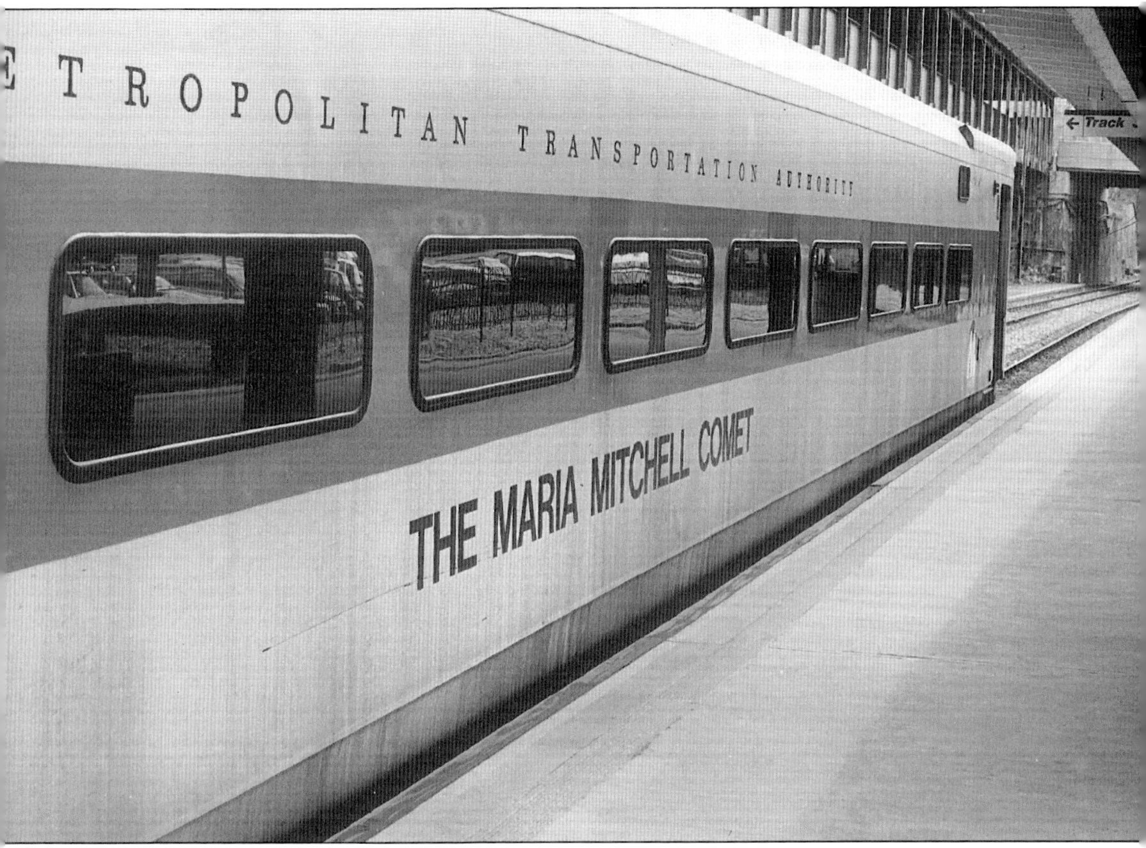

Vassar photographer in Grand Central Station photographed these railroad cars, named by the Metropolitan Transportation Authority. Matthew Vassar would have enjoyed the publicity! (Photographs by Dixie Sheridan.)

ACKNOWLEDGEMENTS

The authors are grateful for the support of Pres. Frances D. Fergusson and Vice Pres. for College Relations Susan DeKrey as well as the rich resources of the Special Collections Department of the Vassar College Libraries. We especially want to thank the former curator of Special Collections, Nancy MacKechnie, and Dean Rogers, Special Collections assistant, for their invaluable help. We also thank Patricia Phagen (the Philip and Lynn Straus curator of prints and drawings), Joann Potter (registrar–collections manager) of the Frances Lehman Loeb Art Center, and Diane Zucker and Susan Kowalski of the Office of College Relations. Thanks also go to Mary Alice Hunter and Elisabeth B. Chapman of the Class of 1938, Eileen Hayden (executive director of the Dutchess County Historical Society), the Honorable Albert M. Rosenblatt, and Prof. Robert Pounder. Two Vassar students of the Class of 2000, Jeremy Linden and Amanda Forman, with their student eyes and insights, have added verve to this work.

All photographs are courtesy of the Special Collections Department of the Vassar College Libraries and the Office of College Relations, except where otherwise noted.